Reproductive Rights in New York and New Jersey

Reproductive Rights in New York and New Jersey

Abortion, the Empire, and the Garden

Jonathan F. Parent

LEXINGTON BOOKS
Lanham • Boulder • New York • London

Published by Lexington Books
An imprint of The Rowman & Littlefield Publishing Group, Inc.
4501 Forbes Boulevard, Suite 200, Lanham, Maryland 20706
www.rowman.com

Unit A, Whitacre Mews, 26-34 Stannary Street, London SE11 4AB

British Library Cataloguing in Publication Information Available

Library of Congress Cataloging-in-Publication Data

Names: Parent, Jonathan F., author.
Title: Reproductive rights in New York and New Jersey : abortion, the Empire, and the Garden / Jonathan F. Parent.
Description: Lanham : Lexington Books, [2018] | Includes bibliographical references and index.
Identifiers: LCCN 2018010945 (print) | LCCN 2018009890 (ebook) | ISBN 9781498555548 (Electronic) | ISBN 9781498555531 (cloth : alk. paper)
Subjects: LCSH: Abortion--Government policy--New York (State)--History. | Abortion--Government policy--New Jersey--History. | Reproductive rights--New York (State)--History. | Reproductive rights--New Jersey--History.
Classification: LCC HQ767.5.U5 (print) | LCC HQ767.5.U5 P37 2018 (ebook) | DDC 362.1988/809747--dc23
LC record available at https://lccn.loc.gov/2018010945

∞™ The paper used in this publication meets the minimum requirements of American National Standard for Information Sciences Permanence of Paper for Printed Library Materials, ANSI/NISO Z39.48-1992.

Printed in the United States of America

To my parents, Lynne and Jack,
whose support was boundless.

Contents

List of Figures

Acknowledgments

From their inception early in my grad school career, the ideas that would become this book were nurtured and developed by Julie Novkov, and I owe her a tremendous debt. Similarly, Patty Strach and Udi Sommer always had an eye on my project serving as more than a dissertation and faithfully guided it in that direction.

I am also indebted to Emily Roderick and Kathryn Tafelski at Lexington Books, as well as the anonymous reviewer who agreed to provide invaluable feedback on this project. A version of the New York case study appears in the *Journal of Law and Courts* and the comments from that journal's referees were also of tremendous value in improving the overall project. A research grant from Le Moyne College allowed me to spend a very fruitful summer revising this work and my wonderful colleagues there deserve credit for this book as well.

Finally, this book would not exist without Kelsi-Leandra Lane's endless encouragement and patience. A hearty thank you as well to William J. Brennan (the cat) for keeping me company during long hours of writing and revision.

Chapter One

The Empire, the Garden, and Abortion

Policy decisions can be made in all three branches of government, whether at the federal or state level, albeit in different ways. Of course, attentive Saturday morning cartoon viewers of *Schoolhouse Rock* in the 1970s and 1980s were familiar with Congress' role in how "a bill becomes a law," though the ABC Network's version of policy development may have been somewhat simplistic. Through measures such as executive orders and instructions to cabinet officials (Howell 2003), the President too can take a very active role in influencing the shape and impact of laws, as well as via less direct means, such as the famous "power to persuade" (Neustadt 1991). The courts also play a critical role in determining policy in practically all issue areas (Dahl 1957; Murphy 1964; Epstein et al. 2001; *inter alia*). Where policy is made can itself have important implications not only for outputs themselves, but also for the form and implementation of change. A law passed by Congress may very well have an immediate impact on the groups or individuals most directly affected by a particular statute; however, the executive has considerable discretion regarding how the relevant law is executed. Similarly, a change in the makeup of the federal legislature might result in repeal or significant alterations to the enactments of a previous governing body. Policy change located in the courts, for its part, faces a different set of challenges and can take a decidedly different form. One need look no further than the landmark U.S. Supreme Court decision in *Brown v. Board of Education* which, as Rosenberg (1991) suggests, had little real impact on the reality of school segregation until well into the 1960s when the executive began more aggressively enforcing the Court's ruling. Understanding where change takes place is therefore critically important for a full account of why policies today exist in their present form. This book speaks directly to this issue by providing an account of policy change in two states, with a focus on what will lead the courts to play a primary or secondary role in that change.

Public law scholars have devoted considerable attention to the interaction between the courts and the other branches of government, most notably in the form of the separation of powers model, which itself can be subdivided into a number of approaches. Additionally, this view has been challenged from the perspective of traditional positivist accounts flowing from the attitudinal and strategic models most closely associated with the works of Segal and Spaeth (2002), Maltzman et al. (2000), and Epstein and Knight (1998). Finally, Lovell (2003), Graber (1993), and Whittington (2007) have put forward what may be broadly termed the legislative deferral hypothesis, arguing that rather than competing for policy making authority, elected officials often empower courts when they wish to avoid the consequences of legislating in controversial issue areas. This study proposes another theoretical approach developed through an investigation of abortion policy making in New York and New Jersey between 1970 and 2010. What this analysis reveals is that the path to policy change differed markedly in the two states, despite their similarities on a number of measures and the almost identical outcomes of this process, with the courts in the latter taking a much more active role in the policy making process than those in the former.

The question at the heart of this work then is, when will courts be more or less likely to be the primary location of policy change? To address this issue the following study will examine the developments in abortion policy making described above. More specifically, this work will provide some insight into the question of why the judiciary was so much more engaged in this process in New Jersey than its counterparts in New York. For a number of reasons discussed in greater detail below, traditional explanations of court behavior are insufficient in accounting for this difference, suggesting that other factors were likely at work. The theory on offer here argues that this divergence is a result of the timing of institutional involvement in the abortion question and the subsequent framing of this issue in terms conducive to its treatment by either the legislature or the courts. Because the first meaningful change in New York's law was the result of legislation, most importantly the passage of a liberalization law in 1970, this issue was framed in political terms, a view reflected in the major opinions of the New York State Court of Appeals for the forty years following legalization. By contrast, New Jersey's law was not altered until 1973 with the U.S. Supreme Court's decision in *Roe v. Wade*, as well as a number of subsequent decisions both from that state's High Court as well as several important federal rulings. The result of this early litigation was that the same issue came to be framed in legal terms in New Jersey, resulting in a string of landmark cases that consistently set policy on reproductive rights, often in opposition to laws passed by the state legislature.

Most research concerning the role of courts in creating policy has focused on the question of whether or not the judiciary is capable of producing meaningful change. A perennial source of debate among socio-legal scholars has been whether this institution has either the will or capacity to help a variety of interests or groups alter the status quo in line with their policy preferences. Some have argued that the courts are a "hollow hope" that are largely powerless to act absent support from the elected branches or the wider public (Barnum 1985; Dahl 1957; Flemming and Wood 1997; Funston 1975; Mishler and Sheehan 1993; Rosenberg 1991). Others have suggested that litigation can play an important role in articulating grievances, educating the public and policy makers, and framing issues in terms of constitutionally protected rights (McCann 1994; Scheingold 2004; Waaldijk 2000; Zemans 1983). Despite the existence of a large body of work addressing the ability of courts to affect change, there has been very little inquiry into the question of when policy will be altered through the actions of judges or justices rather than via elected lawmakers. The development of abortion policy in New York and New Jersey between 1970 and 2010 offers an excellent opportunity to investigate the question of when courts rather than the elected branches will create social policy. Indeed, these states were chosen as they offer a number of advantages for this type of case study because they share a host of characteristics in common, from their racial, religious, and other demographic makeup to similar political, legal, and even economic history and traditions.[1]

Beyond the advantages of considering judicial development in New York and New Jersey, the abortion question itself is an excellent issue for the examination of the differing roles played by courts in developing policy for two main reasons. The first of these is that this issue has tended to be one that has seen quite an extensive record of involvement by the courts and therefore a lack of judicial involvement would be all the more striking.[2] In addition to this, abortion has seen very little variation in terms of public opinion since the *Roe* decision in 1973, unlike other social issues such as same-sex marriage, gun control, and capital punishment, which have seen dramatic swings in the percentage of Americans supporting or opposing these policies over the last several decades (Gallup 2013b; Jones 2013). Indeed, the percentage of Americans answering that abortion should be illegal under all circumstances rose by a single point between 1975 and 2013, while those supporting access to the procedure under certain circumstances dropped by a mere three percent over the same period (Gallup 2013a). As previous research (Barnum 1985; Flemming and Wood 1997; McCloskey 2010; Mishler and Sheehan 1993) has demonstrated that courts are often responsive to the policy preferences of the public, the fact that this has remained more or less constant for the last forty years suggests that differences in the behavior of the courts on this issue are not the result of changes in public opinion.

ALTERNATIVE EXPLANATIONS FOR THE ROLE OF THE COURTS

The study presented in the following chapters will devote considerable attention to demonstrating that most conventional approaches to explaining the behavior of courts in determining policy fail in accounting for the observed differences between that institution's role in formulating abortion laws in New York and New Jersey. It is therefore worth briefly summarizing why alternative explanations for the divergent role of the judiciary in these two states besides the framework described in this study are insufficient. Most obviously, a traditional, variable-based positivist account fails at this task for several reasons. Many of the demographic, social, and political characteristics that most social scientists often look to as explanatory independent variables are very similar in both states and are therefore unlikely to provide much insight into the puzzle this study seeks to address; that is, the highly active role the courts played in altering policy in New Jersey compared to their counterparts in New York.[3]

The apparent reluctance of the New York Court of Appeals to engage in abortion policy making is also notable as this body has often been responsible for very significant changes in public policy. Some notable examples include *People v. LaValle* (2004), which struck down New York's capital punishment statute; *People v. Ferber* (1981), which found the state's child obscenity law unconstitutionally vague; and *People v. Onofre* (1980), which invalidated New York's 1965 sodomy law. Many of these cases involved relatively antiquated laws that had been more or less ignored by the legislature at the time the decisions were rendered, such as *Onofre* or *People v. Acme Markets, Inc.* (1975), which struck down an 1881 Sunday closing law. Other landmark cases in the Court's jurisprudence involved state departmental policy, as with *Matter of Griffin v. Coughlin* (1996), which invalidated the Department of Corrections policy mandating participation in a religiously based substance abuse program as a condition of visitation rights. Still others simply required agencies or other government bodies to do something, as was the case in *Campaign for Fiscal Equality v. State* (1994) requiring a specified level of funding for public schools. Nevertheless, there is little reason to suspect that the courts in New York are any more or less inclined to wade into the political fray than their counterparts in New Jersey.

Structural and institutional features of the states' governments similarly do not seem to be sufficient to explain the divergent role of the courts in developing abortion policy. Indeed, these structures are largely comparable in New York and New Jersey as both states have strong governors by national standards (see Salmore and Salmore 2008; Schneier et al. 2010) and maintain highly professionalized legislatures (see Maestas 2000; Squire 2008). While there are some differences between the states' constitutions, most notably for the purposes of this study the mandate in Article XVII of New York's document that the provision of health care be the responsibility of the legislature, the relevant section has been interpreted by the courts both to uphold as well as strike down laws passed by the Senate and Assembly. In *Aliessa v. Novello* (2001), for example, the New York Court of Appeals struck down a law denying Medicaid benefits to resident aliens, reasoning that Article XVII required the allocation of such funds; however, in *Khrapunskiy v. Doar* (2009) it upheld a state statute denying Supplemental Social Security benefits to noncitizens on the basis that the same provision allowed the legislature to determine who was and was not entitled to that funding. *Lee v. Smith* (1977), for its part, saw the Court strike down a Social Services Agency decision to deny state aid to disabled persons who received federal Social Security Insurance, while in *Brownley v. Doar* (2009) the Court wrote that "Article XVII is not intended to mandate that public assistance must be granted on an individual basis in every instance or command" (842). The Court of Appeals frequently argued that the health care provisions in the New York State Constitution allowed the legislature a wide berth in setting abortion policy, as will be demonstrated in chapter 3; however, these cases demonstrate that Article XVII was used as often as not to overturn the policy choices of the legislature.

The only remaining potentially relevant structural differences between the governments of New York and New Jersey are the off-year election of members of the legislature in the latter and the ability for parties to cross-endorse the candidates of other parties in the former. While cross-endorsement may have a bearing on the electoral calculations of members of New York's legislature—though this is far from a settled question (see Ward 2006)—it is difficult to see how this would affect the likelihood of the courts to engage in policy making. Similarly, given that New Jersey Supreme Court Justices are, like their northern counterparts, unelected, there does not seem to exist any mechanism by which off-year elections would make the Court any more likely to engage in policy making in the Garden State. Indeed, the timeline of policy decisions by institution presented in chapter 3 reveals no relationship between court action on abortion and election years.

One common explanatory approach employed by law and courts scholars when accounting for differences in the behavior of courts, whether across time (Segal and Spaeth 2002; Kaheny et al. 2008; Spriggs and Hansford 2001), levels within the judicial hierarchy (Zorn and Bowie 2010), or between jurisdictions (Goldman 1975; Flemming et al. 1998; Weiden 2011), has been the policy preferences and ideologies of judges. While there exists surprisingly little systematic research on the ideological makeup of state supreme courts, both the New York Court of Appeals (see Bonventre and Powell 1994; Bonventre 1992; Brace et al. 2000) and the New Jersey Supreme Court (see Salmore and Salmore 2008; Wefing 1997; Lehne and Reynolds 1978) have traditionally been seen as among the most progressive in the country. The case studies presented in chapters 2 and 3 would seem to bear this out as only two decisions during the entire forty years covered upheld laws or executive agency policies that restricted abortion access (*Planned Parenthood of NYC v. State* in New Jersey and *Hope v. Perales* in New York). So while both Courts would seem to have rather liberal orientations toward social policy, including abortion, their roles in policy development differed significantly. Given that the High Courts of both states have tended to be understood as very socially liberal by national standards, it seems unlikely that the policy preferences of the judges and justices staffing the courts of last resort are sufficient to account for the divergent roles of the judiciaries in creating abortion policy.

Finally, scholars (Brace and Hall 1995, 1997; Hall and Brace 1992; Hall 1987) have argued that the method states use to select judges has a significant impact on their behavior once in office. As noted above, there are at least five commonly employed methods states use to staff their courts; however, in both New York and New Jersey, members of the High Court are nominated by the governor and confirmed by the Senate. There are nevertheless some relatively minor differences between the states' top courts. While both consist of six associate judges and justices—New York being unique in referring to its inferior court members by the latter term—and one chief, New Jersey's Supreme Court members are initially nominated to seven-year terms before being reconfirmed by the Senate until the mandatory retirement age of seventy. New York's Court of Appeals judges, by contrast, are appointed to fourteen-year terms and are not subject to further review by the Senate. Prospective nominees are proposed to the governor by the Commission on Judicial Nomination, which consists of "twelve members of whom four shall be appointed by the governor, four by the chief judge of the court of appeals, and one each by the speaker of the assembly, the temporary president of the senate, the minority leader of the senate, and the minority leader of the assembly" (NYS Constitution, Article VI, §2). Judges in New Jersey may be removed from office if they are impeached by a simple majority in the General Assembly and convicted by a two-thirds vote in the Senate. Alternatively, if the governor determines "that it appears that any Justice of the Supreme Court or Judge of the Superior Court is so incapacitated as substantially to prevent him from performing his judicial duties" (NJ Constitution, Article VI, §6), he or she may remove a sitting justice, subject to the approval of a three-member commission appointed by the chief executive. Removal from the bench in New York requires either a vote of two-thirds of both houses of the state legislature or a request by six members of the Court of Appeals, subject to approval by the Commission on Judicial Conduct.

As with the other structures of government in New York and New Jersey, it seems unlikely that either the selection method or the removal procedures of state judges and justices would have a meaningful impact on the behavior of the courts, either in developing abortion policy or in accounting for the lack of observed meaningful change from that branch in the former. Indeed, the two states' judicial systems have much more in common with each other than they do with the majority of other states, thirty-eight of which choose their Supreme Court justices through some form of election, whether partisan, nonpartisan, or retention (American Judicature Society 2013), making their highly divergent role all the more noteworthy. While New Jersey's renomination procedure could conceivably result in some form of political repercussion for a Justice issuing a particularly unpopular decision, no member of the state's Supreme Court ever faced this prospect during the period included in this study. In any event, despite this difference in the appointment process in the two states, it was the New Jersey court that was considerably more likely to challenge the laws passed by the legislature, further suggesting that reconfirmation did not play a role in influencing the behavior of that body.

THEORETICAL FRAMEWORK

To answer the question posed above regarding when courts are likely to take the lead in policy development, and more specifically the central role of the courts in New Jersey's development of abortion policy and their comparative absence from the same developments in New York, the following study will employ a theoretical framework that draws on previous scholarship on path dependence as well as some of the more recent work in Law and American Political Development (APD). In terms of the former, the case studies considered here reveal that the initial occupation of an issue area by either the judicial or elected branches tended to result in that institution persisting as the primary location of policy development. For example, the liberalization law passed by the legislature in New York in 1970, coupled with a series of early decisions treating the abortion issue by that state's High Court, set in motion a developmental path that would see a highly disengaged judiciary that never meaningfully altered the choices made by elected officials. By the same token, a palpable lack of engagement with the issue by the legislature in New Jersey in the early 1970s, in combination with several key court decisions in that decade, set that state on a path that saw a robust role for the judiciary whose decisions ultimately determined most of that state's abortion policy. The specifics of how the interactions between the courts, both federal and state, and the elected branches in New York and New Jersey led to this divergent role for the judiciary will be described in much more detail in the case studies presented in chapters 2 and 3; however, the theory on offer here can be summarized by the following points: (1) during the early stages of policy change, the field of potential discursive frameworks surrounding a given issue that will structure the understandings of policy makers in all three branches of government is much broader than at later points in the process; (2) this field will be significantly narrowed once substantive change has occurred and will tend to reflect the narrative most closely associated with the institution that initiated the change; and (3) the conceptualization of a given issue that is adopted by the courts, and hence its role in developing policy in that area, will be largely structured by the discursive framework that was determined by the initial change. In terms of the specific cases considered in this study, the initial "choice" of issue frames employed to discuss abortion can be loosely categorized as either "legal" or "political." Moreover, while the adoption of one or the other frame was critically important for the role the courts would play in altering policy, they were also clearly present in the other two branches of government as well.

The process by which this adoption took place, therefore, is a dynamic one that requires consideration not only of the dialogue within and between courts, but in the context of the wider policy making community. It is also critical to view this development across time as the succession of decisions by the relevant legal institutions serves both to reinforce and further legitimize the initial issue conceptualizations, as well as provide evidentiary support for the argument offered here regarding the importance of institutional first movement and path maintenance. Indeed, the mechanism that served as the driving force behind the differential role of the courts in the two states was the framing of the abortion question that became predominant among the judiciaries in New York and New Jersey. Bobbitt (1982) provides a rough approximation of the interpretive approaches that can be seen in the two cases. In terms of the former, the New York Court of Appeals, beginning in the early 1970s, tended to take what the author terms a "prudential" view of the issue, which tends to focus, among other things, on the proper functions of the various structures of government; in this case, that the abortion issue was best left to the elected branches. The New Jersey Supreme Court, as well as the relevant panel decisions from the Third Circuit Court of Appeals, however, tended to adopt a "doctrinal" view, which emphasizes adherence to precedent and places greater value on the views expressed by legal commentators.[4]

The major contribution of work from the Law and APD tradition can be found in Brandwein's (2011) argument regarding the relationship between ideas and institutions and her rejection of the view that these characteristics ought to be thought of as operating independently of each other. In addition, the framework proposed here is informed by what Kahn (2006) calls the "Social Construction Process," albeit in a somewhat modified form. Specifically, while Kahn argues that doctrinal development is informed both by forces endogenous as well as exogenous to the courts, in this case meaning the larger social context, this understanding instead views the primary external influence as coming from the other branches of government. Finally, borrowing from Novkov's (2011) concept of legal archeology, this study aims to trace "the flow of discursive framings of ideological commitments from legal language to political and cultural discourse and vice versa" (356). An issue initially framed in legal terms will be much more likely to be treated by the courts than if that same issue had been first articulated in more "political" terms. Where this theoretical approach diverges from much of the previous work in the Law and APD field (see for example Orren 1991; Nackenoff 2006; Keck 2004, 2006; Gillman 1993, 1999; *inter alia*), then, is that the level of analysis used to account for the behavior of judges and courts is shifted from considering doctrinal or policy development within the judiciary alone to the policy making community as a whole, defined as all three branches of government.

To elaborate on the characteristics of path dependence that inform this theoretical approach, it should be noted first and foremost that the particular aspect of policy development that is responsive to these pressures is the way in which the abortion question was framed in New York and New Jersey, both at the outset of policy change as well as going forward. It would at this point be helpful to more fully describe the concept of issue framing as it is used here. Despite the relatively large body of research utilizing the concept, a widely accepted definition is surprisingly elusive. Jacoby (2000) characterizes framing as "the way that policy controversies will be presented to the public" (751) while Nelson and Oxley (1999), who have written extensively on the topic, call frames "alternative definitions, constructions, or depictions of a policy problem" (1041). Following Wedeking (2010), issue framing will be defined throughout this study as "a small collection of related words that emphasize some aspect of an issue at the expense of others" (617). Specifically, throughout chapters 2 and 3, it is clear that both elected officials and members of each state's judiciary consistently employed certain key phrases that can loosely be categorized as "political" or "legal," depending on how abortion was discussed early on in the process. By way of example, an emphasis on concepts such as "rights," "equal protection," and "overbroad language" that are common to jurisprudential discourse are found much more frequently in the court opinions and executive messages in New Jersey than in New York. Conversely, more emotive and politically charged language such as "back-alley abortions," "imposing morality," and "value judgment" tended to be found more often in these same institutions in the Empire State. It should therefore come as little surprise that the institutional location of policy making tended to be situated in the courts of New Jersey more often than those of New York. While the branch of government, and the norms and mandates that are associated with it, that first altered policy is highly relevant in accounting for the location of policy change going forward, it bears emphasizing that the force driving why the courts in New Jersey, but not in New York, came to predominate in developing abortion policy was the language and issue frames that informed the debate in the legislatures and the judiciary. Simply put, the articulation of abortion first in legal or political terms, at an early stage when one or the other could have shaped the views and thinking of judges, largely set the tone going forward and was subsequently reinforced by successive decisions. Faithful to the arguments of path dependence scholars, then, timing matters, though in the case of the theoretical approach proposed here, not primarily in the sense of policy direction but in terms of issue framing.

Some scholars working within the path dependence tradition have nevertheless argued that "ideas," broadly understood, can be responsive to these pressures, though the argument presented in this work conceptualizes this phenomenon somewhat differently. Acharya (2004), for instance, suggests that norms, in this case as they relate to the development of regionalism in Asia, developed along a path dependent trajectory, while North (1994) and Paul (2008) highlight the ways in which culture too can be influenced by factors such as increasing returns and self-reinforcing sequences. Neither norms nor culture, however, captures the same concept of framing as it is used throughout this study. The former tends to focus on behavior and values while the latter suggests a more all-encompassing set of traits associated with a shared history, language, etc. Instead, the frames that are responsive to path dependent pressures described in the following analysis are concerned with ways of understanding and thinking about policy problems and controversies by the various actors within the courts, as well as the elected branches. Indeed, Llewellyn (1934) provides a concise, but rather accurate description of this phenomenon when he describes legal reasoning as "involv[ing] not patterns of doing (or of inhibition) merely, but also accompanying patterns of thinking and of emotion" (18). So while some previous work in the path dependent tradition has treated ideas as one of a number of concepts that may be subject to this type of influence, the theoretical framework presented here offers an understanding of framing that is somewhat distinct from this scholarship.

Beyond this focus on issue framing as particularly responsive to path dependent pressures, some of the other predictions and assumptions of this approach are also used to inform the theoretical framework described here. The specific details of this approach are explored at length in the case studies that follow, though Mahoney's (2000) description of path dependence serves to illustrate well how this view frames the present study. Describing the major approaches researchers have taken to understanding this behavior, he writes that:

> [w]ithin the framework of path dependence, scholars often consider two dominant types of sequences. First, some path-dependent investigators analyze *self-reinforcing sequences* characterized by the formation and long-term reproduction of a given institutional pattern . . . A second basic type of path-dependent analysis involves the study of *reactive sequences*. Reactive sequences are chains of temporally ordered and causally connected event. These sequences are "reactive" in the sense that each event within the sequence is in part a reaction to temporally antecedent events. Thus, each step in the chain is "dependent" on prior steps (508, 509 emphasis in original).

This study will identify both types of sequences, as each appears to be at play in the cases considered in the following chapters. Specifically, the initial location of decision making either in the legislature or the judiciary can be seen as the first in a reactive sequence of events that was followed precisely because of this early choice. Subsequent developments then became self-reinforcing, making a change in paths increasingly more costly as the process progressed.

Paul Pierson further elaborates on the manner by which policy development is structured by initial decisions and choices early on and maintained for extended periods until eventually switching to another path. Specifically,

> path dependent processes involve three distinct phases—three stages in a temporal sequence: (1) the initial "critical" juncture, when events trigger movement toward a particular "path" or trajectory out of two or more possible ones; (2) the period of reproduction, in which positive feedback reinforces the trajectory initiated in phase one; and (3) the end of the path, in which new events dislodge a long-lasting equilibrium (Pierson 2000b, 76).

What an examination of abortion policy development in New York and New Jersey over a forty year period reveals is that early involvement by one institution had a profound impact on what role the courts would later play.

Two caveats bear mentioning here for the sake of clarification. The first is related to institutional first movement and self-reinforcing sequences described above, and how these are understood throughout the analysis presented here. In terms of the former, the claim is not that an institution's initial involvement in the development of a given policy is a sufficient cause for that institution's continued predominance as the process continues. Instead, this institutional location must be consolidated over time, with the mechanism producing that consolidation being the continued and repeated use of the frame that was first used to articulate the conflict or controversy. The second point that should be emphasized is the difference between norms as they are discussed by some proponents of path dependence such as Campbell (2002), Solinger (2005), and Guiraudon (2000), and frames as they are understood here. While there are some similarities between the two concepts inasmuch as they both refer to relatively ephemeral qualities such as practices and ideas, the focus in this study is on frames as they are understood by Wedeking (2010) and Brandwein (2006), though the latter uses the term "knowledge claim." Indeed, norms typically refer to patterns of behavior that are associated with given groups, societies, or some other identifiable organization. Quoting Yee, Grafstein succinctly defines a norm as "a generally accepted principle or guideline" (1997, 1042). The proposition that norms may be responsive to path dependent pressures therefore has some utility for the theory on offer here, though it is not synonymous with frames and it is the latter concept that is the focus of the theoretical framework proposed in this study.

In this sense, the theoretical framework proposed here is not one that considers path dependence as a phenomenon occurring exclusively in the judicial branch, but rather through the dialogue between the elected branches and the courts as well as between previous and subsequent courts. Critical moments, then, took place within the executive, legislative, and judicial branches and are most significant in the sense that they guided the dialogue and framing of the abortion question, though in some cases they also had the practical effect of keeping some issues off the court's agenda. In terms of the latter, for example, Governor Carey's veto of the parental consent bill in 1976, discussed in much more detail in chapter 3, precluded the possibility that the court would issue a ruling on that particular restriction, as did the passage of the 1978, 1979, and 1980 budgets without Medicaid funding bans in New York. The actions and framing choices of the elected branches as they relate to the understanding of abortion adopted by the courts at critical moments will be discussed in more detail in the following chapters, though as suggested by the theory on offer here, this ongoing dialogue following the initial involvement of the legislature in New York and the courts in New Jersey had a highly significant impact on the role the courts in both states throughout the entire period considered in this study.

As mentioned above, the second part of the theoretical approach proposed in the present study draws on some of the insights of work in the Law and APD tradition. Central to this argument is the conceptualization of institutions and ideas as inseparable or, as Brandwein (2011) puts it, the notion that "stable sets of ideas are inherent to mandates and hence to institutions" (190).[5] Kahn, for his part, writes that "[i]t is possible to identify social constructions in a case and line of cases and see which social constructions are accepted and rejected by the Court" (2006, 87). In a similar vein, Lieberman (2002) notes that "any political moment or episode or outcome is situated within a variety of ordered institutional and ideological patterns, each with its own origins and history and each with its own logic and pace" (701). The point, in any event, is that institutional behavior is structured around the ideas, values, and conceptualizations of the actors who collectively guide them. Furthermore, these conceptualizations can be identified, and the influence they have on the behavior of the courts observed, through the use of frame analysis not only of the written opinions offered by judges and justices, but of all of the members of the policy making communities of the two states. In the case of abortion policy making in New York and New Jersey, the lens through which judges saw this policy issue, both as developed within the courts as well as in concert with the elected branches, structured their actions and subsequently guided the substantive role the courts were to play.

Bringing these two intellectual traditions together yields a theoretical approach that focuses both on the importance of institutional first movement and the issue framing that shapes how courts deal with particular policy areas. This approach assumes, as Brandwein (2011) argues, that ideas shape institutions, but also that the norms and patterns of behavior that characterize different institutions will themselves influence how issues are resolved. As Kahn and Kersch (2006) suggest, courts are both "inward" and "outward" looking in that they are shaped by distinctly legal phenomena—the Constitution, stare decisis, etc.—as well as external factors as diverse as the other branches of government, the media, and the wider public. What the theoretical framework on offer here adds is that, not only do these endogenous and exogenous factors matter for how courts come to view policy questions, but that the institution that first alters the status quo will have a disproportionate influence on the frames that are adopted by judges and consequently their roles as more passive or active participants in policy change. This leads courts to treat the issues that come before them in a unique way, and through a particular lens that can itself influence how those outside of the court come to view issues as well. This mutually constructed understanding can be seen in the case studies presented in the following chapters. In the New York case, elected officials were the first to create policy dealing with abortion, and the courts that dealt with the issue subsequently came to view the question as one best suited for resolution by those same officials. In New Jersey, however, the courts were the first institution to formulate abortion policy and therefore came to understand the controversy as one of legal rights rather than a political question.[6] This in turn led the latter to become the dominant institution in this issue as the framing process adopted by the courts continued to be reinforced with each successive decision.

In any event, the theoretical approach employed in the present study does not seek to explain the decision making of courts—be they the U.S. Supreme Court or state courts of last resort—through an exclusively path dependent lens. Instead, the argument offered here is that the issue frame adopted by courts is likely to be influenced by the institution that first addresses a particular issue or controversy. In the case of abortion policy making in New York, this institution was the legislature, while in New Jersey it was the courts. This institutional first movement subsequently helped frame that issue as one properly worked out by the elected branches in the former, while in the latter, abortion gradually came to be seen as a rights rather than a political question. To be clear, this is not to suggest that policy change first located in the elected branches necessarily requires that subsequent development must also be undertaken by those institutions. Indeed, it would clearly remain possible for the courts under those circumstances to assert a more active role depending on the specific details of a given issue, a radical change in the behavior of judicial or political actors, or some other external shock. This is particularly true at critical moments during the policy development process. What this does mean is that institutional first movement will make the issue frame adopted by the courts considerably more likely to take a legal form if the first meaningful policy change occurs in that branch or, conversely, a more political tone if that change is initiated by the elected branches. Following from one of the major characteristics of path dependence theory, the likelihood of a change in the behavior of the courts as an active or passive participant also decreases as further changes in policy continue to be located in one or the other branch; what Mahoney (2000) calls a self-reinforcing sequence. The point here is that while institutional first movement is highly important, it is not strictly deterministic but deals more in terms of probabilities, with the chances of the judiciary changing its behavior becoming less likely the further the established path progresses.

In what he calls the "configurational approach," as it applies to small-*n* case studies, Ragin (2000) suggests a comparison of cases that bear many similarities, but differ in one key aspect. To illustrate the point, the author offers the following example:

> [A] White, suburban, middle-class, male professional with three children and a mortgage who votes for the Republican Party differs by only a single trait from a person with all these same characteristics but who votes for the Socialist Labor Party. Thus, from a variable-oriented viewpoint, they are very similar. Still, it might be very different to be trapped in an elevator with one versus the other. This qualitative difference captures the essence of viewing cases as configurations: Two cases may be similar in most ways but because they differ on one or more key aspects, their differences may be one of kind, not simply one of degree (71).

Examining the development of abortion policy in New York and New Jersey, we see very much this same pattern. Two Northeastern states that share a host of characteristics, including even their policies on abortion, though one key and highly relevant difference exists: the institution that is largely responsible for those policies as they exist today. Following the configurational approach, this study will systematically identify the variables that might be expected to result in the location of policy making within different institutions. Once these have been accounted for, the analysis of the cases themselves, within their respective contexts, will help reveal why courts in New

Jersey played such an active role in policy development in contrast to their counterparts in New York.

To accomplish this, it is necessary to briefly discuss some of the assumptions that frame the methodology described above. First, it is assumed that different characteristics that social scientists have identified as traditionally influencing the policy making process, particularly in the realm of social issues such as abortion, will influence the location of decisions. These include factors such as religion, political orientation, partisan affiliation, race, structure of government, public opinion, etc. For example, a state such as Oklahoma, with a large number of evangelical Christians, self-identified Republicans, and a decidedly socially conservative political tradition, might be expected to see more legislation limiting abortion access emanating from its legislature because publicly taking a pro-life position is unlikely to harm the electoral fortunes of many lawmakers. A state like Florida, on the other hand, often understood as the proto-typical swing state, might be expected to see more decision making on this issue in the courts, as legislators are reluctant to take a position that might alienate either pro-life or pro-choice constituencies, both of which may be necessary for reelection.[7] Indeed, this assumption is very much at the heart of the legislative deferral model discussed above as Lovell (2003), Graber (1993), and Whittington (2007) all to some degree argue that elected officials will have an incentive to pass decision making responsibility to courts in cases where choosing either position on a controversial issue will negatively affect their electoral interests. The point here is that these pressures are more likely to be felt by lawmakers facing a more moderate electorate than those whose constituents are largely homogenous in their policy views, a situation more likely to be present at the state level where district populations are smaller and presumably less heterogeneous.

Related to this is a second assumption, drawn largely from Ragin's configurational approach. If traditional explanations for differences in the location of policy change between two polities can be shown to be insufficient as explanatory factors for these differences, some other factor must be responsible. As Sir Arthur Conan Doyle once wrote through the words of his Sherlock Holmes character, "when you have eliminated the impossible, whatever remains, however improbable, must be the truth" (1890, 111). While nineteenth-century English literature may not fully capture the rigors of modern social scientific methodology, the sentiment is largely the same inasmuch as the second assumption of the present study reflects the idea that systematically eliminating variables as potential explanatory factors will be useful in identifying what is responsible for the phenomenon of interest. This is, admittedly, a somewhat unorthodox strategy; however, because the aforementioned traditional explanations of policy making behavior do not prove adequate in accounting for the difference in the roles of the courts in New York and

New Jersey, as will be demonstrated in the following chapters, it is necessary to approach the problem through a relatively novel methodological scheme.

A third assumption is that the more characteristics and history governmental units, in this case American states, share, the more likely they are to behave similarly in their policy making development, both in terms of outcomes as well as institutional location. Conversely, even small differences in these characteristics may result in different policy making processes. For example, an ethnically homogenous country like Japan will follow a different policy making process than a highly diverse country such as South Africa. The presence of a greater diversity of constituencies in the latter will exert influence on its government differently than would be the case in the former. Indeed, this influence can be seen in the constitutions of the two countries, with South Africa devoting considerably more attention to the protection of group rights in its document[8] than its Japanese counterpart (see Constitution of Japan, 1947 and The Constitution of the Republic of South Africa, 1996). Maioni (1998) also makes a similar point regarding the importance of governmental structure and formal arrangements in her analysis of the development of healthcare policy in Canada and the United States. Despite the historical, cultural, linguistic, and demographic similarities between the two countries, differences in their governmental structures resulted in vastly different outcomes in this area. By the same token, antecedent historical developments will influence the trajectory and institutional location of policy change. Put considerably more succinctly: history matters. Returning to the examples of South Africa and Japan, the history that led up to the adoption of each country's respective constitutions deeply influenced the character of each, which in turn manifests in the way policy change occurs. In the Japanese case, the Constitution was adopted under the supervision of American military occupation following that country's defeat in World War II and therefore contains strong prohibitions against the use of military force. This in turn has meant that a considerable amount of foreign policy as it relates to bilateral treaties and the use of force abroad has been the subject of much litigation. For its part, South Africa's history of gross human rights violations during the Apartheid era led to one of the most expansive and inclusive Bill of Rights among modern democracies, a fact which has resulted in a number of sweeping decisions by that country's Constitutional Court, often to the chagrin of the elected branches (Roux 2009).[9]

A brief description of how issue frames are understood and identified is important as this approach will form the basis of the analyses presented in the case studies discussed in chapters 2 and 3 and is of critical importance to the theory on offer here. As mentioned earlier, identifying rhetorical frames is a surprisingly difficult task and scholars often disagree on what does or does not fall into this category. This definition of a frame fits well with the purpose of this study as it is assumed that there are a limited number of potential types of frames that may be used to articulate claims related to abortion. Considerations such as foreign policy, tax rates, or the right to bear arms, for example, are unlikely to be found with much regularity when discussing reproductive rights.[10] Indeed, as Greenhouse and Siegel (2012) point out, prior to the *Roe* decision, the field of potential narratives on both sides of the abortion question was considerably broader than it was following the 1973 ruling, though a focus on framing the issue in terms of rights or as a political debate pitting the interests of women against those of "potential life" had become apparent. Wedeking's definition therefore seems appropriate inasmuch as a choice existed for much of the period considered in this study between "rights talk" and more "political" language, even after the U.S. Supreme Court handed down its landmark decision. Moreover, as suggested by the theoretical framework proposed here, which of these two choices came to prominence within the policy making communities in New York and New Jersey, broadly speaking, was largely a product of which institution altered the status quo first and would have an important bearing on where subsequent developments were to be located.[11]

A second component of frame analysis relates to the manner in which the identification of one or the other framing choice, and its maintenance over time, will be demonstrated in the following empirical chapters. Here again Brandwein (2006) provides a useful guide, though some alterations to her prescription for proper frame identification are made here in order to tailor it to the needs of the present work. Specifically, the focus of much of the analysis that follows will take into account three main qualities that may fairly be said to represent both the establishment as well as the maintenance of a particular narrative throughout the abortion debate in both states. The first of these involves "isolat[ing] the underlying interpretive framework . . . explain[ing] how it enables and constrains meaning . . . [and] link[ing] the underlying framework to its sponsoring interpretive community" (Brandwein 2006, 235). The second will consider the identification of these "interpretive communities," defined in terms of affiliated academic or professional groupings. For the purposes of this study, however, interpretive communities are defined as specific branches of government. In addition, these groupings are considered to operate within particular policy making communities, which are understood here to be those of New York and New Jersey.[12] Finally, the analyses of frames will discuss why "a win or loss at each stage in [a knowledge claim's] career" (235) is significant for its continued reproduction.

Finally, a brief description of how the data that makes up the following chapters was collected is at this point warranted. The major events in the development of abortion policy in New York and New Jersey, as well as the relevant documents, were accumulated through several sources. Initially, a ProQuest Historical Newspaper search of all *New York Times* articles between 1970 and 2010 including the terms "abortion" and "New York" or

"New Jersey" was performed and analyzed for any references to changes in abortion policy. Supplementing this was a search of the same terms in the LexisNexis legal database, including all decisions from state courts in New York and New Jersey, as well as federal district and Second and Third Circuit Courts of Appeal. Finally, where gubernatorial vetoes had been issued of abortion legislation, copies of the accompanying messages were obtained from the New York State and New Jersey public libraries, the latter being requested and sent via regular post. This collection of data and historical records allows for the organization of the major events in the development of abortion policy to be placed in temporal order and facilitates the identification of major decision points by each relevant institution. This ordering is well-suited to address the question posed at the outset regarding the passive or active role of the courts in policy development, as well as demonstrating the utility of the theoretical approach on offer here.

NEW YORK AND NEW JERSEY IN COMPARATIVE CONTEXT

The choice of these two states follows from what Gerring (2007) calls "most-similar" cases, meaning those where a particular pairing is selected precisely because of their similarities on a host of measures, with the exception of the variable of interest. As the following section reveals, New York and New Jersey clearly fit this definition as they share many characteristics with the exception of the role of the judiciary in developing abortion policy. Indeed, Gerring argues that "most-similar" cases are particularly valuable when "a researcher moves from an exploratory to a confirmatory mode of analysis" (131). In other words, the primary purpose of this type of investigation is exploratory and hypothesis-generating. Following the identification of an anomalous finding, in this case the highly differential role of the courts in policy development, Gerring suggests using what John Stuart Mill called a "method of difference" to account for why otherwise similar units of analysis might produce this divergent result.

Perhaps most obviously, New York and New Jersey are both Northeastern states located in what the U.S. Census Bureau considers the Mid-Atlantic region. Demographically the states are also quite similar, as can be seen in figures 1.1, 1.2, and 1.3 below. Specifically, the racial makeup of the two states is comparable, with New Jersey having a slightly lower minority population than New York. Nevertheless, the difference between the average percentage of White, Black, and Latino residents in both states does not exceed 4 percent according to data from the U.S. Census over the course of the four decades between 1970 and 2010. Changes in these racial characteristics also followed similar trends over this same time period, with both New York and New Jersey seeing steady declines in their White populations, moderate increases in the percentage of Black residents, and a rapidly rising proportion of those identifying as Latino. The latter's urban population has been consistently higher than the former—averaging 91.3 percent versus 86 percent, respectively—though both are significantly higher than the national average of 76.4 percent over the same time period.[13]

Figure 1.2 evinces some notable differences between the two states; with the most obvious being the relatively higher average income in New Jersey as compared to New York. Similarly, the Empire State had a higher percentage of its population living below the poverty line than the Garden State. This fact is almost certainly attributable to the vast income inequality that exists in New York City, the highest level of all major cities in the United States, resulting in a larger proportion of the population living in poverty (Glaeser et al. 2008). In any case, the importance of income for abortion policy making is less than clear, with some studies (Wetstein and Albritton 1995; Wetstein 1996) finding that this measure is negatively related to support for abortion restrictions, while others (Carmine and Woods 2002; Gober 1994) found more mixed results. Additionally, public support for the pro-life and pro-choice positions has remained virtually identical in New York and New Jersey between 1970 and 2010, suggesting that income has not influenced the public's views on this issue in the two states. Education levels, for their part, have been similar in both, with the percentage of those with a bachelor's or advanced degree being comparable, though New York has led New Jersey in high school graduation rates on average.

Finally, and arguably most importantly in light of the issue area that is the focus of this study, the religious characteristics of both states are remarkably similar, as can be seen in figure 1.3. Specifically, the percentages of the populations identifying as Evangelical Protestant are essentially identical, while New York has a slightly larger proportion of Mainline Protestants. By the same token, New Jersey's population is three percent more Catholic than New York's, though both are well above the national average. The propor-

Year	% White		% Black		% Hispanic		% Urban	
	NY	NJ	NY	NJ	NY	NJ	NY	NJ
2010	71.5	74.1	17.5	14.6	18.0	18.8	87.9	94.7
2000	70.0	74.4	17.0	14.4	15.1	13.3	87.5	94.4
1990	74.4	79.3	15.9	13.4	12.3	9.6	84.3	89.4
1980	79.5	83.2	13.7	12.6	9.5	6.7	84.6	89.0
1970	86.8	88.8	11.9	10.7	8.0	4.3	85.6	88.9
Average	76.4	80.0	15.2	13.1	12.6	10.5	86.0	91.3

Figure 1.1. Race and Urbanization in New York and New Jersey *Source:* U.S. Census

Year	Income				Education (Percent of Population)					
	Mean Income (In Dollars)		% Below Poverty Level (Family)		High School Graduate		Bachelor's Degree		Advanced or Graduate Degree	
	NY	NJ	NY	NJ	NY	NJ	NY	NJ	NY	NJ
2010	54,659.00	68,342.00	10.8	7.0	84.7	87.4	32.4	34.5	14	12.9
2000	43,393.00	55,146.00	11.5	6.3	79.1	82.1	27.4	29.8	9.8	11
1990	23,710.00	24,354.00	13	7.6	74.8	76.7	23.1	24.9	9.9	8.8
1980	24,465.00	27,772.00	13.4	9.5	67.8	67.4	17.9	18.3	--	--
1970	10,609.00	11,403.00	11.1	8.1	78.5	52.5	11.9	11.8	--	--
Average	31,367.00	37,403.00	11.96	7.7	77	73.2	22.5	23.9	11.2	10.9

Figure 1.2. Income and Educational Attainment in New York and New Jersey
***Source:* U.S. Census**

tion of Jewish people in the two states is identical, and similarly much higher than that in the country as a whole, though significantly more New Yorkers identify as unaffiliated than those in New Jersey. The U.S. Census does not collect data on religious affiliation and therefore the percentages reported in table 1.3 are only for the year 2008 and come from Pew Forum. Nevertheless, this data suggests that New York and New Jersey are quite similar in terms of religious identification, further illustrating the demographic comparability of the two states. This characteristic is particularly relevant as religion has been demonstrated by a wide range of scholarship to be highly predictive of attitudes toward abortion (see, for example, Brace et al. 2002; O'Connor and Berkman 1995; Legge 1983; Roh and Haider-Markel 2003; *inter alia*). In addition, much of the support for abortion restrictions in New York and New Jersey was led by the Catholic Church throughout the entire period covered in this investigation.

Politically, both states have traditionally been viewed as Democratic Party strongholds and liberal Northeastern states. In the ten presidential elections between 1970 and 2010, New York and New Jersey were won by the same party's candidate all but twice, once in 1976 and again in 1988, both years in which the Republican candidate carried New Jersey while the Democratic candidate won New York. Ideologically, a 2010 Gallup poll reported that 26.6 percent of New Yorkers identified as "liberal" compared to 24.2 percent of New Jersey residents, while 30.6 percent identified as "conservative" in the former compared to 34.6 percent in the latter. By contrast, 20.3 percent of all Americans chose the "liberal" moniker and 39.8 percent answered that they thought of themselves as "conservative." In terms of partisanship, 50.5 percent of respondents in New York claimed to be "strong" or "weak" Democrats while 46.6 percent of New Jerseyans fell into one of these categories. Conversely, "strong" or "weak" Republicans made up 32.0 percent of New York's population, compared to 35.8 percent in New Jersey. Again comparing these to national averages, the Democrats enjoyed the sup-

Religion (Percent of Population)					
State	Evangelical Protestant	Mainline Protestant	Catholic	Jewish	Unaffiliated
New York	11.0	16.0	39.0	6.0	17.0
New Jersey	12.0	13.0	42.0	6.0	12.0
National	26.0	18.0	24.0	2.0	16.0

Figure 1.3. Religious Affiliation in New York and New Jersey *Source:* Pew Forum 2008

port of 43.7 percent of all Americans while the GOP was favored by 40.4 percent. The academic literature has also borne out the view of New York and New Jersey as highly ideologically similar. Erikson et al. (2007), for example, places both at almost the same position on the left-right spectrum, while Wright et al. (1985) claim that:

> The political complexions of several of the more populous states (California, *New York, New Jersey*, Pennsylvania, Michigan, and Ohio) are quite similar. These states are tightly clustered within a relatively small range on the partisanship axis and vary in ideology only along the most liberal third of the spectrum (482, emphasis added).

Finally, Brace et al. (2004) examined the levels of ideological change in all fifty states between 1974 and 1999, finding that both New York and New Jersey saw "no variation" in this measure during that twenty-five-year period, suggesting that the comparable ideological makeup of the two states reflected in the Gallup data can likely be extended over the course of the time frame covered in the present study.

New York State and New Jersey are also both heavily influenced by their proximity to New York City, by far the country's largest metropolitan area. Fully thirteen of the Garden State's twenty-one counties are considered suburbs of New York City, all of which also fall into the media market of the city according to the Nielsen Media Group (Polidata 2002a). Twelve of New York State's 61 counties are also considered part or suburbs of New York City, as well as falling within that media market, though well over half of the state's population—12 million people—live in these areas (Polidata 2002b). In addition, over 200,000 New Jersey residents worked in New York City in 2009 (Bernstein 2012), further emphasizing the cultural and economic ties between the two states.

Despite the demographic, cultural, and ideological similarities between New York and New Jersey, there are nonetheless some important differences in the operation of politics between the two states. As in every state in the

Union, with the exception of Nebraska, both states have a bicameral legislature, an independently elected chief executive, and a court of last resort. New Jersey's General Assembly and Senate are both smaller than their counterparts in New York, with the former having eighty members and the latter forty to New York's 150 and sixty-three, respectively. In addition, New Jersey's assembly districts each consist of two members, unlike the single-member districts in New York, though both are elected every two years. Senators in New Jersey are elected in a "2-4-4" cycle, with the two-year term falling after the U.S. Decennial Census in order to ensure proportions remain reflective of population changes, while all state legislators in New York are elected to two-year terms.

More informally, though, legislators in New Jersey are generally understood to be more independent than those in New York, as power tends to be more concentrated within the leadership of the latter (Ward 2006). Owing to the state's smaller size, lawmakers in Trenton also spend less time in the capital than those in Albany (Salmore and Salmore 2008). The latter are compensated at a higher level as well, earning $79,500 a year compared to $49,000 per annum in New Jersey, though both are paid considerably more than their fellow legislators in most states (Empire Center 2012). Finally, New Jersey is one of only five states to hold elections in odd-numbered years, the others being Virginia, Kentucky, Louisiana, and Mississippi (Salmore and Salmore 2008).

As evidenced in figure 1.4, partisan control of the Assembly and Senate in New York has also been considerably more stable than the same bodies in New Jersey, with the upper chamber in the former seeing a Republican majority for all but two years between 1970 and 2010 and the Assembly being dominated by Democrats from 1974 to the present. New Jersey, by contrast, has seen considerably more turnover during the same period with the Assembly changing hands four times and the Senate three, including one two-year period during which the latter was split evenly with both parties holding twenty seats and control of the chamber being shared between each party's leadership. Both states, however, have seen roughly the same number of Republican and Democratic governors. It is worth noting that, in terms of the abortion question, party labels were of little predictive value regarding this issue until well into the 1980s, a fact which is borne out in the New York case where restrictions on the procedure were as likely to be supported by Democrats as by Republicans. Nevertheless, it was during this period that the vast majority of the state's abortion policy was set. For New Jersey's part, much of the legislation restricting abortion access that was struck down by the courts in that state was passed during the relatively brief period in the mid to late 1990s when all three elected institutions were controlled by Republicans. Finally, while Republicans had come to be associated with the pro-life position and Democrats with the pro-choice view in both states by the mid-

1980s, the GOP took a considerably more moderate view of the issue in New York and New Jersey than the national party. Indeed, neither state party's platforms ever explicitly took a position on abortion during the forty years considered here and the Republican governors of both states were always seen as relatively moderate, a fact which will be demonstrated in greater detail in chapters 2 and 3. In any event, the partisan makeup of the two states' legislative chambers did not seem to influence the likelihood of the courts weighing in on the abortion question, though given the importance of the court's interaction with the elected branches for the theory on offer here, a consideration of these political factors is nonetheless instructive.

In addition to the racial, religious, educational, cultural, and political similarities between New York and New Jersey, and of equal importance to the present study, both states have virtually identical abortion policies. Since the 1973 U.S. Supreme Court decision in *Roe v. Wade*, many states have passed a host of limits on the procedure, with most of these having been considered, and in some cases passed, in the two cases presented in the following study. These have included bans on public financing and/or Medicaid funding, late-term abortion restrictions, parental notification and/or consent, mandated counseling—including required information on fetal pain, negative psychological consequences, and the purported link between abortion and breast cancer—mandatory waiting periods, requirements regarding facilities that may perform the procedure, restrictions on nonsurgical abortions, conscience exceptions, and laws restricting private insurance coverage. None of these, however, are currently in force in New York or New Jersey, making both states somewhat unique in their lack of abortion restrictions as most states currently maintain at least some of these provisions. Indeed, the only differences between the abortion policies of the two states is the requirement in New Jersey that a physician perform the procedure and that it take place in a hospital after the fourteenth week of pregnancy (Guttmacher Institute 2013); both relatively minor restrictions compared to those in place in other jurisdictions.

More specifically, the most common abortion restrictions among all states are: parental involvement laws, bans on Medicaid funding, late-term abortion bans, and mandatory waiting periods. Besides New York and New Jersey, there are only seven states that do not currently enforce any of these.[14] Interestingly, the courts have been responsible for the lack of most of these restrictions with only Hawaii, Washington, and New York having failed to pass any of these four most common abortion limits, making the latter a rather remarkable outlier. Figure 1.5 illustrates this point with reference to six types of abortion laws passed by states in the forty years since *Roe*, including parental involvement laws—which may include either a notification requirement, consent requirement, or both—bans on Medicaid funding, mandatory counseling often aimed at dissuading women from undergoing the

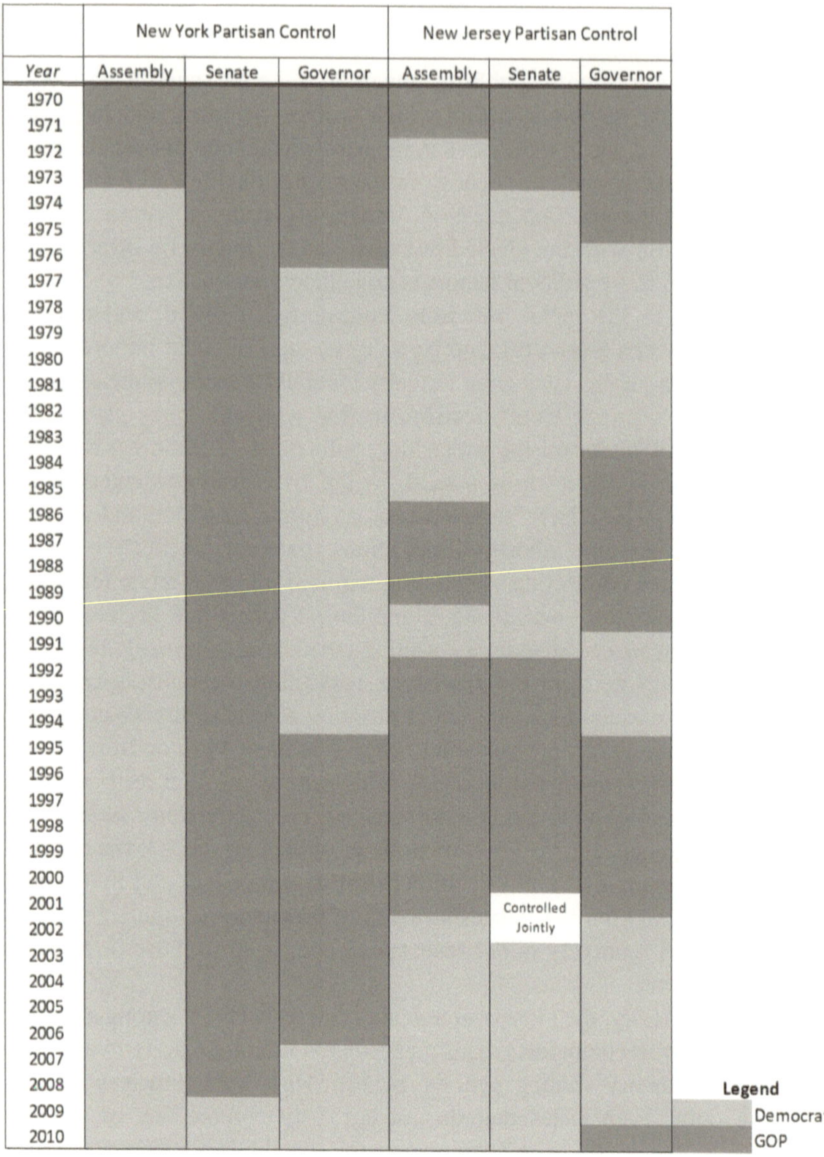

Figure 1.4. Partisan Control of State Government (1970–2010)

procedure, required waiting periods ranging from eighteen to seventy-two hours, bans on late-term abortions, and limits on private insurance coverage. New Jersey is more typical of states that do not maintain restrictions on abortion, with the courts having struck down both the parental notification and public financing bans that were passed in the 1990s and 1980s, respectively. Because the question at the heart of this study is concerned with why courts create policy treating a controversial social issue in some jurisdictions but not in others, the list of comparable states is quite limited. This list becomes even shorter when controlling for states with similar demographic, political, and social characteristics. For example, Washington State, like New York, has not seen any meaningful policy on abortion created by the judiciary, while California courts, like their counterparts in New Jersey, have weighed in on the matter on several occasions, striking down both a parental notification law and a ban on Medicaid funding. These two West Coast states have considerably different religious and racial characteristics, however, which would complicate any comparison. Similarly, New York and Illinois have a comparable racial makeup, though the latter has almost double the per capita number of Evangelical Protestants (19 percent of the population compared to 11 percent in New York) and a considerably smaller Catholic presence (32 percent to New York's 39 percent) (Pew Forum 2008). Finally, the geographical, cultural, and economic similarities between New York and New Jersey further speak to the utility of examining these states as the potential influence of these characteristics can be more easily controlled.

As the case studies in chapters 2 and 3 demonstrate, the absence of most of the aforementioned restrictions in New York and New Jersey is almost entirely the result of judicial decision making in the latter and legislation or vetoes from the elected branches in the former. The combination of two states that share a host of characteristics, policy development in the same issue area, and entirely different routes to policy change affords an excellent, and likely rare, opportunity to investigate the question of why and when courts will create social policy. While policy development related to education in Texas and same-sex marriage in Illinois may be capable of providing insight into this same question, the sheer number of potentially relevant variables would make disentangling cause from effect or relationships from correlations a nearly impossible task. The unique circumstances of two demographically similar states from the same region reaching the same policy outputs on the same issue through vastly different institutional paths, however, has the potential to inform our understanding of the behavior of courts generally, and the location of policy change in particular.

The structure of the court systems in New York and New Jersey is also largely comparable, with both consisting of courts of first instance, intermediate appellate courts, and a court of last resort.[15] As mentioned earlier in this chapter, judges serving on the New York Court of Appeals and the justices of the New Jersey Supreme Court are both appointed by the governor and subject to confirmation votes in the upper houses of both state legislatures. The constitutions of the two states also contain provisions mandating retirement at the age of 70. The selection method of trial court judges does differ

State	Parental Involvement	Medicaid Ban	Mandatory Counseling	Waiting Periods	Late-Term Ban	Private Insurance Limits
Alabama	■	■	○	■	□	○
Alaska	■	□	■	○	□	○
Arizona	■	□	○	■	■	○
Arkansas	■	■	■	■	■	○
California	□	□	○	○	○	○
Colorado	■	■	○	○	○	○
Connecticut	○	□	○	□	○	○
Delaware	■	■	○	○	○	○
Florida	■	■	○	○	□	○
Georgia	■	■	■	■	■	○
Hawaii	○	○	○	○	○	○
Idaho	■	■	○	■	□	■
Illinois	□	□	○	○	□	○
Indiana	■	■	■	■	■	○
Iowa	■	■	○	○	□	○
Kansas	■	■	■	■	■	■
Kentucky	■	■	○	■	□	■
Louisiana	■	○	■	■	■	○
Maine	■	■	○	○	○	○
Maryland	■	○	○	○	○	○
Massachusetts	■	□	○	□	○	○
Michigan	■	■	■	■	■	○
Minnesota	■	□	■	■	○	○
Mississippi	■	■	■	■	■	○
Missouri	■	■	■	■	□	■
Montana	□	□	○	□	■	○
Nebraska	■	■	■	■	□	■
Nevada	□	■	○	○	○	○
New Hampshire	■	■	○	○	■	○
New Jersey	□	□	○	○	□	○
New Mexico	□	□	○	○	■	○
New York	○	○	○	○	○	○
North Carolina	■	■	■	■	○	○
North Dakota	■	■	■	■	■	■
Ohio	■	■	■	■	■	○
Oklahoma	■	■	■	■	■	■
Oregon	○	□	○	○	○	○
Pennsylvania	■	■	■	■	○	○
Rhode Island	■	■	○	○	■	□
South Carolina	■	■	■	■	■	○
South Dakota	■	■	■	■	■	○
Tennessee	■	■	○	□	■	○
Texas	■	■	■	■	○	○
Utah	■	■	■	■	■	■
Vermont	○	□	○	○	○	○
Virginia	■	■	○	■	■	○
Washington	○	○	○	○	○	○
West Virginia	■	□	■	■	□	○
Wisconsin	■	■	○	■	□	○
Wyoming	■	■	○	○	○	○

■	Law in Effect
□	Law Enjoined
○	No Law

Figure 1.5. Abortion Restrictions by State

between the two states, however, with the former being chosen in partisan elections while the latter are appointed by the governor and confirmed by the senate, as with the state Supreme Court. Terms for trial court judges also differ both within and between the states, ranging from three years for municipal court judges in New Jersey to fourteen years for supreme court justices in New York, though most serve for ten years in the latter and seven years in the former (National Center for State Courts 2013). Intermediate appellate court judges and justices are chosen in the same manner as members of the court of last resort in both states, that is, by gubernatorial nomination and confirmation by the senate, with nominees being initially suggested by the nomination commission in New York. New Jersey, however, does not have geographically defined appellate divisions, whereas New York has four (American Judicature Society 2013). The appellate courts in the latter are also divided into the Appellate Divisions of Supreme Court, which hear appeals from city, town and county trial courts from all four divisions, and the Appellate Terms of Supreme Court, which deal with civil and criminal cases originating in the City of New York (New York State Unified Court System 2013).

FINDINGS AND THE PROCEEDING STUDY

Returning to the theoretical framework proposed at the beginning of this chapter, that the initial institutional location of policy change will influence how courts view specific policy questions and that subsequent dialogue between the judiciary and the other branches, as well as the internal discourse within the courts themselves, will influence when and how judges formulate policy, a consideration of the New York and New Jersey cases reveals the following findings. These may be stated formally as:

1. *Institutions and institutional behavior, ceteris paribus, are largely shaped by the ideas and norms by which they are constituted.*
2. *Judicial behavior in a given issue area will be influenced by the ideas and understandings of the institution that first developed policy in that area.*
3. *Subsequent decisions will tend to reinforce the initial issue conceptualizations established early in the process of policy development.*

While the case study portions of this inquiry will examine these findings in much greater detail, a brief explanation of the rationale behind each is warranted here. The first suggests that the manner in which a given branch of government will conceptualize a question or controversy will be shaped by the norms inherent in that institution's mandate. For example, the elected branches will tend to understand issues in terms of electoral considerations, the feasibility of implementation, the social consequences of policies, etc. Courts, however, will tend to think of issues through the language of rights, adherence to precedent, and formal concepts such as due process, equal protection, etc. The second finding is closely related to the first in that it serves as somewhat of a qualifier. While the first claim may seem tautological inasmuch as institutions would normally be expected to follow the norms and ideas inherent to their mandates, the second argues that this understand-

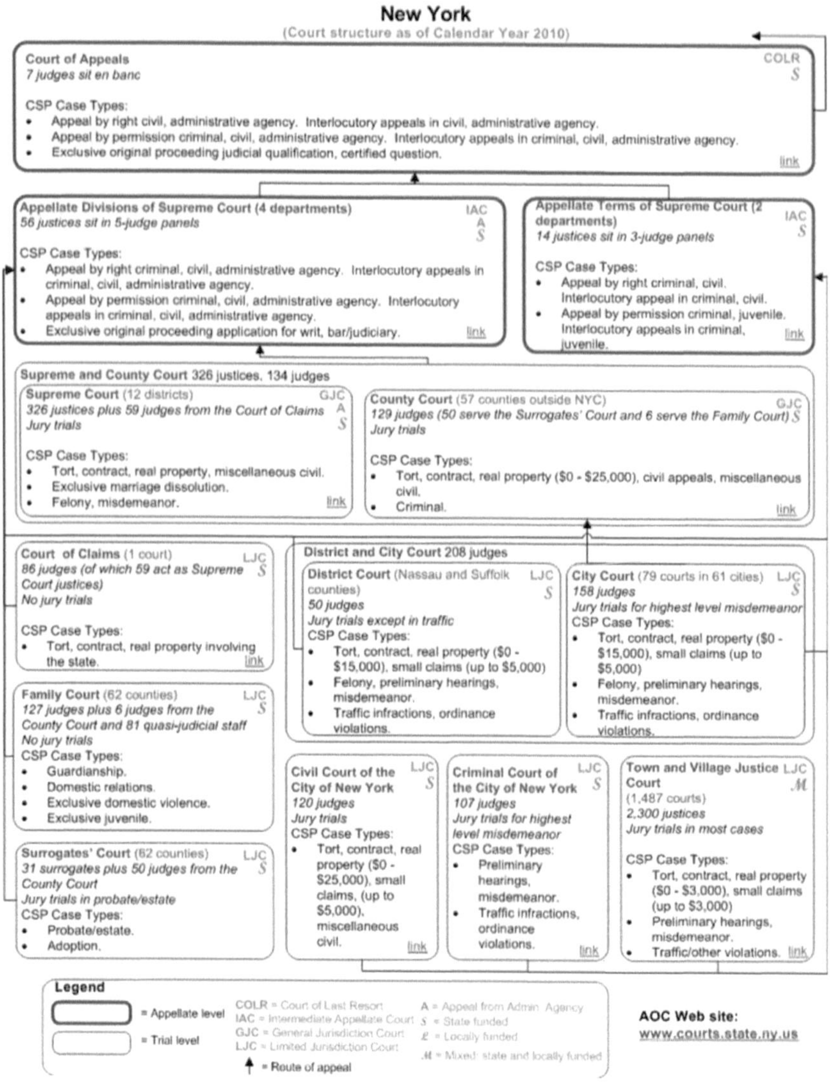

Figure 1.6. Court Structure in New York State *Source:* National Center for State Courts

ing can be influenced meaningfully by the actions and framing choices of another branch *if* that branch is the first to alter the status quo. In this sense, the second portion of the proposed theoretical framework draws largely from the path dependence tradition and argues that institutional first movement will have a significant impact on the role of the courts as these adopt the

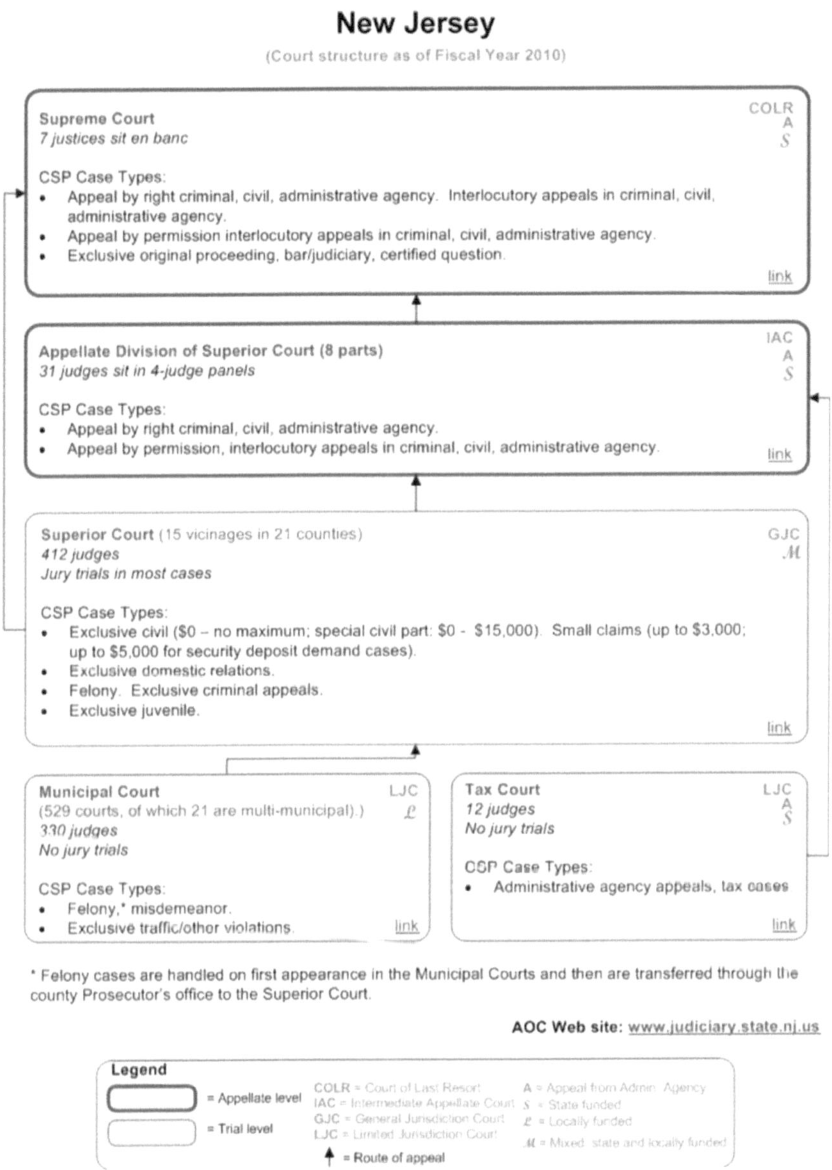

Figure 1.7. Court Structure in New Jersey *Source:* National Center for State Courts

understandings that first framed the issue or controversy. Indeed, one of the most striking differences between the development of abortion policy in New York and New Jersey was the institution that initiated policy change. Despite the fact that a case challenging the 140-year-old law in the former had begun making its way through the federal courts in 1969, the legislature passed a statute legalizing the procedure essentially at the discretion of a woman and her doctor up to the twenty-fourth week of pregnancy in 1970; three years before *Roe*. Two years later, the Assembly and Senate repealed the liberalization bill, though this was vetoed by Governor Rockefeller. An analysis of the early court decisions treating the abortion question reveals that the judges of the state's Court of Appeals largely adopted the notion that this issue belonged properly in the elected branches and used much of the language associated with that institution. In New Jersey, by contrast, federal courts, and later the *Roe* decision itself, were the first substantive change to that state's abortion laws. What the early rulings in that context reveal is a much different conceptualization of the issue; one based around language such as fundamental rights, substantive due process, and equal protection.

The foregoing description provides a very cursory overview of how these two portions of the theoretical approach described in this study function in conjunction with each other, though a much more thorough analysis will be presented in chapters 2 and 3. Specifically, a form of process tracing is employed that identifies an initial important event, followed by a consideration of how subsequent events were shaped by the qualities of the antecedent development. More formally, process tracing as it is understood here is defined as "an analytic tool for drawing descriptive and causal inferences from diagnostic pieces of evidence—often understood as part of a temporal sequence of events or phenomena" (Collier 2011, 824). Within the broad umbrella of process tracing is also found what Collier (2011) refers to as "recurring empirical regularities." Borrowing from Waltz, Collier describes this approach as concerned "not simply [with identifying] . . . a relationship that has been found, but . . . one that has been found repeatedly" (824). As will be seen in the case studies that follow, there is indeed a clearly identifiable relationship between both the language employed by the courts and the elected branches when treating the abortion question, as well as the institution primarily responsible for policy change. It is argued here that these observations are not coincidentally related, but that the issue frames first used to discuss abortion informed the role that the courts would play going forward. To reiterate, if the issue was initially conceptualized in legal terms, it would be much more likely to be subsequently developed by courts. Conversely, if it was first discussed in "political" terms, the courts were far more inclined to defer to the choices of the elected branches.

Finally, the third component of the formal theoretical framework described above draws on path dependence theory in that sequences are seen as self-reinforcing, with each decision tending to make similar decisions more likely to take the same shape. Note that this does not refer necessarily to the direction of the ruling, but to the language and understandings that formed the basis of those previous decisions. Indeed, the Court's ruling in *Hope v. Perales* (1994) upheld an abortion restriction that had been passed by the legislature despite having previously issued "pro-choice" decisions in *Byrn v. New York City Health & Hospitals Corporation* (1972) and *Matter of Roman Catholic Diocese of Albany v. New York State Dep't of Health* (1985). Instead what these decisions have in common is their shared view of abortion as a "political" question and deference to the elected branches. It is due to this continuity that the courts in New York played such a minor role in the development of abortion policy in that state, despite some evidence that the policy preferences of many of the judges would have compelled them to vote in another direction.

This self-reinforcing sequence can be seen in the elected branches as well. While there is obviously no equivalent to written opinions akin to those issued by courts, an analysis of the veto messages of Governors Rockefeller and Carey as well as statements from members of the Senate and Assembly reveal that they, too, were thinking about and conceptualizing the abortion question in terms of more "political" considerations such as the social consequences of restrictions on the procedure, the passionate debate within the wider public, and the role of the state in regulating private behavior. While it may not be surprising that political actors were thinking and writing in "political" terms, the same documents in New Jersey demonstrate a tendency toward much more "legal" language from the governor and other elected officials. The point, in any event, is that the dialogue between the elected branches as well as the various courts, both between levels of government and across time, evinces a common theme that can clearly be traced back to the initial involvement of the legislature.

The story, of course, is quite the opposite in New Jersey. In the years leading up to *Roe*, and indeed for a significant time following that decision, the legislature seemed to be making every effort to avoid creating policy dealing with the abortion issue. The situation after 1973 was so uncertain in the state, and the legislature's reluctance to engage the topic so entrenched, years went by during which doctors and women seeking the procedure in New Jersey were unsure as to whether abortion was even legal. This uncertainty prompted a number of public requests, by physician's associations as well as the governor, for some sort of policy from the legislature, though the General Assembly and Senate stubbornly refused to heed these appeals. Finally, the executive was forced, reluctantly, to issue guidelines on the state's official policy, though these were often vague and contradictory. It was not until 1979 that the legislature finally passed any substantive bill related to abortion, a collection of restrictions including a mandatory 24-hour waiting period, a parental notification provision, and a series of reporting requirements, though this was vetoed by Governor Byrne. It would not be until almost twenty years later that the legislature again acted, this time passing a late-term abortion ban that was also vetoed, this time by Governor Whitman.

By contrast, the courts in New Jersey took an early lead in developing abortion policy, and continued playing a preeminent role throughout the forty years covered in the present study. In 1972, a federal District Court held in *Young Women's Christian Association of Princeton, New Jersey v. Kugler* that the state's nineteenth-century abortion law was unconstitutionally vague, a finding upheld by the Third Circuit Court of Appeals in 1974. Two year later, the New Jersey Supreme Court ruled in *Doe v. Bridgeton Hospital Association* that "quasi-public" hospitals were required to perform abortions, a decision both the governor and the legislature had steadfastly avoided up to that point. The 1980s and 1990s similarly saw a steady stream of decisions from both state and federal courts on issues as diverse as state financing of abortions to parental involvement laws to injunctions against clinic protesters. Indeed, the latter, as well as the *Bridgeton Hospital Association* and *Kugler* decisions were not even in response to legislation enacted by the Assembly and Senate, but were the culmination of court actions brought against private citizens and institutions, where policy treating these groups was undertaken for the most part by the legislature in New York.

This, of course, is not an exact science. The identification of the frames used to discuss the abortion question in the two states is not readily quantifiable and there are not a finite number of key words or phrases that can be found with precision in the cases examined in this study. Nevertheless, patterns do emerge. Particularly in the written opinions offered by the high courts in both states, there is an undeniable tendency among the judges of the New York Court of Appeals to focus on issues such as the consequences of prohibiting abortion as well as the proper location of the question within the elected branches. The justices of the New Jersey Supreme Court, for their part, rested their decisions much more frequently on the constitutionally protected right to abortion, equal protection concerns regarding access to the procedure—particularly for low-income women—and deficiencies in the relevant statutes related to overbroad language. Referring again to Collier's (2011) "recurring empirical regularities," the purpose of the case studies presented in chapters 2 and 3 is to identify the framing patterns that occur consistently, relate these to their initial source, and describe why these phenomena resulted in the differences between the role of the courts in these two states.

Having outlined the theoretical approach on offer here as well as discussing the choice of abortion policy in New York and New Jersey as appropriate for answering the question at the heart of this inquiry—that is, what factors will tend to lead courts to take on the primary role of policy development in a given issue area—the following analysis will be divided into four main sections. The following chapter will present the case study of abortion in New

Jersey, with an emphasis on the decisions and interactions of the various institutions of government. The goal of this portion of the study will be to assist in identifying what role each branch played, how they responded to each other's actions, and the ways in which institutional first movement and reinforcing sequences largely shaped the behavior of the judiciary. Chapter 3 will be structured in much the same way; though will of course focus on the development of abortion policy in New York. To further refine the theory presented in this book, as well as offer some context outside of the abortion issue in these two states, chapter 4 will present four somewhat abbreviated case studies of the development of capital punishment policy in New York and New Jersey as well as abortion in Minnesota and Wisconsin. Finally, chapter 5 will synthesize the conclusions drawn from the preceding case studies, address some of the issues that remain from the analysis of New York and New Jersey, and suggest some future areas of research. In addition, the final chapter will also discuss in greater detail the implications of the present study for the separation of powers approach, as well as our understanding of judicial policy making more generally. Throughout the following chapters, though, the overall focus will be an explanation of why the theoretical approach described here—that the initial institutional location of policy change will influence the issue framing of abortion adopted by the courts, and consequently their role as passive or active participants in the policy making process—provides the best explanation for the divergent role of the judiciary in New York and New Jersey in this area.

NOTES

1. A more complete description of these is offered later in this chapter.
2. Indeed, an extensive body of case law exists in this issue area including landmark U.S. Supreme Court rulings such as *Roe v. Wade*, *City of Akron v. Akron Center for Reproductive Health*, *Webster v. Reproductive Health Services*, *Planned Parenthood of Southeastern Pennsylvania v. Casey*, and *Gonzales v. Carhart*, to list only a few examples.
3. Nevertheless, these demographic and political variables have been considered in a number of regression analyses using the involvement of the courts or legislatures of New York and New Jersey as dependent variables. No significant relationship was demonstrated. Copies of all regression analyses and details regarding dependent and independent variables are available by request from the author.
4. This is not, in any way, meant to suggest that one or the other interpretive view was more or less likely to be found in either jurisdiction across cases or time frames. Quite the contrary, in the sense that the argument advanced here is that a particular interpretive framework will be influenced more by the actions of the other branches as well as early rulings than by the presumptive commitments to certain approaches to constitutional interpretation on the part of judges or justices of a particular court.
5. A point of clarification is warranted here. While ideas themselves can be, and indeed sometimes are, regarded as "institutions" in their own right (see Bell 2012 for a more thorough discussion of this), the term as it is used throughout this work refers to institutions as the particular branch of government at issue unless otherwise specified.
6. The term "political" as it is understood throughout this study has two somewhat different, though related, meanings. In terms of issue framing, it refers to concepts loosely defined as

"policy processes" and ideas such as the feasibility of implementation and public welfare. At the same time, it also makes reference to "political" institutions, specifically the executive and legislative branches. This distinction will be made explicit where differentiation is relevant to the larger point.

7. Indeed, this is precisely what we do find. The Oklahoma legislature has, as of this writing, banned late-term abortions and abortions post-viability with a health and life exception, requires abortions be performed in hospitals, bans Medicare funding, requires parental consent and notice, and requires pre-abortion counseling (Guttmacher Institute 2013), with few of these provisions having been litigated. Conversely, Florida has seen a host of litigation on the abortion issue (see *In Re T.W* [1989], *Florida v. Barquet* [1972], *Operation Rescue v. Women's Health Center* [1993], *North Florida Women's Health and Counseling Services v. Florida* [2003], and *Florida v. Kawana* [2003]).

8. The South African Constitution, for example, is the first, and to date only, to explicitly protect the rights of LGBT individuals.

9. See, for example, *Japan v. Sakata et al*; Sup. Ct. G.B. 1959, *Japan v. Sakane et. al.*; Sup. Ct. G.B. 1969, *Uno et. al. v. Minister of Agriculture and Forestry*; Sup. Ct., 1st P.B. 1982, *Ito et. al. v. Minister of Agriculture and Forestry*; Sapporo Dist. Ct. 1973, *inter alia*, and *S. v. Makwanyane* 1995 SALR 391, *S v. Williams* 1995 SALR 632, *Carmichele v. Minister of Safety and Security*, 2001 SA 938, *Lesbian and Gay Equality Project v. Minister of Home Affairs*, 2006 SALR 524, *J v. Director-General, Department of Home Affairs*, 2003 (5) SALR 621, *inter alia*.

10. Lest these examples be thought absurd, it bears noting that even a policy controversy as iconically domestic as the civil rights debate of the 1950s and 1960s did on several occasions invoke international considerations related to the Cold War (Dudziak 2004).

11. It is worth noting here that the frames described throughout this work refer to overall issue conceptualizations and not particular legal doctrinal views.

12. For the most part, these include the executive, legislative, and judicial branches of state government, though on some occasions, these will be meaningfully influenced by the actions of federal-level institutions, most importantly the U.S. Supreme Court and the Second and Third Circuit Courts of Appeal. The dynamics of these federal and state interactions, when they occurred, are discussed in much greater detail in chapters 2 and 3.

13. All data in tables 1 and 2 are from the Decennial U.S. Census. Some definitions, such as "urban" and "rural" classifications, were changed between 1990 and 2000. Additionally, questions have not necessarily been consistent across decades either, with the "Hispanic" option, for example, being added to the short form version in 1980.

14. Specifically, California, Connecticut, Hawaii, Illinois, Oregon, Vermont, and Washington.

15. See figures 1.2 and 1.3 for a comparison of both systems.

Chapter Two

The Development of Abortion Policy in New Jersey

Litigation treating the abortion question is far from a unique phenomenon. Both state and federal courts have issued a wide array of rulings on the constitutionality of restrictions on the procedure, injunctions against clinic protesters, and other controversies touching on reproductive rights. In this sense, New Jersey is far from an outlier, though the judiciary in that state was particularly inclined to strike down statutes limiting access to abortion services.[1] While New York also saw a number of court decisions on the issue, these never meaningfully altered the choices that elected officials had made. Indeed, virtually all of the key decisions concerning abortion in the Garden State, as well as other states and the country at large, from Medicaid funding for the procedure, to parental notification, to bans on so-called "partial-birth abortions," were made by the seven justices of the New Jersey Supreme Court. In some cases, New Jersey represents something similar to what Lovell (2003), Graber (1993), and Whittington (2007) predict in terms of policy making around a controversial and potentially politically damaging issue such as abortion, though in others this account also appears insufficient. While elected officials often sought to avoid formulating clear policy decisions and instead left the task of policy making in this area to the unelected branch, there were clearly other periods during which the legislature seemed genuine in its efforts to regulate abortion, though the courts continued to play a highly active role.

The New Jersey case nonetheless evinces some differences in how the path of judicial predominance came to be established when contrasted with the absence of this role for the courts in New York. Perhaps the most obvious of these is likely attributable to the nature of the two branches themselves. While elected officials are able to initiate policy change more or less at their own discretion—they can choose to include or exclude a particular issue from their agenda at specific points in time—the courts are by nature reactive and, while both states' High Courts can decline to review specific cases, are only able to involve themselves in the policy making process once litigation is begun by an outside party. In addition, judges are bound by several features unique to the judicial branch that impose some constraints on that institution that are not present among legislators, including adherence to precedent, the possibility of a higher court overturning a given decision, and questions related to their lack of electoral accountability.[2] In terms of the former, this suggests that legislators may have more control over when in a particular sequence they become involved in policy making, as was the case when lawmakers in New York essentially preempted the courts in 1970 with passage of the liberalization law. The latter, however, did not seem to have any meaningful impact on how judges treated the abortion issue in New Jersey as most of the major decisions were handed down by the state Supreme Court and were not appealable to their federal counterpart. Nevertheless, the fact remains that in practical terms, the courts in both states were similarly situated in that litigation had begun to challenge existing abortion laws—the only difference being that the legislature in New York acted while that same institution in New Jersey did not. The point here is that it seems highly likely that the law in the former would have been struck down just as it was in the latter, meaning that policy change would have taken place in both states one way or the other. For the purposes of the theoretical framework proposed here, the reasons why one institution initiated this change is somewhat less important than what this first movement meant over time as subsequent policy development took place. Indeed, one of the main features of the theory described in the introduction to this work is the importance of the actions—or inactions—of the other branches for the behavior of the courts. So while change may occur somewhat differently if first undertaken by the courts rather than the elected branches, it is the location of the change itself that is most important here.

A final point bears emphasizing here related to how the New Jersey case differs to some extent from that in New York. Consistent with the theoretical framework on offer here, the major difference between the two states in terms of explaining the differential role of the courts in abortion policy development is the institution that was responsible for initiating change. Because of the differences between how courts and legislatures create policy discussed above, though, this begs the question of whether an unwillingness on the part of the elected branches is sufficient to require an active role for the courts. The answer, at least as it relates to the abortion question in New York and New Jersey, would seem to be a qualified yes, depending on the particular aspect of this issue that is being considered. In terms of the legality of the procedure, there would seem to be little doubt that absent legislative action, the courts would eventually create policy in this area, as evidenced by the *Abramowicz* case in New York, *Young Women's Christian Association of Princeton, New Jersey v. Kugler*, discussed below, and ultimately *Roe* itself. The same would seem to be true of the clinic protest cases where both states saw considerable litigation related to limits on these activities, though only New York developed a statutory response to the problem. Other issues, such as parental involvement laws, financing restrictions, and late-term abortion bans, however, required legislative action before the courts had an opportunity to create—or fail to alter—policy created by the elected branches. Recalling that the question this study endeavors to answer is under what circumstances courts can be expected to create policy, the fact that the first issue addressed in both states was whether abortion was to be legalized meant that legislative failure to provide an answer necessarily required the courts to play the role of first mover. The argument on offer here is that this first movement, and the frame it helped to establish going forward, was critically important in explaining the passive or active role of the judiciary.

To properly identify what exactly constitutes a legal frame, some parameters should at this point be clarified. The following chapter will highlight the importance of the political frame that came to dominate discourse on and off the court in New York, identified primarily as references to the practical impact of various policies on women's health, emotionally charged appeals on both sides—whether in the form of warnings about "back-alley" abortions in the case of pro-choice interests or allusions to eugenics or simply the killing of what they considered a human being by those on the pro-life side—or, in the case of the judiciary, an insistence that the issue was one best resolved by the elected branches. Identifying a legal frame, however, is somewhat more difficult, particularly in the case of state Supreme Court decisions, which would seem by their very nature to necessarily speak in a "legal" tone. Nevertheless, two themes that are apparent throughout the following case study suggest that actors within the policy making community in New Jersey as a whole viewed abortion in much more legalistic terms than their counterparts in New York. The first of these is the broadest and can be found in a focus on what might be termed "constitutional" principles. For example, a judicial opinion highlighting due process or equal protection violations clearly has its origin in the language and concepts of the law, in particular the state and federal constitutions. While it may seem axiomatic that judges would think and speak in these terms, a comparison with the focus of the opinions from the New York case suggest that this is not necessarily the case. Indeed, in the major rulings from that state's Court of Appeals, references to these principles were often conspicuously absent, omitted in favor of arguments emphasizing proper institutional roles and the impropriety of the courts addressing the abortion question. In addition, this focus on legal concepts was found consistently across institutions in New Jersey, with lawmakers and executive branch officials also tending to frame their arguments in the language of rights and constitutional protections.

The second theme that is found throughout the following analysis, and suggests that a much more legal frame was apparent throughout the forty years of policy development covered here, concerns references to concepts that clearly originated in the courts. Perhaps the most obvious of these, specifically as it relates to the abortion issue, is the "undue burden" test developed by Justice O'Connor that formed the basis of the *Casey* decision in 1992. Three major cases were decided in New Jersey following the landmark U.S. Supreme Court ruling, two of these from that state's High Court, all repeatedly referenced O'Connor's standard. Similarly, in several decisions concerning clinic obstruction cases, the Court relied heavily on the "time, place, and manner" test first articulated in *Cox v. New Hampshire* (1941) and subsequently applied in a number of abortion protest decisions from the U.S. Supreme Court.[3] Finally, concepts such as "suspect classes" and statutory overbreadth undoubtedly had their origins in the legal community and are found throughout the major abortion decisions in New Jersey. Again, while a reliance on these types of considerations and understandings may not be terribly surprising given the nature of the common law system, these same frames were surprisingly absent from the landmark New York cases, as well as many of the federal decisions discussed below. By way of example, many of the clinic obstruction cases focused much more on the behavior of the protesters themselves in determining whether the injunctions were proper remedies, while the New Jersey Supreme Court instead relied on the more abstract ideas of "time, place, and manner" considerations. The point, in any event, is that the identification of a legal frame as it is understood here can best be understood both as the absence of deference to the choices of the elected branches, and the use of concepts that clearly had their genesis in the legal community. In addition, these frames were prominent not only in the courts but in the public statements of elected officials as well.

This combination of timing and the adoption of a largely legal rhetorical framework, and its importance in accounting for the predominance of the courts as policy makers in New Jersey is apparent throughout the following case study. Put simply, by the time the policy making community in New Jersey had become active in altering the state's abortion laws, whether through the courts or through the actions of the elected branches, the field of potential "knowledge claims" had been significantly influenced by the *Roe* decision in 1973. The argument on offer here is that this fact made the framing of reproductive rights as a legal issue much more likely than was the case in New York. Beyond this, however, the following chapter also reveals that the justices of the New Jersey Supreme Court not only adopted a decidedly more legal narrative, but also developed a uniquely local approach to the question that differed markedly from much of the jurisprudence at the federal level. Specifically, while most of the debate on the federal bench centered on concerns related to substantive due process, issues associated with equal protection violations played a much more central role at the state level. This is not to say that ideas and understandings originating from federal cases did not influence or were not considered by members of New Jersey's High Court; indeed, they made frequent references to issues such as undue burdens and time, place, and manner considerations. These approaches instead tended to supplement rather than steer the series of decisions reached by that state's judiciary. So while *Roe* undoubtedly played a highly significant role in shaping how abortion was to be understood in New Jersey to a much greater extent than in New York, the truly critical moments in abortion policy development in the former were the early state court decisions that were to be so crucial in establishing and subsequently reinforcing the primacy of that institution in setting policy on reproductive rights.

This chapter will begin with an overview of the major events that took place in New Jersey between 1970 and 2010 dealing with abortion and the policy making process that resulted in laws very similar to those found in New York. Indeed, New Jersey saw seven substantive areas of policy development in this area either in the courts or via elected lawmakers; specifically, the legality of the procedure itself, parental involvement laws, limits on abortion funding, injunctions against clinic protesters, regulations regarding where abortions could be performed, access to RU-486, and late-term abortion bans, with only the last of these being absent in New York. Throughout this narrative, particular attention will be paid to the critical moments throughout the policy making process as well as the rhetorical frames employed by members of all three branches of state government. This fact is central to the theory proposed here as it is the dialogue between the courts and the elected branches that to a large extent explains why the "legal" view informed the issue conceptualizations adopted by judges in New Jersey to a much greater extent than those in New York. Finally, a brief overview of these developments in the context of federal courts will be offered.

THE EARLY YEARS

New Jersey, along with the other thirteen colonies, had no laws dealing with abortion at the time of the founding, and it was not until well into the nineteenth century that legislation began to be enacted in this area. New Jersey's legislature first passed a law in 1849 making it a misdemeanor for "any person or persons maliciously or without lawful justification, with intent to cause and procure the miscarriage of a woman then pregnant with child, shall administer to her, prescribe for her, or advise or direct her to take or swallow any poison, drug, medicine, or noxious thing," as well as banning other forms of abortion "without lawful justification" (Nix. Dig. 177, § 103). New Jersey's law was unremarkable for the time, and very much in line with others that had been passed by state legislatures in the first half of the nineteenth century in that it sought primarily to address the harm caused to women as a result of the often dangerous substances that were commonly employed to produce abortions. Perhaps foreshadowing the role the court would later play in the abortion debate in the following century, the New Jersey Supreme Court heard a case later that year dealing with abortion—though it did not mention the statute passed a mere month before the case was decided—and ruled, in *State v. Eliakim Cooper*, that an abortion performed before "quickening" was not an indictable offense. This view was well within the legal mainstream of the time, with the "quickening" distinction being common in many American and British laws and court opinions (Mohr 1979).

The 1849 law was litigated following the *Cooper* decision, though it was not directly challenged. In 1858, the New Jersey Supreme Court heard the case of *State v. Leonard Murphy*, which presented the question of whether the law forbidding the advisement of a woman to administer an abortifacient had been violated if the woman had not in fact ingested the substance. The court found that, while the law lacked specificity, it clearly was the intent of its drafters to ban not only the ingestion of "noxious poisons" but also the advisement to do such, thereby affirming the conviction of Mr. Murphy. Perhaps more interestingly, however, the court in its *Murphy* decision reiterated that it understood the primary objective of the law to be the protection of women from the potentially dangerous effects of abortifacient drugs, writing that "[t]he design of the statute was not to prevent the procuring of abortions, so much as to guard the health and life of the mother against the consequences of such attempts . . . [The] statute regards her as the victim of crime, not as the criminal; as the object of protection, rather than of punishment" (114, 115). Indeed, the 1849 law did not identify the woman procuring an abortion as guilty of any offense, but instead only persons who advised her to take abortion-causing substances or administered these to her. New Jersey's nineteenth-century law, then, was well in line with the norms of the day (Mohr 1979) and differed little in its intent than that developed in New York in the same era, an understanding well-articulated by the court decisions discussed above.

The 1849 law was amended in 1872 to include a ban on the use of "instrument or means whatever with the like intent [of causing a miscarriage]" (Chapter 337, Public Laws of 1872), though like the previous statute made no mention of the stage of pregnancy at which such abortions were to be proscribed. The state Supreme Court heard another case in 1881 seeking to clarify the meaning of the 1849 statute, this time with the defendant claiming that the law did not apply if the substance administered to a pregnant woman was not capable of producing a miscarriage. In *State v. Herman W. Giedicke* [43 New Jersey Law 86 (1881)], the Court found that any "noxious thing," regardless of its ability to cause a miscarriage, was covered by the abortion statute and its amendment and that the sentence of a $500 fine and two years of hard labor did not constitute cruel and unusual punishment. Interestingly, Justice Scudder, who authored the 1881 decision, also included in his opinion a clarification that the "design of the statute was not so much to prevent the procuring of abortions, however offensive these may be to morals and decency, as to guard the health and life of the female against the consequences of such attempts" (*State v. Herman W. Giedicke* 86). Further clarification of the meaning of New Jersey's abortion statute was also offered in *Adelaide E. Powe v. State* [48 New Jersey Law 34 (1886)] when it was found that knowledge of a woman's pregnancy when administering an abortifacient was not necessary for conviction under the law.[4]

New Jersey had also joined other Northeastern states in passing versions of the infamous "Comstock Laws" in 1868 and 1869, though these were not amended to include references to abortion, as well as contraception, until 1898 (Reagan 1997). Specifically, Chapter 235 of the state's Criminal Code was revised in that year to provide that:

> [a]ny person who, without just cause, shall utter or expose to the view of another, or have in his possession, with intent so to utter or expose to view, or to sell the same, any obscene or indecent book, pamphlet, picture, or other representation, however made; or any instrument, medicine, or other thing, designed or purporting to be designed for the prevention of conception, or the procuring of abortion, or who shall in any wise advertise, or aid, or assist in advertising the same . . . shall be guilty of a misdemeanor (Chapter 235, § 53 {Public Laws of 1898}).

The abortion provisions added to the Comstock Laws in 1898 were never challenged in court; however, two more cases were heard by the New Jersey Supreme Court dealing with abortion in the early twentieth century, neither of which resulted in any substantive change to the statutes passed in the previous eighty years. The first of these was *The State v. Charles D. Mandeville* [88 New Jersey Law 418 (1916)], a case which challenged the conviction of Dr. Mandeville of providing abortifacient substances to his pregnant patient in violation of the 1849 law on the basis that the grand jury had not been averred of the fact that the drugs in question were "noxious" as per the language of the statute. The second case, *State of New Jersey v. William H. Bricker* [98 New Jersey Law 58 (1922)] questioned the admissibility of the dying testimony of a woman who had not survived an attempted abortion as the declaration had not been made under a sense of impending death. In both cases, the conviction of the defendants had been upheld, though neither had challenged either the 1849 abortion law nor the Comstock Law passed in 1898.

THE MODERN ERA AND THE SEEDS OF JUDICIAL PREDOMINANCE

As figure 2.1 reveals, the first alteration to New Jersey's abortion laws came as a result of federal court decisions, most importantly, *Young Women's Christian Association of Princeton, New Jersey v. Kugler* and *Roe v. Wade*. The former struck down the state's nineteenth-century abortion ban on a number of grounds and was subsequently upheld by a Third Circuit Court of Appeals decision in 1974, while the latter of course indirectly invalidated New Jersey's law on the basis of that case's trimester framework. What is perhaps most immediately apparent from this figure, however, is the sheer number of cases addressing the abortion question. Indeed, there are eleven instances of these rulings, eight from state courts, while a mere four laws were passed with three of these ultimately being struck down.[5] All of these cases, with the exception of *Planned Parenthood of NYC v. State*, also represented meaningful policy change. In addition, the state court column is the only one that does not reflect rather protracted periods of inactivity, with the other three containing no less than an eighteen-year gap between major policy movement. The details of each of these events are discussed in much more detail in the following sections, though the overall trend of the dominance of state court action is unmistakable.

Changes to New Jersey's abortion law were not seriously attempted until the late 1960s, around the same time that New York, as well as a number of other states, began rethinking their nineteenth-century statutes with the legislature forming the Crane Commission to report on the possibility of revising the law in 1968 (Waggoner 1970). The result was the drafting of a bill by William Crane, a Bergen County member of the Assembly, which would have allowed abortions in the state in cases of rape or incest, to preserve the health—mental or otherwise—of the woman, and in cases of unmarried women under the age of sixteen. The bill was never brought to a vote, however, and the consensus seemed to be that it would not have passed in either the Senate or Assembly, both of which were firmly controlled by Republicans. In addition, Governor Cahill, who had assumed office just two months before the Crane Commission reported to the legislature, had stated publicly that he would veto any liberalization bill as a violation of his Roman Catholic faith (Sullivan 1970). Indeed, the following year, Cahill's Attorney General issued a directive that state Medicaid funds could not be used to pay for abortions in New York following that state's liberalization bill in 1970 (Washington Post 1971).

Year	Courts (State)	Courts (Federal)	Legislature	Executive
1970				
1971				
1972		Kugler		
1973		Roe v. Wade		
1974			Conscience Law	
1975			Medicaid Ban	
1976	Bridegton			
1977	PP of NYC			
1978				
1979				Byrne Veto
1980				
1981				
1982	Byrne			
1983				
1984				
1985	Cannizzaro			
1986				
1987				
1988				
1989				
1990				
1991	Loce			
1992				
1993				
1994	Felicissimo			
1995				
1996				
1997			Late-Term Ban	Whitman Veto
1998				
1999			Parental Not.	
2000	Farmer	Farmer		
2001				
2002				
2003				
2004				
2005				
2006				
2007	Acuna			
2007				
2008				
2009				
2010				

Figure 2.1. Major Developments by Branch in New Jersey

The same month that Senate and Assembly leaders were deciding whether or not to place Crane's bill on the agenda, the first lawsuit to ever directly challenge New Jersey's law was being brought in federal court, backed by, among other groups, the ACLU and the YWCA (Waggoner 1970). While in 1967 the New Jersey Supreme Court "recommended" that the legislature reconsider the vaguely worded 1849 abortion law, explicitly stating in the opinion that, although the law had to be within the bounds of the constitution, the ultimate decision about where to draw the line should not be "pass[ed] . . . to the judiciary" (*State v. Baird* [50 NJ 378] at 383), it had never actually overturned the statute.[6]

The first major ruling by a court in New Jersey dealing with abortion took place in 1972 when a federal District Court for the District of New Jersey ruled that the state's 1849 law banning the procedure was unconstitutionally vague, violated the right to privacy established in *Griswold*, and impermissibly infringed on a doctor's right to free speech by mandating that the counseling of a woman to obtain an abortion constituted a felony. Specifically, in *Young Women's Christian Association of Princeton, New Jersey v. Kugler*, a three-judge federal District Court panel concluded that the "New Jersey abortion statute, 2A:87-1, is unconstitutionally vague on its face and as applied; that it chills and deters the plaintiff-physicians in the exercise of protected First Amendment activities; and that it violates plaintiff-physicians' rights under the Fourteenth Amendment to freely practice the profession of their choice" (1062). The issue, however, became largely moot the following year with the U.S. Supreme Court's decision in *Roe*, though the Third Circuit Court of Appeals did hear the case in 1974 and upheld the decision of the District Court (see *YWCA v. Kugler* 463 F.2d 203). Perhaps most significantly, this decision, though it addressed a statute authored almost 125 years before the New Jersey legislature would offer another law dealing with abortion rights, took issue primarily with the vague nature of the statute's wording, a finding that would presage many of the court's future rulings on laws restricting abortion access.

Kugler and *Roe* then represent something akin to what Mahoney (2000) calls a "first cause," primarily in terms of the case being the first legal rulings on the matter that directly challenged the status quo.[7] Interestingly, beyond striking down the law itself, the District Court's decision in the former case employed a rationale that would be adopted in most subsequent rulings dealing with a challenge to statutory restrictions on abortion in New Jersey in both state and federal courts, finding the statute unconstitutionally vague. That being said, *Kugler*'s significance for future decisions, at least in terms of the interpretive framework it articulated, was not nearly as important as the state cases that would follow. Indeed, as the subsequent decisions reveal, rather than taking their cues from federal jurisprudence on the matter, the state courts in New Jersey often struck down abortion laws on entirely different grounds than their counterparts in Washington. The fact that *Kugler* was never cited in any of the state-level decisions further speaks to the fact that much of the jurisprudence that developed in New Jersey was at least doctrinally distinct from parallel developments at the federal level, though some of this is likely attributable to the *Roe* decision handed down the following year. It is nevertheless significant that the first change in policy took place in the courts, particularly in contrast to the same developments in New York, a point that will be discussed further regarding the roles of the legislative and executive branches in terms of their conceptualization of the abortion question.

Two themes the opinion in *Kugler* did share with many of the abortion decisions the New Jersey Supreme Court would later issue, though, were a concern for overbroad statutory language and a lack of deference to the legislature. In terms of the former, Judge Furman wrote that the defendant's argument that state prosecutors were often deferring to the medical judgment of physicians was "a frail foundation [for the] contention that the statute has thereby been rendered sufficiently specific to conform to the stringent requirements of the Fourteenth Amendment" (1066). A reluctance to offer the legislature broad latitude was also apparent in the opinion, which argued that "[w]hile the legislature may validly leave the task of determining the scope and contours of broadly worded statutes to the judiciary . . . this is hardly susceptible when the intent or purpose of the statute is left obscure" (1063). The point here being that the first major change to New Jersey's abortion law not only took place within the courts, but was framed, even by this federal level decision, in distinctly legal terms, many of which were to be found in subsequent cases from the state's High Court.

A major theme of legislative action in New Jersey dealing with reproductive rights in the early 1970s might better be understood as inaction. While proposals for reform of the state's abortion laws had been put forward as early as 1968 with the formation and recommendations of the Crane Commission, no bill was ever brought to a vote in either chamber prior to the legalization of abortion nationwide in 1973. Indeed, archival sources from the time repeatedly emphasize the reluctance of lawmakers to address the issue, with one *New York Times* piece quoting Assembly Speaker Thomas Kean admitting that "[n]ot many legislators want to vote on abortion, but they may have to" (Sullivan 1973a), while another cited a claim by the state Attorney General's office that it was "plunging through the legal thicket that has grown up around abortion because of the legislature's unwillingness to deal with a thorny political issue in an election year" (Phalon 1973).

This lack of will on the part of New Jersey lawmakers was evident early in the 1970s when several bills were put forward by members of the Assembly which, even in some cases by their own admission, had no realistic chance of becoming law. Two excellent examples of this can be seen in the Kennedy and Hawkins bills, which were offered as attempts to clarify the state's position on abortion following the *Roe* decision; the former allowing the procedure only in cases where the life of the mother was in danger, while the latter was an almost verbatim copy of the liberal New York statute passed in 1970. Neither, of course, were seen at the time as realistic possibilities for reforming state law as the Kennedy proposal would almost certainly have been ruled unconstitutional, while the liberal Hawkins bill had little support in either chamber and would in any event have been vetoed by Governor Cahill. The reluctance of the legislature to address the matter finally became sufficiently problematic that guidelines on what would or would not be permitted in the state finally fell to the executive, despite repeated requests by the Attorney General for action from the Senate and Assembly. When a bill dealing with abortion finally was passed by both houses in 1974 that allowed hospitals to deny abortion services on moral or religious grounds, it was the first in what would be several examples of legislation that was arguably designed either to be interpreted by the courts or struck down entirely. Specifically, the law was worded in such a way as to encompass all state hospitals, regardless of whether or not they were religiously affiliated, a provision about which Governor Byrne expressed serious reservations, though he did ultimately sign the bill. Borrowing from Lovell's (2003) analysis of labor laws in the late nineteenth and early twentieth centuries in which he considers the omission of amendments that might address constitutional deficiencies in proposed legislation to be reasonable evidence of intent at deferral, we see in the 1974 conscience bill the legislature's refusal to include the McGahn amendment, which would have limited the law's scope to include only sectarian facilities. As discussed below, the early 1970s saw intense pressure on lawmakers by the Catholic Church to oppose abortion and it seems reasonable to suspect that legislators, many of whom represented districts with large Catholic populations but may not have been aware of their constituents' actual policy preferences, had every incentive to bolster their pro-life voting records while being assured the law would be unlikely to survive a court challenge.

Roe did not, however, at least for many in the Garden State, make the legal status of abortion entirely clear. Following the decision, Attorney General Kugler issued another directive instructing state attorneys not to prosecute doctors performing abortions to preserve the life of the woman, adding that "the medical judgment by the physician may be exercised in its broadest sense and in the light of all factors—physical, emotional, psychological, familial, and the woman's age—relevant to the well-being of the patient" (Sullivan 1973a). The Attorney General also added that, according to his reading of the Supreme Court's decision, women did not possess a constitutional right to abortion but that the decision must be concurred with by a physician "based upon the best clinical judgment that an abortion is necessary," though he added that he did not intend to "second guess" decisions of individual doctors (Sullivan 1973a). In this sense, the state's chief law enforcement officer seemed somewhat reluctant to define exactly what would or would not be permitted in New Jersey in terms of abortion access, a sentiment echoed by several top medical executives. Specifically, the executive director of the Medical Society of New Jersey stated that the Attorney General's directive seemed at odds with the "full implications" of the *Roe* decision, which he claimed took into account both the health as well as the "comfort" of the woman (Sullivan 1973a). The president of the New Jersey Hospital Association, for his part, argued that Kugler's use of the term "well-being of the patient" significantly broadened the circumstances under which abortions could be performed beyond the physical health or life of the pregnant woman and was sufficiently in line with the intentions of the Supreme Court's decision (Sullivan 1973a).

Anti-abortion activists, in the face of a legislature clearly reluctant to offer any legislation limiting the practice or challenging the Supreme Court's decision at the margins, shifted their focus from pressuring government officials to attempting to persuade local hospitals not to perform abortions. A series of protests and letter-writing campaigns targeted at state hospitals and led by the New Jersey Right to Life Committee, urged these not to perform the procedure and achieved limited success by convincing at least two non-sectarian hospitals[8] —Riverside Boonton and Newcomb Vineland—to refuse to provide abortion services (Wechsler 1973). The actual impact of this campaign may have been negligible, however, as the state had 140 hospitals at the time with only eighteen, following New Jersey Right to Life's campaign, refusing to perform abortions. Indeed, much was made of the Atlantic City Hospital Board of Governor's decision in May of 1973 to begin providing abortion services, despite intense pressure including a telephone campaign and continuous pickets of their offices by anti-abortion activists, making it the only facility in Southern New Jersey to offer legal abortions (*New York Times* 1973a).

Also in 1973, the ACLU brought a suit in Superior Court that sought to challenge the 1971 directive by the state's Attorney General which denied Medicaid funding for abortions, as well as requiring Bridgeton Hospital Association and Newcomb Vineland to provide the service. The plaintiffs in the case were two women from Cumberland County whom the ACLU claimed were being denied their constitutional right to abortion as the two hospitals in their vicinity did not provide the procedure, while their denial of Medicaid funding further restricted their access to abortions (Boylan 1973). The Superior Court judge ruled in favor of the plaintiffs and ordered the two hospitals to perform the abortions; however, he refused to rule on the Medicaid question, an issue that would be resolved several years later in a separate case. This decision was overturned on appeal, however, only several hours before one of the women was scheduled to undergo the procedure (*New York Times*

1973b). The question of whether nonsectarian hospitals could be compelled to perform abortions was eventually resolved by the New Jersey Supreme Court in the case of *Doe v. Bridgeton Hospital Association* (1976), the first case in which a New Jersey state court addressed the issue of limits to abortion access, when the Court ruled that, despite the status of these facilities as private institutions, the exclusive services they provided as well as the state funds they received made them "quasi-public" and therefore subject to the provisions of the state and federal constitutions. Indeed, the Court wrote that the "federal constitutional right to an abortion during the first trimester is now well-settled" (490) and could not be abridged by the hospitals serving the relevant counties.

Bridgeton though dealt only peripherally with a challenge to a state law as the case focused primarily on the denial of two Central New Jersey hospitals to offer abortion services. Finding that the facilities were "quasi-public" due to their role as the primary providers of healthcare for the residents of the nearby counties, the state Supreme Court reversed the lower court's holding and mandated that the hospitals must offer the procedure as first trimester abortions were protected under the U.S. Constitution, writing that "[t]he federal constitutional right to an abortion during the first trimester is now well-settled . . . For the state to frustrate that right by its action would be violative of the constitutional guarantee" (at 647). Additionally, while the case, which was originally brought in 1974, was being litigated in the state Superior and Appellate courts, the legislature passed a conscience law allowing individuals and facilities that objected to abortion on moral, philosophical, or religious grounds to refuse such services. On appeal to the state Supreme Court, the respondents asked that the Court include a ruling on this statute on the grounds that it permitted them to refuse abortion services due to the moral convictions of the members of the Board of Trustees of the hospital. While the Court refused to consider the general constitutionality of the conscience law, it did find the law inapplicable to the Bridgeton and Newcomb hospitals as "to empower a non-sectarian non-profit hospital to refuse to permit its facilities to be used for elective abortions would clearly constitute state action" (at 490). The case was eventually appealed to the U.S. Supreme Court, though certiorari was denied, effectively rendering the state Supreme Court's decision the final word on the matter. While *Bridgeton* represents an important case insofar as it was the state Supreme Court's first direct ruling on the abortion question, as well as signaling the Court's willingness to hand down decisions supportive of abortion rights, it did not directly address the constitutionality of a state law treating the matter, and it was not until six years later when the question of Medicaid funding for abortion reached the High Court that it would finally deal with this question directly.

As mentioned above, the legislature in 1974 passed a conscience protection law, which was signed by Governor Byrne, and offered a relatively broad definition of what individuals and institutions were to be covered by the statute. Specifically, the bill mandated that no individual "shall be required to perform or assist in the performance of an abortion or sterilization" and that no hospital or other medical facility would be required to provide procedures or services for such operations (N.J.S.A.2A:65A-1). Interestingly, Governor Byrne had expressed serious reservations about the law, based largely on the broad language of the bill that allowed any medical facility, including nonsectarian ones, to refuse abortion services, and even went so far as to suggest that he doubted the statute's ability to withstand a constitutional challenge. The Governor ultimately did sign the bill, though, claiming that refusing to do so would "frustrate the wishes of our citizens" (Waggoner 1974a). The potential constitutional difficulties related to the inclusion of all medical facilities in the law were not lost on members of the legislature either as Senator Joseph McGahn, a Democrat from Atlantic City, during the floor debate leading up to the vote in the upper chamber proposed an amendment which would have narrowed the scope of the bill to include only religiously affiliated facilities, though the amendment was ultimately defeated (Waggoner 1974a). These concerns were indeed well-founded as the New Jersey Supreme Court ultimately did strike down the portion of the law that allowed nonsectarian hospitals to refuse abortion services in the *Bridgeton* decision, though the other provisions of the statute were never challenged.

As was the case in many states following the *Roe* decision by the U.S. Supreme Court, the controversy over abortion in New Jersey soon moved to the question of whether or not state funds could be used to cover the procedure for those eligible for Medicaid. The issue arose initially in the form of a lawsuit on behalf of sixteen women who had obtained abortions in New York in 1971, before the procedure was legal in New Jersey, and sought reimbursement from the state. The claim was denied in Superior Court, a decision that was subsequently upheld by the Appellate Division in a 1976 opinion delivered by a three-judge panel. The plaintiffs in the case had argued that denial of the funds amounted to an equal protection violation as the policy had a disproportionate effect on poor women and that the refusal to reimburse the women unconstitutionally infringed on the right to abortion guaranteed in *Roe*, though these claims were rejected by the Appellate Division panel. The case was finally appealed to the New Jersey Supreme Court, which also refused to order the reimbursement sought by the plaintiffs.

A ban on Medicaid funding for abortions did pass the State Senate by a vote of 22–14 in 1974, though the Assembly version of the bill was stalled in committee and never made it to the floor for a vote that year (New York Times 1974a). The lower house did bring the bill to a vote the following year, however, and passed the ban on state financing of nontherapeutic abortions by a margin of 46–18. The new law was immediately challenged by the New Jersey chapter of the ACLU on the grounds that it violated both the federal Social Security Act as well as the Fourteenth Amendment's equal protection guarantee. In terms of the former, the suit alleged that the Act "defines permissible medical assistance to include 'medical care, or any other type of remedial care . . . furnished by licensed practitioners . . . whether furnished in the office, the patient's home, a hospital, or a skilled nursing home or elsewhere'" (Waggoner 1976), while the New Jersey law, as well as denying Medicaid funding, also mandated that abortions be conducted only in hospitals. The ACLU suit also claimed, as it had in its challenge dealing with out-of-state abortions, that denying Medicaid funding for the procedure made an unconstitutional distinction between poor women and those who could afford to pay for their abortions privately. The initial ruling in the federal District Court in Trenton, handed down by Judge George Barlow, temporarily restrained enforcement of the law and set February 2, 1976, as the date for a full hearing and an opportunity for the state to demonstrate why the law should not be further enjoined (Waggoner 1976). The hearing was not held until March, however, when Judge Barlow issued a permanent injunction against enforcement of the law until the U.S. Supreme Court issued a ruling on the constitutionality of bans on Medicaid funding of abortion (Waggoner 1977a). Such a ruling did indeed come the following year when the Court handed down its *Maher* decision in 1977 and Judge Barlow lifted the injunction in light of the new precedent (Waggoner 1977b).

The Medicaid funding ban is also instructive in revealing the issue framing that seemed to have already taken root in the state following the *Roe* decision. Following the bill's passage out of the Committee on Institutions, Health, and Welfare by a 3–1 vote, the lone dissenter, Senator Alexander J. Menza (D-Union County), was quoted as claiming that the "Legislature is deliberately moving a series of bills that will effectively do away with a woman's right to an abortion. It's just another attempt to erode the Supreme Court's decision" (*New York Times* 1974b). By the same token, Senator Martin Greenberg (D-Essex County) decried the bill following its passage in the upper house as "pick[ing] and choos[ing] between those who have rights and those who don't," while fellow Democrat and Senate Majority Leader Matthew Feldman stated that "whether you are pro-abortion or anti-abortion is quite beside the point . . . [as the bill is] clearly unconstitutional" (Waggoner 1974b). Indeed, a tendency to speak in terms of rights and constitutional considerations was not limited to opponents of the bill, with Senator Anthony Scardino (D-Bergen County), a supporter of the measure arguing that "[n]o one is denying them anything . . . they still have their right to have an abortion" (*New York Times* 1974b). To be sure, not all members of the state's legislature spoke in terms of abortion in constitutional or rights terms—the bill's sponsor, Senator Joseph Merlino (D-Mercer County) claimed that "having [Medicaid] pay for abortions is perverse. Abortions cannot be said to save life. If anything, they destroy it" (Waggoner 1974b)—though the fact remains that many in the elected branches, regardless of their position on the issue, seemed considerably more inclined to employ language taking a decidedly legal tone. In this sense, the legislature was clearly taking many of its cues from the "sponsoring interpretive community" of the judiciary, in this case the U.S. Supreme Court.

The foundation for what would culminate in the Court's landmark *Byrne* decision was laid in 1977 when it agreed to hear the case of *Planned Parenthood of New York City v. State*, where the Division of Medical Assistance and Health Services' decision not to fund the out-of-state abortions of 550 New Jersey women was challenged on federal Equal Protection grounds, as well as a violation of Title XIX of the Social Services Act. Judge Bischoff, delivering the opinion of a unanimous Appellate Court the previous year, responded to this claim by writing that:

> [W]e underscore the plain fact that the right of the women in question to have abortions in the first trimester of pregnancy is not here involved, for all the abortions involved have been performed. Nor are we confronted with a claim that the needy or disadvantaged are entitled to have the State assume the burden of providing them with abortions should they desire to have them . . . All that is involved is the claim of plaintiff, a New York clinic, that it is entitled to be paid for its services out of New Jersey Medicaid funds (*Planned Parenthood of New York City v. State of New Jersey* 138 [N.J. Super. 450] at 454).

The 1976 ruling also rejected the claim that the *Roe* decision ought to apply retroactively, citing *State v. Nash* [64 N.J. 464, 470 (1974)], which had laid out a three-part test considering (1) the degree to which the rule was furthered by retroactivity, (2) the level of reliance which had been placed on the old rule by its administrators, and (3) the implications of a retroactive application on the administration of justice. Finally, the Appeals Court highlighted that the plaintiffs in the suit had no reasonable expectation at the time they procured their abortions that these would be reimbursed by New Jersey's Medicaid fund.

The case was eventually appealed to the New Jersey Supreme Court and was consolidated with a number of other similar cases where a total of 550 Medicaid-eligible women who had obtained abortions in New York prior to 1973 sought reimbursement from the state. In *Planned Parenthood of New York City* the Court upheld the decision of the Appellate Division panel, though a somewhat wider array of questions were addressed by the Supreme Court. Specifically, the appellants again argued that the decision in *Roe* should be applied retroactively, that abortions were not illegal in New Jersey at the time that the women obtained the services in New York, that federal statutes require reimbursement, and that denial of the funds violated the equal protection clause of the Fourteenth Amendment. The Court rejected all four claims on the basis that (1) prior holdings dealing with the retroactive applicability of rulings had found that these applied only in criminal cases, and not in instances where monetary reimbursement was sought, (2) no court decision had been reached or statute passed in New Jersey prior to 1973 that legalized nontherapeutic abortions, (3) the federal mandate that states provide Medicaid funding for services applied only to procedures that were legal and commonly practiced in the issuing state, and (4) the U.S. Supreme Court's decision in *Maher v. Roe* (1977) had found that indigence alone could not be considered a suspect class and that therefore there had been no equal protection violation in the present case. Interestingly, the Court did however acknowledge that an equal protection claim might be sustainable under the New Jersey State Constitution, and that its decision should not be interpreted as a judgment on the ban on Medicaid funding for nontherapeutic abortions that had been passed by the state legislature in 1975.

Justice Pashman's concurring opinion in particular suggested that such a guarantee might be sustainable under a similar provision of the state Constitution. Much as Justice Harlan's dissenting opinion in *Plessy v. Fergusson* has been understood by some scholars (see Lawrence 1995; Schmidt 2008; *inter alia*) to have helped lay the groundwork for the Court's eventual rejection of the separate but equal doctrine in *Brown v. Board of Education*, Justice Pashman's opinion in *Planned Parenthood of NYC* served to presage the New Jersey Supreme Court's ruling in *Right to Choose v. Byrne*. Indeed, Pashman wrote that "[T]he [present] case is not a proper vehicle for deciding whether the equal protection guarantees in the New Jersey Constitution include the right to decide whether to carry a pregnancy to term unburdened by the intrusion of state economic incentives designed to induce desired behavior" (61). While agreeing with the majority's reasoning that *Maher* was controlling and that the U.S. Constitution did not afford indigent women a right to abortion funding, Pashman went on to write that "it is noteworthy that with respect to significant rights, New Jersey's version of equal protection may be more exacting than the traditional rational basis test used in federal cases when a non-fundamental interest is affected" (61). In addition, just as the U.S. Supreme Court had not made mention of Justice Harlan's dissent in *Brown*, the New Jersey High Court also failed to reference Pashman's opinion in its 1977 ruling.[9]

As state financing for abortions was making its way through the court system in New Jersey, the state joined Louisiana, Missouri, Indiana, and Minnesota in passing a bill requesting that Congress establish a constitutional convention with the goal of securing a "right-to-life" amendment (Waldron 1977a). Indeed, the bill passed the Senate by a wide margin of 27–6 amid intense pressure from pro-life groups who had bombarded the legislature with mail, telephone calls, and nearly round-the-clock protests at the Capitol. Opponents of the measure argued that such a convention would have the potential to alter a number of provisions in the Constitution as it would be nearly impossible to limit delegates to focusing on a single issue (Waldron 1977a). The bill had been supported by a national pro-life group called Americans for a Constitutional Convention, which argued that, because Congress seemed unwilling to act in order to pass a right-to-life amendment, a more productive strategy would be a state-by-state approach aimed at garnering the two-thirds of states necessary for assembling such a convention (Waldron 1977b). While the requisite number of states have never passed bills calling for a constitutional convention—of any kind—the possibility seemed at least realistic enough in the late 1970s that a surprisingly large number of state lawmakers seemed to take the issue seriously. In any event, the passage of the bill in New Jersey seems to have been an almost entirely political move with little risk to legislators seeking to appeal to pro-life constituents and interest groups.

While the ban on Medicaid funding for abortions remained intact into 1979, a number of cases that year had begun to chip away at the law, challenging it on a number of grounds and on behalf of a wide array of plaintiffs.[10] The first such case involved a Newark woman who sought state financing for an abortion on the basis that she feared her child would be born with serious and potentially life-threatening birth defects, with Superior Court Judge David Furman finding that the state's limit on such financing only in cases where the life of the mother was endangered was overly narrow. Later that year, the same judge ordered that Medicaid funds be provided to finance the abortion of a twelve-year-old rape victim in Camden; however, Judge Furman also ruled against the claims of two pregnant women from New Brunswick who were receiving benefits from New Jersey's Aid to Dependent Children program (Waggoner 1978b). The New Jersey Supreme Court weighed in on the matter shortly after the Superior Court decision and refused to set aside Judge Furman's ruling, though Chief Justice Hughes did not address the broader question of the constitutionality of the state's Medicaid ban, saying that more litigation on the matter was needed. Interestingly, the Court did take the opportunity to clarify that it did not view the state's interest in the statute as one related to fiscal concerns, but rather as addressing "the moral issue of the state paying for something so many people think is wrong" (Waldron 1978).

Judge Furman did finally strike down New Jersey's Medicaid funding ban as a violation of federal law in January of 1979 in a class action suit brought on behalf of a number of Medicaid-eligible women, including the New Brunswick women whose claims had been denied the previous year. Several members of the state legislature that year also proposed a bill that would have been one of the most restrictive in the country and included provisions requiring that parents or guardians of girls under eighteen be notified before they obtained an abortion, prohibiting the use of saline solutions in the procedure as well as banning any abortion after fetal viability, and requiring women to sign forms before undergoing an abortion demonstrating that they had been informed of the physical and psychological damage that might result after the procedure. The bill was sponsored by Assemblyman Thomas Deverin of Carteret and Senator Joseph Maressa of Atco, both Democrats, and was referred out of both the Assembly and Senate committees that first considered it (Waldron 1979). Another bill requiring only that women be informed of the risks of abortion was proposed by Assemblywoman Mildred Barry Garvin, Democrat of East Orange, though it never made its way out of committee (Waldron 1979). Despite the fact that the Deverin-Maressa bill was widely believed to have the support of a majority in both Houses of the New Jersey legislature (Waldron 1979), it was never brought to a vote, though some of its provisions would later be debated in a more piecemeal fashion in the following years.

Indeed, a similar bill did pass the state Senate in November of 1979 by a margin of 27–9 that mandated that women seeking abortions wait twenty-four hours after offering their "informed consent" and also required parental notification before the procedure could be performed on a minor. The Assembly had passed essentially the same piece of legislation in the previous session in a 51–17 vote; however, the Senate version had made several changes to this bill that required concurrence from the Assembly but, like the Deverin-Maressa bill, was never brought to a vote there (Davis and Wycliff 1979a). Likewise, a bill had passed the Assembly in June of that year that would have made it a criminal offense, punishable by up to ten years in prison, for the killing of an infant who had survived an abortion (Davis and Wycliff 1979b), though again the measure never made it to the floor for a vote in the Senate. The two Houses finally did pass a measure in December of 1979 requiring a twenty-four-hour waiting period after the signing of a consent form for women before proceeding with an abortion, prohibiting the procedure in clinics after the twelfth week of pregnancy, requiring parental notification before an abortion could be performed on a minor, and some additional reporting requirements (Assembly Bill No. 1285 [3rd OCR]). Originally, the bill had also declared the state's position to be that life began at conception; however a Senate amendment had struck that portion of the statute, a change that was eventually agreed to by the Assembly (Waldron 1979b). The bill was ultimately vetoed by Governor Byrne (Waldron 1980) who indicated that he did not believe that the law was constitutional and no serious attempt was ever made to override the veto, despite the fact that the measure had passed both Houses with well over the two-thirds required. As with the Medicaid ban, comments by lawmakers following passage of the package bill in 1979 again highlighted that those in the elected branches continued to view the abortion issue as a constitutional question. Senator Feldman, as he had five years earlier, spoke out against the law, arguing that "[t]he Supreme Court has told us that a woman has an absolute right to an abortion during the first two trimesters . . . [it] does not give us the right to create unnecessary obstacles which infringe upon the woman's right to privacy" (Sullivan 1979).

The message that accompanied the veto is instructive inasmuch as it revealed very clearly the "legal" frame through which Byrne appeared to view the abortion question. The Governor wrote, for example, that "I feel it inappropriate for me to approve a bill which will substantially impair a woman's constitutionally recognized right to privacy in the matter of abortion" (1). Further elaborating on these concerns, Byrne went on to write "there are still questions about the constitutionality of the bill. After careful consideration, I have concluded that the cumulative effect of the provisions of Assembly Bill No. 1285 would not be to regulate reasonably but rather to erode substantially the right of a woman to choose to have an abortion in this state" (1). Finally, the Governor took issue with the bill's conflict with existing state law, arguing that "[o]ther areas of concern include the procedure for parental notification, the twenty-four hour waiting period and the requirement that all abortions after the twelfth week be performed in a hospital. This latter requirement is in direct conflict with the pertinent regulations of the State Department of Health and the Board of Medical Examiners which permit licensed independent clinics to perform abortions" (2). While the message made several passing references to policy concerns regarding the likely impact of the parental notification provision on the health of minor women and the chilling effect of some of the reporting requirements, the overall theme of Byrne's veto was based on what may fairly be considered legal issues. The point again is that the rhetorical framework adopted by the Governor was one more closely related to the interpretive community of the courts than it was to what might be expected from elected officials.[11]

The Medicaid funding ban was finally struck down by the Court, which did ultimately adopt the course that Pashman had suggested in *Planned Parenthood of NYC* and considered the ban on Medicaid funding of abortion in light of the state constitution in the 1982 case of *Right to Choose v. Byrne*. In a direct challenge to the state's law that began in 1979, the Court found that the denial of Medicaid funds for therapeutic abortions in which the health of the mother was threatened amounted to a violation of the state Constitution's Equal Protection guarantee in Article I, Section I, though the majority refused to extend this right to women seeking elective abortions. Specifically, Justice Pollock wrote for the majority that "[t]he right to choose whether to have an abortion, however, is a fundamental right of all pregnant women, including those entitled to Medicaid reimbursement for necessary medical treatment" (305). *Byrne* is notable for its heavy reliance on "legal" reasoning, again in contrast to the tone found in many of the landmark cases in New York. By way of example, the majority in that case argued that "[a]s to that group of women [to whom the statute denied Medicaid financing], the challenged statute discriminates between those for whom medical care is necessary for childbirth and those for whom an abortion is medically necessary" (305). Furthermore, Pollock wrote that "[b]y granting funds when life is at risk, but withholding them when health is endangered, the statute denies equal protection to those women entitled to necessary medical services under Medicaid" (306). The Court in *Byrne*, then, was making a clear and forceful case for an understanding of abortion as a "fundamental right" that the state was bound to respect.

Pollock also wrote in terms of "equal protection" for women dependent on Medicaid, something the federal courts had refused to do, and was wary of a statute that discriminated between women seeking abortion and those opting to carry their pregnancies to term. Much as Judge Furman had ten years earlier in *Kugler*, the Court in *Byrne* also evinced an unwillingness to offer the executive and legislative branches much latitude in dictating access to the procedure. Specifically, Pollock wrote that these "two branches properly enjoy wide latitude in making fiscal decisions, but the State may not use its treasury to persuade a poor woman to sacrifice her health by remaining pregnant. Statutes such as N.J.S.A. 30:4D-6.1 'can be understood only as an attempt to achieve with carrots what government is forbidden to achieve with sticks'" (308). Finally, while the majority refused to invalidate the law entirely on the basis of its overbreadth, it did interpret the statute in a much more expansive way than it had originally been written. Concluding the opinion, Pollock writes that "N.J.S.A. 30:4D-6.1 violates equal protection of the laws under the New Jersey Constitution by limiting funds to abortions medically necessary to preserve the mother's life. We construe that statute to require Medicaid funding of all abortions that are medically necessary to preserve the mother's life or health" (318). To the extent that it is possible to identify "interpretive communities," it would seem that the norms and discursive frameworks expressed in the above quotes are those most closely associated with the courts, placing little emphasis on the prerogative of the elected branches to choose among policy options.

While the Court made it clear that Medicaid funding was only mandated for "medically necessary" abortions, it is worth reiterating that following a Chancery Court decision overturning the ban on Medicaid funding of abortions in 1979 (165 N.J. Super. 443), the state Department of Human Services had issued guidelines articulating what this term was to mean that encompassed an extremely broad range of considerations, which, in practice, allowed for state funding for eligible women for virtually any abortion to which a doctor consented. It seems highly unlikely that the justices of the state Supreme Court were unaware of these guidelines and were conscious of the fact that this ruling would in practical terms mandate Medicaid assistance for any qualifying women seeking to terminate their pregnancies. Nevertheless, the majority argued that the state did have a rational interest in protecting potential life and that the purpose of the Medicaid program was to provide assistance to the indigent for necessary medical care, which did not include elective abortions. As he had in *Planned Parenthood of NYC*, Justice Pashman again concurred in part and dissented in part in the 1982 ruling, arguing that "[t]here is no medically valid distinction between therapeutic abortions and so-called elective abortions" (320). The lone dissent in the case, authored by Justice O'Hern, essentially echoed the U.S. Supreme Court's opinion in *McRae* that indigence was not a suspect class and that only a rational basis level of scrutiny was therefore required. Consequently, because the state could rationally claim that it had an interest in protecting potential life, the plaintiffs could not sustain an equal protection violation (335, 336). Despite his disagreement with the majority, it is notable that even the dissent offered in the case focused largely on "legal" concerns such as the appropriate level of scrutiny and the identification of "suspect classes." Finally, Justice O'Hern disagreed with the majority's claim that, for purposes of government financial assistance in obtaining an abortion, there was not a sufficient distinction between "medical necessity" and "preservation of life," writing that "[t]o be unable to distinguish these two is to misunderstand one of the central mysteries of existence" (337).

The jurisprudential development between 1972 and 1982 is interesting as well in terms of the initial timidity with which the courts treated the abortion issue, though this type of gradual legal development is by no means unique to the present case. In *Bridgeton Hospital* and *Planned Parenthood of New York City*, the court began in the former with a very narrow ruling that applied only to the two hospitals involved in the case, though demonstrated an unmistakable inclination toward a skeptical view of restrictions to access to abortion services. Specifically, Justice Schreiber wrote in the former that "[m]oral concepts cannot be the basis of a non-sectarian non-profit eleemosynary hospital's regulations where that hospital is holding out the use of its facilities to the general public" (647). Following from the argument offered in the case regarding the "quasi-public" nature of the hospitals involved, the Court went on to claim that "[n]either the trial court nor the defendants have suggested that the regulations prohibiting elective abortions were adopted to further any medical standards. Medically there is no valid distinction which justifies permission to utilize hospital facilities and equipment for therapeutic, but not elective abortions" (647). Interestingly, these formulations are somewhat less distinctly "legal" than those found in *Byrne*, focusing instead on the impropriety of "moral concepts" as a guide to what procedures would or would not be allowed in the facilities and the lack of a medical distinction between different types of abortion.[12] In its Per Curiam opinion in *Planned*

Parenthood of NYC v. State, the Court did not go as far as Justice Pashman had, writing that "plaintiff for the first time urges that we interpret the implied equal protection guarantee of Article 1, Section 1 of the State Constitution to be more demanding than that of the federal constitution . . . Under these circumstances we deem it inappropriate to consider and pass upon the question" (54). So while the interpretive framework that would eventually come to dominate the decisions of the courts in New Jersey, one based on a "legal" understanding of the abortion question, would not be fully articulated until the landmark *Byrne* ruling, a pattern of declining to defer to the choices of extra-legal actors, in the case of *Bridgeton*, or of suggesting that the state Constitution might be a viable avenue for claims foreclosed by federal decisions did much to set the stage for more robust decisions in the following decades.

It would at this point be useful to summarize the developments within the courts and the legislature thus far in the context of the theoretical framework proposed in this study. If *Kugler* and *Roe* are to be understood as a "critical moment" in terms of relationship between the elected and judicial branches, *Byrne* may also be regarded as a similarly, and likely more important, crucial juncture, inasmuch as it was the first time a state law had been overturned.[13] Indeed, this move had to that point been unprecedented as *Kugler* had been a federal court decision, *Bridgeton Hospital Association* had dealt only with the ability of individual healthcare facilities to refuse abortion services, and *Planned Parenthood of NYC* had actually upheld the executive's choice not to reimburse Medicaid funding for the procedure. The 1982 decision also represents an example of jurisprudential path dependent development, similar to that described by Orren (1991), though via a somewhat different mechanism. In the first place, *Byrne* fits in well with previous decisions in the state dealing with abortion as it not only served to demonstrate that the Court would be willing to strike down laws dealing with reproductive rights passed by the legislature, it added significantly to the growing body of case law in New Jersey that served to locate policy making on this issue within the judicial branch. To continue the *Plessy/Brown* metaphor, *Byrne* may finally be thought of as something of a midway point in the Court's development of abortion law, which began with *Kugler*, *Planned Parenthood of NYC*, and *Bridgeton* and culminated in *Planned Parenthood of Central New Jersey v. Farmer* (2000), discussed in much greater detail in the following section, much as *Plessy* and *Grutter* flank *Brown* in the development of law treating citizenship and equality. Indeed, Jack Balkin (2005) makes precisely this point in discussing these landmark federal cases in similar path dependence language, suggesting that conceptualizations of critical questions of law—in this case, issues of race—often develop over long time frames and in response to ever-evolving legal understandings. While *Bridgeton* was the first state-level case to frame the abortion issue as a legal question in New Jersey,

Byrne reinforced this conceptualization and, as will be discussed below, both *Farmer* cases ultimately solidified the predominance of the courts in this area.

Recall, however, that the argument presented here is not that the location of policy making in the courts is strictly a result of path dependence in its traditional sense, whether legal or political. As with the New York case discussed in the following chapter, it is not the branches of government individually that constitute the level of analysis, but rather the policy making community of the state as a whole. The assumption here is also that the field of potential rhetorical narratives is considerably wider in the early stages of policy development and that the institution that first alters the status quo will be better positioned to establish an interpretive framework and thereby is more likely to be the location of further change. Unlike in New York where the legislature had acted at a time when the abortion question was still open to a relatively large array of potential issue frames, the *Roe* and *Kugler* decisions seem to have reduced this field, a point made by Greenhouse and Siegel (2012) in terms of the former, and supported by some of the statements from officials in the elected branches. So while the explanation of the divergent role of the courts in New Jersey can be found primarily through a consideration of the actions, and in some cases inactions, of state level officials both within and outside of the judiciary, these developments were nevertheless influenced by some narrative frameworks that were first articulated by federal judges, including those on the Third Circuit Court of Appeals in the *Kugler* case and the U.S. Supreme Court in *Roe*.

In contrast to the earnestness demonstrated by the courts to involve themselves in the policy making process around abortion in the 1970s, and their consequent early occupation of that issue "niche," the legislature appeared for their part complicit in allowing this dominance. The significance of this from the perspective of the theoretical framework proposed here is clear as the legislature quickly became marginalized as an institutional player in the development of abortion policy. In other words, by initially ignoring the issue, and later crafting laws with little chance of surviving judicial review—or in the case of the 1979 package bill being vetoed by the governor—the legislature effectively ceded the abortion question to the courts, and did not return to it for nearly twenty years. Specifically, two "critical moments" can be identified on the legislative end of the equation, the first being an unwillingness to act following the recommendations of the Crane Commission, signaling a reluctance to address the issue at all and thereby initiate the creation of the norm of judicial dominance. The second was the passage of the obviously constitutionally flawed conscience law and Medicaid restriction, which represented the first real instances of efforts to legislate in this issue. In this sense, there was clear cooperation between these two branches as the courts did not simply decide on their own initiative to take on the primary role of policy making surrounding the abortion question but were assisted by lawmakers who either avoided the issue or transparently invited judicial review. Nevertheless, from the perspective of the theory proposed here, the failure of the legislature to offer any policy guidance or alter its laws prior to *Roe* was likely the most important feature of the 1970s associated with this branch. This again is in stark contrast to New York, where, as the following chapter will demonstrate, the rhetorical framework that would characterize the opinions of the Court, and for that matter, the executive, can be traced back to passage of the liberalization law in 1970, leading to a very different focus in the opinion offered two years later in that state's *Byrn* decision.

The first twelve years of abortion policy development in New Jersey saw considerable movement in this issue area in all three branches of government, though by 1982, the path of judicial predominance had been relatively well established. Prior to *Roe*, it seems that the potential list of narrative frames though which abortion could have been viewed was much broader than it became following that decision. This can be seen in some of the statements made during the hearings by the Crane Commission in the late 1960s. Alan Guttmacher, for instance, argued that "[w]e cannot separate medical and social well-being . . . In order to allow doctors to practice good medicine, abortion should be removed from the penal code and placed under the Medical Practice Act" (Westfield Leader 1968, 8). At the same time, Ruth Russel Gray, president of the New Jersey Coalition on Abortion, took a decidedly more legal tone, stating "[t]he right of a woman to determine her reproductive life without interference from the state is fundamental" (Westfield Leader 1968, 8). Finally, Felix Vann of the American College of Obstetricians and Gynecologists told the hearing that "therapeutic abortion is a medical procedure and should depend upon a full consideration of the patient's health and personal situation, taking into account her social, cultural and economic environment" (Westfield Leader 1968, 8). The point here being that prior to any substantive alterations to New Jersey's laws, the legal frame that would come to dominate in the state, and consequently the primary role of the courts, was by no means a forgone reality in the early 1970s. However, the legislature's failure to act, coupled with a series of court decisions in the first decade of this study, eventually resulted in abortion being understood by the policy making community in New Jersey as a legal issue, that is, the language and discursive framing indigenous to the judiciary. The *Byrne* decision, then, may properly be viewed as the first "critical moment" in the path that would lead to the Court's eventual, and near total, domination of abortion in the state as it was both the first instance of the New Jersey Supreme Court striking down a statute limiting access to the procedure and initiated a line of legal reasoning that was unique to the Garden State.

REINFORCING THE PATH

The focus of the abortion debate during the 1980s and early 1990s in New Jersey shifted from questions regarding limits on the procedure to the protest activities of anti-abortion groups in the state. Initially, it was the courts exclusively that dealt with the problem of increasingly aggressive and violent protests with injunctions being issued in cases such as *Planned Parenthood of Monmouth County Inc. v. Cannizzaro* in 1985 and *State v. Loce* in 1991. The legislature did eventually wade into the matter with several members of the New Jersey legislature introducing an abortion clinic access bill in late 1991 that would have created a 100-foot "buffer zone" around any facility providing the procedure (Gray 1991) during a lame-duck session that followed an election that saw the Democrats losing control of both the state Assembly and Senate. The bill followed a report by the Alan Guttmacher Institute that found that, while the number of incidents involving protesters at abortion clinics nationwide had dropped since the mid-1980s, they had increased in New Jersey and were becoming increasingly volatile (Gray 1991). Opponents of the legislation, which would have been the first of its kind in the Northeast, including the ACLU, claimed the law was overly broad and might be used to silence constitutionally protected speech. If convicted, protesters violating the 100-foot buffer zone would face up to six months in prison and a possible $1,000 fine. The bill was voted out of the Assembly Judiciary, Law, and Public Safety Committee, though, despite expectations that it would be voted on by the full chamber in December 1991 (Gray 1991), it was never brought to the floor in either house of the legislature. In addition to arguably being an attempt by the outgoing Democratic majority in the legislature to pass a measure that was unlikely to be taken up by the Republicans the following year, it is worth noting that the bill bore some striking similarities to the series of injunctions that were being issued in New York during the same period; a rare example of the legislative branch being the location of initial debate surrounding abortion policy in New Jersey.

Almost all of the cases with which the courts dealt in the mid to late 1980s and into the early 1990s were centered around judicially imposed restrictions on pro-life demonstrators, who again at the time had become increasingly aggressive and militant. This in and of itself is noteworthy, particularly in contrast to the same issue in New York where much of the policy making initiative aimed at dealing with these protests was located in the legislature. Specifically, we find three major cases addressing the question of the extent to which this type of expression could be limited by the courts, the first of which being *Planned Parenthood of Monmouth County Inc. v. Cannizzaro*. The plaintiff in that case, a clinic located in Shrewsbury, New Jersey, sought an injunction against New Jersey Right to Life barring the group from trespassing on the clinic's property. The anti-abortion group had been staging increasingly aggressive protests on Planned Parenthood's property for a number of years leading up to the litigation during which members of New Jersey Right to Life had blocked entrance to the clinic, left leaflets on cars parked at the facility, verbally harassed employees, and attempted to dissuade women from entering the clinic. Planned Parenthood eventually sought intervention from the court in an attempt to prevent further disruption at their Shrewsbury location. In a 1985 Chancery Court ruling, Judge Selikoff ordered a permanent injunction against the anti-abortion group's protests, limiting their activities to the surrounding public sidewalks, barring them from shouting at employees or clients of the clinic, as well as using sound amplification devices, enjoining them from distributing leaflets in the facility's parking lot, and requiring that protests on the surrounding sidewalks remain separated by at least five feet (544). In his opinion, Judge Selikoff acknowledged the existence of the competing interests of privacy and property claimed by the plaintiffs as well as the free expression claims of New Jersey Right to Life; however, on balance found that the former must yield to the latter, a determination that was upheld two years later by a state Appeals Court.

The second such case, *State v. Loce*, saw a somewhat aberrant trial court ruling by Judge Michael Noonan, which, while convicting the defendants of trespassing, suggested that a claim of "legal necessity" might be sustainable but for the U.S. Supreme Court's holding in *Roe*. Aggressive protests of abortion clinics in New Jersey continued into the early 1990s, perhaps best exemplified by the case of Alexander Loce. Loce, as well as fourteen other anti-abortion protesters, entered a Morristown doctor's office after learning that his fiancé planned to undergo an abortion and locked the doors to the operating room with chains and bicycle locks (Sullivan 1991). The group was eventually arrested and charged with trespassing while Loce's fiancé proceeded with the abortion. Loce and the other protesters challenged their convictions on the grounds that they had acted out of "legal necessity" as the fetus was in fact a human life that they sought through their actions to protect. Judge Michael Noonan of the Morristown Municipal Court eventually heard the case and, while he ruled against the defendants in upholding their trespassing conviction, also wrote in his opinion that he agreed with defense witnesses that life did in fact begin at conception and that the question was indeed justiciable. According to Judge Noonan, it was only the U.S. Supreme Court's ruling in *Roe* that prevented him from finding in favor of Loce, and that he felt a re-examination of that decision's holding should be considered (Sullivan 1991). The case was appealed and, in *State v. Loce* (360 A.2d 792), the Appellate Division upheld the trespassing conviction and rejected Judge Noonan's assertion regarding the justiciability of the life issue. The case was never directly heard by the state Supreme Court, leaving the Appellate Division ruling in place.

The New Jersey Supreme Court would rule on the clinic access issue in *Horizon Health Center v. Felicissimo* (1994), a case which began in Jersey City in 1990 when a Chancery Court judge issued a temporary restraining order against the anti-abortion group Helpers of God's Precious Infants from protesting outside of the center that the trial court later made permanent. The respondents in this case argued that the injunction amounted to an infringement of their free expression rights guaranteed in the New Jersey and federal constitutions, much as they had in previous litigation related to abortion clinic protests, as well as the debate surrounding the access bill proposed in the legislature in 1991. The Court, in a unanimous opinion, rejected this claim, arguing that the state had a compelling interest in protecting access to medical facilities, that the injunction was sufficiently content neutral, and that the interests in protecting private property and ensuring public safety all justified the restrictions placed on the free expression of the pro-life group.[14] While the respondents in the case had based their free speech claims on both the federal and state constitutions, the Court found it unnecessary to consider the latter and based their ruling entirely on the potential First Amendment violation. Interestingly, this decision came the same year as passage of the federal access to clinics act, which would itself be upheld by the U.S. Supreme Court several years later.

Felicissimo is notable for a number of reasons, not least of which being the fact that nearly all of the state's policy making, treating the question of limits on the protest activities of anti-abortion groups, was undertaken by the courts, quite unlike the same issue in New York described in the following chapter. Indeed, the only semblance of a legislative effort to address the abortion protest issue came in 1991 when a bill proposing a 100-foot buffer zone surrounding clinics that offered abortion services was voted out of the Assembly's Judiciary Committee, though it was never brought to a floor vote in either chamber. Aside from this one instance of attempted legislative action, though, both sides of the abortion debate seemed content to keep their activist efforts confined to the courts, while judges seemed equally inclined to set the state's policy on the matter. The Court's role in the clinic access cases also closely mirrors its involvement in the abortion issue in the early 1970s, particularly in relation to the legislature. One of the overriding themes during this period had been the clear reluctance of the Senate and Assembly to issue guidelines regarding what would and what would not be permissible in New Jersey following the U.S. Supreme Court's *Roe* decision. The Attorney General's request to the legislature that such a clarification be offered, which resulted in the Hawkins and Kennedy bills, neither of which were seen at the time as serious attempts to create policy (Sullivan 1973b), reflects this sentiment well. Unlike New York, which had first proposed a clinic obstruction bill in the early 1990s, and passed a state version of the federal Freedom of Access to Clinic Entrances (FACE) law in 1998, the New Jersey legislature never enacted any laws addressing this issue. The courts, therefore, may not have been the initiator of the shift in focus toward the issue of aggressive pro-life protesters, however, the unwillingness of the Senate and Assembly to engage in policy making in this area once again left this task, perhaps only implicitly, to the judicial institutions in the state.

It is also notable that the clinic access cases were litigated almost entirely in state courts, in contrast to most of the same examples both in New York as well as other neighboring states. Challenges to aggressive protest activities by pro-life groups in the former were for the most part the result of claims brought in federal district courts, resulting in cases such as *New York v. Terry*, *New York State NOW v. Terry*, and *Pro-Choice Network v. Schenck*. Similarly, efforts to protect women seeking abortions from harassment by militant anti-abortion activists in Pennsylvania were also undertaken via litigation at the federal level.[15] What this reveals is that efforts to address the problem were likely to occur in New Jersey in some form, whether legislatively, as they did in New York through passage of that state's FACE law, or through the courts via judicially imposed injunctions against these protests. Reflecting the increasingly independent jurisprudential development of abortion regulation in New Jersey, an analysis of the decisions issued by the state Supreme Court demonstrate that the rationale upon which these rulings were based differed notably from that of their federal counterparts, who tended to be more concerned with the degree to which these protests represented an actual barrier to access.

Justice Clifford's majority opinion in *Felicissimo* illustrates this point well. Demonstrating features critically important to the theoretical framework proposed here, the Court wrote that "[t]he New Jersey Constitution does not guarantee explicitly a fundamental right to health. Yet . . . [w]e conclude that because New Jersey has valued it so highly, the preservation of health constitutes at least a significant government interest" (144, 145). In contrast to the language that was so common within the major decisions of the New York Court of Appeals, stressing that the state Constitution explicitly delegated health policy making to the legislature, and Clifford's observation of the absence of such a provision in New Jersey's document is striking. Rather than looking to the Constitution for guidance on the matter, then, the Court instead relies on its previous jurisprudence in *Byrne*. Additionally, while the opinion devotes considerable attention to the free speech issue, as that was, after all, the basis upon which the respondent claimed that the injunction was unconstitutional, much of it is also concerned with the abortion question. In particular, Clifford writes that "although the federal constitutional right to abortion, see *Roe v. Wade*, 410 U.S. 113 is not protected against private interference, see *Bray v. Alexandria Women's Health Clinic*, 506 U.S. 263 '[t]he State has a legitimate interest in seeing to it that abortion, like any other medical procedure, is performed under circumstances that insure maximum safety for the patient' *Roe*, Supra" (145).

The majority of the Court's opinion in *Felicissimo*, however, is devoted to two considerations that it seems fair to characterize as distinctly "legal," that of "time, place, and manner" issues and the question of whether the injunctions were sufficiently content neutral. Addressing the former, Justice Clifford wrote that "[w]e agree with the courts referred to above that restrictions prohibiting trespass on and prohibiting blocking or obstructing access to abortion or family-planning clinics are narrowly tailored to meet significant government interests" (151). The Court also offered a lengthy discussion of the content neutrality question, concluding that "the injunction restraining the Helpers and those acting in concert with them is content neutral. In issuing the injunction the trial court did not act with the purpose to suppress anti-abortion messages; the injunction can be justified without reference to the content of defendants' speech" (142). While these types of considerations are far from unusual in many similar cases related to clinic obstruction injunctions, both in many of the Second and Third Circuit Court decisions as well those from other states, the important point here is again found in the contrast between the dominant theme of the opinions emanating from the New Jersey Supreme Court and those from the New York Court of Appeals. Indeed, federal-level clinic obstruction cases from the Third Circuit were as likely to employ more "political" language as they were the "legal" tone of the New Jersey cases. In this sense, the state courts here reflected a more consistent tone than their federal counterparts, and one very different from the comparable decisions in New York. Looking then at the "underlying interpretive framework" articulated in *Felicissimo*, we clearly find an opinion that looked to sources closely related to previous legal reasoning employed by other courts, a consideration of the relevant sections of the state and federal constitutions, and the application of tests laid out by the U.S. Supreme Court as to acceptable purposes for restricting speech.

In addition to the rhetorical frames that formed the basis of that decision, previous rulings from the state's High Court also figured prominently in *Felicissimo*. While the case could easily have been decided entirely with reference to the content neutrality of the injunction, which it did at some length, Judge Clifford also saw fit to further elaborate the Court's position on abortion, drawing a direct line between that decision and *Byrne*. Looking again to the claims of the legal path dependence model, as they relate to the theoretical framework proposed here, Hathaway writes that "self-reinforcing or adaptive expectations . . . lead actors to react to current conditions in ways that enhance the likelihood that similar conditions will persist in the future" (2001, 109). *Felicissimo*, in that sense, both reinforces the judicial path entrenched in *Byrne*, and adds to the predominance of judicial decision making surrounding abortion, even in a case where this reinforcement was neither legally nor ideologically necessary. Of course, references to previous decisions are not sufficient to establish a path dependent process as it is understood here. The Court tersely quotes its decision in *Byrne*, writing that "'we recognize that New Jersey accords a high priority to the preservation of health' *Right to Choose v. Byrne*" (144), evincing an understanding of a previously established narrative framework in reduced form. Indeed, Brandwein (2011) suggests that an interpretive framework that has not been accepted by a knowledge community, in this case the New Jersey Supreme Court, will be characterized by further elaboration focused on describing the claim in greater detail. Justice Clifford's opinion, however, makes no such effort, largely taking for granted the idea, established in *Byrne*, that the state places a high degree of emphasis on the preservation of health, here understood to be access to abortion.

As the following chapter reveals, similar cases in New York stressed that the state Constitution delegated health policy to the legislature. Nevertheless, there is no reason to suspect that these provisions were truly controlling in terms of requiring the Court of Appeals to defer to the elected branches when it came to the abortion question as a series of other cases decided by that Court had found a completely different meaning for these clauses, as discussed in chapter 1. Instead, what is important is that the judges on the New York High Court, in addition to employing much more "political" language to justify their rulings, also found a basis in the state Constitution to support the legislature's leading role on the issue. The *Felicissimo* decision, like *Byrne* and *Bridgeton* before it, spoke at length about the weighing of the government's interest in protecting access to the "right" to abortion articulated in *Roe* and balancing the competing constitutional protections of free speech and reproductive rights. As with *Byrne*, this decision further demonstrates the difference in the issue frames the courts took in New Jersey, and as a result, the different role that institution saw for itself in the Garden State.

In terms of temporal ordering, *Cannizzaro*, *Loce*, and *Felicissimo* share some of the same features as the *Bridgeton*, *Byrne*, and *Farmer* sequence, while also representing some important differences. Specifically, the clinic access cases can be understood as "self-reinforcing sequences" in the sense that they served to build upon the institutional role of the courts as the dominant venue for policy making surrounding abortion. While *Bridgeton* and *Byrne* had previously established this norm for the judiciary in terms of determining what types of restrictions would—or rather, would not—be permissible in the state, *Cannizzaro*, *Loce*, and *Felicissimo* broadened the scope of that norm to include policy making that limited the activities of anti-abortion activists. This series of cases not only added to the list of sub-issues that were subsequently framed from that point forward as legal questions, but also resulted in the courts occupying an additional "niche," to borrow Pierson's (2004) term, which could just as easily have been taken up by the legislature, as it had in New York. Indeed, the New Jersey Supreme Court explicitly cited both *Bridgeton* and *Byrne* in its *Felicissimo* opinion (at 145) as instances where the court had properly identified its role as a venue for healthcare policy making generally, and the abortion question specifically. At the same time, the clinic access cases also played something of a "first cause" role by proposing, and subsequently reinforcing, a novel legal understanding that courts in New Jersey should act in issue areas where the legislature had remained silent.[16]

MAINTAINING THE JUDICIAL PATH

While the mid-1990s saw little movement on the abortion issue in either state courts or the legislature apart from the *Felicissimo* decision, a Republican-dominated Senate and Assembly passed two major pieces of legislation restricting abortion access in the latter part of that decade. The first of these came in 1997 when a bill banning the dilation and extraction abortion method was approved by the legislature with fifty-eight Assembly-members supporting the measure to twelve opposing it, while the Senate passed the bill by a similarly wide margin of 25–13 (Preston 1997b). The law would have banned late-term abortions in all cases except when the life of the mother was in danger, a strict requirement that led Governor Christine Todd Whitman to announce that she would veto the bill without an amendment widening the exception to include the mother's health as well. Opponents of such an amendment argued that it would create a loophole rendering the ban meaningless, with the bill's Assembly sponsor Clare M. Farragher, a Republican from Freehold, stating that "[i]t [late-term abortion] is not a health issue . . . What we are saying is that this is wrong. It is a procedure that ends in death" (Preston 1997a). The bill also contained no specific medical terms, which opponents argued could lead to a ban on the "dilation and evacuation" procedure, a much more common type of abortion used after the twelfth week of pregnancy (Preston 1997a).

Governor Whitman did indeed veto the bill, returning it to the legislature with two proposed amendments, the first narrowing the time frame after which late-term abortions could be banned to when the fetus could sustain life independent of the mother, and the second including an exception to preserve the health of the woman (Preston 1997c). In her veto message, the Governor told legislators that the bill "subjects physicians to punishment for performing a procedure that the bill fails to define with the necessary clarity" (Whitman 1997). The Senate and Assembly voted to override the veto, however, with the upper house managing the two-thirds majority needed by a single vote. Senator Andrew R. Ciesla, a Republican from Brick Township, provided the crucial twenty-seventh vote despite having initially opposed the measure after receiving a number of telephone calls from constituents urging him to support the override (Preston 1997c). In a matter of hours following the vote, the ACLU filed a lawsuit challenging the bill in federal court with Judge Anne E. Thompson issuing a temporary restraining order against the new law. Governor Whitman also declined to defend the law, arguing that she and her Attorney General had concluded that the legislation was unconstitutionally vague, while the legislature promised to hire its own counsel (Preston 1997d). While the initial restraining order was set only for ten days, this was later extended by Judge Thompson to June of 1998 in order to offer both sides a chance to prepare their cases. In the meantime, the Medical Society of New Jersey issued new guidelines for the performance of the dilation and extraction procedure despite the fact that the law provided for a fine of $25,000 and the revocation of the medical license of any doctor performing this type of abortion (Goodnough 1997).

Whitman's message in 1997 was almost entirely focused on the constitutional deficiencies of the late-term abortion ban. Beginning with a brief statement regarding her opposition to "partial-birth abortion," the Governor went on to write that:

> I am advised by the Office of the Attorney General, the Office of Legislative Services, and my Chief Counsel that the "Partial-Birth Abortion Ban Act of 1997" is unconstitutional in several respects. First, the conduct that the bill purports to prohibit is defined so broadly as to sweep within its ambit not a single clearly identified procedure but, potentially, several commonly practiced medical procedures . . . Second, because the ban applies throughout pregnancy, and severely restricts medical options by applying to several distinct procedures, it is unconstitutional under United States Supreme Court precedent narrowly circumscribing the authority of the State to "place a substantial obstacle in the path of a woman seeking an abortion before the fetus attains viability" . . . Third, because the sole exception to the ban is for cases in which a partial-birth abortion is necessary "to save the life of the mother," the ban violates settled precedent holding that even when a fetus is viable, the state must permit abortions that are "necessary, in appropriate medical judgment, for the preservation of the life or health of the mother" (2, 3).

Indeed, the veto message made reference to no fewer than five state and federal cases dealing with abortion, including *Roe* and *Casey*, in explaining why Whitman believed the bill to be unsustainable. The final portion of the message recommended alterations to the proposed statute that the Governor claimed would remedy these constitutional deficiencies, all of which were of course rejected by the legislature when they voted to override the veto. Whitman's veto clearly relies heavily on language and issue frameworks that are much more common to courts and the legal community than to elected officials in the executive branch. In terms of the theoretical framework proposed here, there would seem to be considerable evidence that the policy making community in New Jersey, including the legislature, the governor, and the courts, had all focused their rhetorical narratives on "legal" formulations, a fact, it is argued, that is largely explicable by the lack of meaningful engagement with the abortion question prior to 1973.

The restraining order issued in 1998 was made permanent when Judge Thompson finally ruled the law unconstitutional in December of 1998, ultimately agreeing with the Governor that the late-term abortion ban was too vaguely worded. Additionally, the ruling argued that the New Jersey law effectively banned abortions that were protected under the *Roe* decision and had the potential to endanger women's health by prohibiting what was in many cases the safest method for ending a pregnancy (*Planned Parenthood of Central New Jersey v. Verniero* 41 F. Supp. 2d 478 [1998]). The district court ruling was eventually upheld by a three-judge panel of the Third Circuit Court of Appeals in the case of *Planned Parenthood of Central New Jersey v. Farmer* (2000). Again, the court pointed out that the law was unconstitutionally vague and that it placed an undue burden on women's access to abortion services, a decision that echoed the one handed down earlier that year by the U.S. Supreme Court in *Stenberg v. Carhart*, a case dealing with an almost identical statute passed by the Nebraska legislature.

In its opinion, the Court evinced palpable frustration with the legislature's apparent unwillingness to offer any real policy guidance on the abortion issue in the late 1990s and early 2000s, particularly when it came to legislation dealing with restrictions on late-term abortion. Judge Maryanne Barry of the Third Circuit Court of Appeals in *Farmer* struck down the ban on the procedure on the grounds that it was unconstitutionally vague and imposed an "undue burden" on women seeking abortions, as well as physicians administering the procedure, expressed this frustration vividly. Indeed, Judge Barry's opinion in the case reads almost as a textbook example of what Lovell (2003) and Graber (1993) would identify as a transparent attempt by the legislature to author a statute the sole intent of which was to defer the issue to the courts. While the legislative counsel in the case—bearing in mind that neither Governor Whitman nor her Attorney General considered the act to be defensible[17] —argued that it was the sole intent of the drafters of the bill to ban the Intact Dilation and Extraction (D&X) method of late-term abortion, the Court wrote that:

> We note only that naming the procedure or utilizing clear medical terminology to define that procedure for the physicians at whom the Act is aimed would at least have indicated the Legislature's supposed intent to simply ban the D&X. There is simply no excuse for the failure of the Legislature to have done so or for the incurably vague Act which resulted from that failure (at 140).

In responding to the legislative counsel's suggestion that the Act ought to be narrowed by the Court, rather than rejected outright, Judge Barry further wrote that "[t]he Act, pure and simple, is not susceptible much less 'readily susceptible' to a narrowing construction. To narrow it to prohibit only the D&X procedure, as the Legislature now says was the sole procedure it intended to ban, would entail a complete rewriting, if not 'brute force.'" (141). Additionally, in what one can only assume was not in fact an attempt at humor, the legislature's attorney argued "that because New Jersey is one of the most 'liberal' states in terms of abortion rights, it is 'clear' that the drafters did not intend to repudiate decades of abortion rights by banning all abortions, but only intended the Act to prohibit the D&X procedure" (140). The Court, apparently unamused, similarly rejected this argument as well. Finally, Judge Barry wrote that the Act amounted to an "undue burden" both for women seeking abortions as well as physicians in violation of the standard articulated by the U.S. Supreme Court in *Casey* by:

> [e]rect[ing] a substantial obstacle because, as already discussed in great detail, it is so vague as to be easily construed to ban even the safest, most common and readily available conventional pre- and post-viability abortion procedures. Separate and apart from whether such a widespread proscription was intended by the drafters, because physicians are unable to determine precisely what the Act bans, they will be chilled from performing suction and curettage, D&E and induction abortions in order to avoid the risk of license revocation and fines (144, 145).

This *Farmer* case is somewhat distinct from the other landmark decisions dealing with abortion in New Jersey in several important ways. The most obvious of these is that fact that it was the first time a federal court had struck down a state statute since the Third Circuit had upheld the district court's ruling invalidating New Jersey's nineteenth-century abortion ban in 1974. While the language in Barry's opinion was similar to many of the state decisions in the preceding twenty years in its focus on concerns such as overbreadth and unconstitutionally vague definitions of the D&X procedure, this "legal" frame was not found in all of the decisions dealing with this issue from the Third Circuit, as will be discussed later in this chapter. For this reason, it may be difficult to characterize the federal *Farmer* case as fitting clearly into the theoretical framework on offer here, either as a part of the self-reinforcing sequence of cases that helped establish abortion as a "legal" question in New Jersey, or as falling squarely within the level of analysis of the policy making community in the state. Nevertheless, the case is important as it obviously came as a result of the actions of the legislature, a body that does of course fall into the aforementioned community. Rather than being explicable as a natural outgrowth of the norm of abortion being a matter for the courts in New Jersey resulting from its initial location there and the development of that frame over time, it seems more likely that the late-term ban at issue in the case was a rare example of legislative deferral to the judiciary in Lovell's (2003) and Graber's (1993) terms. While these two concepts need not be mutually exclusive—and indeed one might expect deferral behavior to be more common in jurisdictions where legal frames have been established than in those, like New York, where they have not—such an argument is not presented here. The passage of the late-term abortion ban in New Jersey is instructive instead for what it reveals regarding the ways in which members of the elected branches were conceptualizing the issue of reproductive rights, as suggested by Governor Whitman's veto, rather than its influence on the discursive framework adopted by the courts.

The second major limit on abortion access that was passed by the New Jersey legislature in the late 1990s dealt with parental involvement and made the state the thirty-ninth to require parental consent or notification before a minor could proceed with an abortion. Specifically, the 1999 bill required doctors to notify the parents or guardians of women under the age of eighteen seeking abortions before proceeding, though including a judicial bypass if the minor could prove she was mature enough to make the decision or if there was evidence of sexual or physical abuse. Indeed, these two provisions were included after legislative leaders consulted with Governor Whitman and she indicated that she would support parental notification only if they were added (Kocieniewski 1999a). Whitman surprised many at the time, despite her involvement in the process leading up to passage of the statute, by signing the measure as she had been consistently viewed as one of the nation's leading pro-choice Republicans. Indeed, many observers believed that abortion rights groups had not put forward much in the way of lobbying efforts precisely because they expected the Governor to veto any parental notification bill, with Elizabeth Volz of the New Jersey chapter of the National Organization of Women stating that "had we known the Governor's position sooner we would have mobilized sooner" (Kocieniewski 1999b).

The ACLU of New Jersey again sought an injunction against the parental notification measure, though this time a Superior Court judge refused their request, arguing that, while abortion rights were guaranteed by New Jersey law, the judicial bypass sufficiently protected women's access to the procedure (*New York Times* 1999). The ACLU filed an emergency appeal of the decision that was upheld by judges on the state's Appellate Division of Superior Court. Justice Gary Stein of the New Jersey Supreme Court granted a temporary restraining order, the day before the law was set to go into effect, however, blocking enforcement of the law until it could be reviewed by the full Court (Hu 1999).

That review took place the following year with the Court ruling, in a 4–2 decision, that the parental notification law violated the Equal Protection guarantee of the New Jersey State Constitution in *Planned Parenthood of*

Central New Jersey v. Farmer (2000). The executive did defend the Parental Notification for Abortion Act, unlike the previously discussed *Farmer* case, arguing that the law advanced the state's interest in protecting minors from their own immaturity, fostering the family structure, and protecting parents' rights to rear their children, all of which were rejected by the State Supreme Court. Specifically, the Court in *Byrne* had rejected the U.S. Supreme Court's "rational basis" versus "strict scrutiny" framework in favor of a balancing test that weighed the governmental interest in the statute against the interests of the affected class, in this case, a minor's right to privacy and as they had in 1982, found that the latter outweighed the former by impermissibly drawing a distinction between young women who chose to carry their pregnancies to term and those who chose abortion. The Court also rejected the judicial bypass provision of the Act, arguing that rather than providing a true alternative to minors seeking to avoid the involvement of their parents, this provision in fact simply created further obstacles to young women seeking abortions and was likely only to delay the procedure further. Finally, it is worth noting that unlike the late-term abortion ban struck down by the Third Circuit Court of Appeals, based on the opinion authored by the Supreme Court, there seems to be considerably less reason to suspect that lawmakers were consciously engaging in an attempt to defer policy making responsibility to the courts when drafting the parental notification law.

Looking more closely at the text of the majority opinion in the New Jersey Supreme Court's *Farmer* decision, written by Chief Justice Poritz, the unique trajectory of the path begun in cases such as *Bridgeton, Planned Parenthood of NYC*, and *Byrne* is clearly evident. Specifically, the Court writes that "[t]he Parental Notification for Abortion Act is designed to impose restrictions on young women who seek an abortion, treating them differently than it treats young women who decide to carry to term" (632). In regards to the provisions of the state Constitution under which the Court argued the Act failed, Poritz stated that "Article I, paragraph 1, of the New Jersey Constitution does not permit the State to impose disparate and unjustifiable burdens on different classes of young women when fundamental constitutional rights hang in the balance" (638). Perhaps more importantly, the majority in the state *Farmer* case devoted considerable attention to rejecting the rationale the state had offered in defense of the statute, again in contrast to the highly deferential tone found in the New York abortion cases. In particular, Justice Poritz argued that "[t]he State has failed to demonstrate a substantial need for the Parental Notification for Abortion Act, or even that the asserted need is capable of realization through enforcement of the Act's provisions. Nor does the State offer adequate justification for distinguishing between minors seeking an abortion and minors seeking medical and surgical care relating to their pregnancies" (638). Finally, the Court claimed that "there is no principled basis for imposing special burdens only on that class of minors seeking an abortion" (638).

The New Jersey Supreme Court's opinion in *Farmer* also helps illustrate both the cumulative effect of its past decisions dealing with abortion, as well as the norm of framing this issue in legal terms that had been entrenched by that point. Specifically, Justice Poritz wrote that:

> At the time the Court decided *Right to Choose*, the Supreme Court of the United States had recently handed down *Harris v. McRae* (1980), which held that the Equal Protection Clause did not prohibit Congress from proscribing the use of Medicaid funds for an abortion except when required to save the life of the mother. We held to the contrary under equal protection principles found in our State Constitution (*Planned Parenthood of Central New Jersey v. Farmer* at 630).

Further elaborating on the understanding that the State Constitution provided a higher standard than its federal counterpart, as well as the framing of the abortion question in terms of rights, the majority opinion went on to claim that:

> [w]e have earlier discussed the importance of a woman's right to control her body and her future, a right we as a society consider fundamental to individual liberty . . . Although we will not repeat that discussion here, we are keenly aware of the principle of individual autonomy that lies at the heart of a woman's right to make reproductive decisions and of the strength of that principle as embodied in our own Constitution. We have not hesitated, in an appropriate case, to read the broad language of Article I, paragraph 1, to provide greater rights than its federal counterpart. Our precedents make clear that the classification created by the statute is deserving of the most exacting scrutiny (*Planned Parenthood of Central New Jersey v. Farmer* at 631, 632).

The point here is that, while it seems possible that the legislature desired to "switch paths" in the case of parental notification, the norm of treating abortion as a right, subject to strict judicial scrutiny, had by that point been entrenched to the point that the Court was unlikely to uphold any serious restriction on reproductive rights. To borrow a term from the social movement literature, abortion in New Jersey had become subject, more so than in New York, to "rights talk" (Glendon 1991; McCann 1994; Scheingold 2004; *inter alia*), the result of a long process that began with *Kugler* and *Roe* and came into its own in *Farmer*.

Indeed, the concept that the state may not burden young women seeking access to abortion services appeared frequently in Portiz's majority decision, with Justice O'Connor's phrase from *Casey* regarding an "undue burden" appearing a full thirteen times in the opinion.[18] Some examples include a statement that "minors who choose abortion are therefore subject to burdens not imposed on minors who do not. The greater the burden on the underlying right, the more difficult it is to sustain the State's classification" (633). In response to the state's claim that the judicial bypass procedure sufficiently mitigated the difficulties resultant from the statute, the majority argues that this provision "impose[s] far greater burdens on minors who, for very good reasons recognized by the statute, are unable to communicate with their parents about their decision" (634, 635). The justices in New Jersey continued to write in terms of abortion as a "right" that may not be impeded by an "undue burden," concepts that seem clearly linked to the sponsoring legal community. This latter term in particular is a concept that is almost entirely indigenous to legal discourse and, while being found frequently in both *Farmer* decisions, was almost entirely absent from the major rulings in New York.

The state *Farmer* case also reveals references to earlier understandings established in previous decisions in reduced form, just as the Court had in *Felicissimo*. Specifically, Poritz writes that "[w]e employ the *Right to Choose* balancing test to determine whether that differential treatment unfairly burdens only one class of young women, thereby violating the State Constitution's guarantee of equal protection" (632). This too reveals that the knowledge claim the Court had developed eighteen years earlier in voiding New Jersey's Medicaid funding ban continued to be the "winning," understanding of how, and perhaps more importantly, where abortion policy making was to be articulated and located. Note that the reasoning upon which the Court relies in the state *Farmer* case also differs markedly from that which had been by that time well established by the U.S. Supreme Court in the evaluation of abortion jurisprudence in *Roe* and *Casey*. In the former, of course, the right to abortion had been found primarily in the Due Process Clause of the 14th Amendment.[19] Similarly, the "undue burden" test developed by the Court in *Casey* likewise relied on the Due Process Clause, with Justice O'Connor writing that "[o]nly where state regulation imposes an undue burden on a woman's ability to make this decision does the power of the State reach into the heart of the liberty protected by the Due Process Clause" (*Planned Parenthood v. Casey* at 874). The *Farmer* decision, however, struck down the state's parental notification requirement on the basis of its violation of the Equal Protection Clause. Also, while Poritz makes reference to the *Casey* decision at several points in the majority opinion, it is primarily discussed as a contrast to the main argument offered by the Court, one relying on the balancing test first described in *Byrne*. We see then not only a relatively unique view of what may constitute an acceptable restriction on abortion access developed on the New Jersey Court, one distinct from the standard developed at the federal level, but one clearly linked to a series of discursive frameworks extending back to Justice Pashman's concurrence in part in *Planned Parenthood of NYC*.

In the same year that the Court struck down the parental notification law, the state Assembly voted on a resolution calling for a constitutional amendment that would effectively reverse the ruling, though it fell short of the three-fifths majority required for passage, garnering 44 yeas to 14 nays with 16 abstentions. The vote fell largely along partisan lines with only two Republicans opposing the measure and one Democrat voting in support of the proposal, in contrast to the original parental notification bill, which had received considerable bipartisan support (Hanley 2000). Interestingly, the proposed amendment did not mention abortion, but rather would have allowed the legislature to pass any bill requiring that parents be informed of "any medical or surgical procedure, or any treatment, irrespective of any right or interest otherwise provided in the Constitution" (Hanley 2000). Had the resolution been approved by the Assembly, as well as by a similar three-fifths majority in the Senate, it could have been placed on the ballot for approval by voters;[20] however, it was never brought to the floor of the Senate during the 2000 legislative session.

The proposed amendment was again brought to a floor vote in the Assembly during the lame-duck session that followed the 2001 general election, which had seen the Republicans lose control of the lower house, as well as the Governor's office, and resulted in an even 20–20 split in the state Senate. This time the proposal passed by a 52–21 margin in the Assembly, though only by a single vote in the Senate, requiring that the measure be approved again in the following session, something that was unlikely given the large Democratic majority which would control the Assembly in 2002 (Mansnerus 2001). Indeed, both Senator Richard Codey, who was scheduled to share the Senate leadership with Republican John Bennett, as well as Speaker-elect Albio Sires, indicated that they had no plans to schedule a vote on the issue in the following legislative session (Mansnerus 2001). The timing of the Assembly vote may also have been important during the 2001 session as it took place after the Senate had already passed the proposal by less than the three-fifths required for ballot access the following year, meaning that members of the lower house were aware that even a three-fifths vote in their chamber would not have been sufficient to bring the issue before voters in November. In any case, the momentum behind the push to amend the New Jersey Constitution to effectively overturn the Supreme Court's decision on parental notification had clearly waned after the 2001 election and the issue was never again brought to the floor in either chamber of the legislature.

Unfortunately, there were considerably fewer examples from the media records at the time of lawmakers speaking publicly about their views on either the late-term abortion ban or parental notification requirement than had been the case in the mid-1970s when the state passed the Medicaid funding restrictions, making analysis of the rhetorical frames of members of the legislature considerably more difficult. Indeed, the vast majority of reports discussing these laws were focused on Governor Whitman and other members of the executive and centered on the former's veto of the late-term ban and her role in negotiating a less restrictive parental involvement statute. Nevertheless, Assemblyman Neil Cohen (D-Elizabeth), lamenting Governor Whitman's failure to veto the measure, stated that abortion rights advocates had "unfortunately, distressingly, become an invisible voice for women's reproductive rights . . . [and] had been seduced into believing the Governor would protect them. Legislators don't feel there's a price to pay for infringing on a woman's rights, and that's disturbing" (Kocieniewski 1999a). In reference to the late-term abortion ban, Assemblywoman Diane Allen (R-Burlington), following Whitman's veto, urged her fellow lawmakers to "find a way that is constitutional and will let any woman follow her God" (Ginsberg 1997). Also echoing a theme similar to that of statements from legislators in the mid-1970s, even supporters of the bill spoke in terms of legal consideration. Assemblywoman Clare Farragher (R-Monmouth), the prime sponsor of the late-term abortion ban, argued that "[i]t is my belief that this does not interfere with a [woman's] right to choose" (Ginsberg 1997). The point here is that actors within the elected branches in the late 1990s continued to frame the abortion question in large part through a legal lens, emphasizing aspects of the parental notification and late-term abortion bans related to the laws' potential constitutional defects and the degree to which they interfered with women's rights.

If *Roe*, and to a lesser extent *Kugler*, are to be understood as "critical moments" at the level of the entire policy making community within New Jersey, as suggested by the previous section, then the late-term abortion ban would seem to represent part of what Mahoney (2000) calls a "reactive sequence" whereby past actions structure the behavior of subsequent actors. Specifically, just as they had with the conscience bill in 1974 and the Medicaid ban in 1975, there is considerable evidence that the "partial-birth abortion" ban statute was designed either to be struck down entirely or be severely restricted by judicial interpretation. The Circuit Court in *Farmer* made several references to *Bridgeton* and *Byrne* as past examples of overbroad legislation that was constitutionally defective, suggesting that this type of behavior had become something to be expected from New Jersey's legislature. Again, it seems unlikely that lawmakers in passing the late-term abortion ban were unaware of these defects and at this point understood well that the courts were likely to rule it unconstitutional. In other words, there seems to have been something of a pattern among legislators of choosing to pass laws that were legally questionable when drafting the conscience and Medicaid ban statutes, though this early in the process, they may not have been completely aware of the fact that these measures would not survive court challenges. By 1997, however, it seems difficult to imagine that members of the Assembly and Senate believed that restrictions on abortion access, particularly those as broad as the late-term abortion ban, would be sustained in court. The reactive sequence here, bearing in mind that the level of analysis remains the policy making community as a whole, can be understood as a continuation of the back-and-forth between a legislature seemingly avoiding robust efforts to engage the abortion question in a meaningful way, at least in the case of the late-term abortion ban, and courts that had become increasingly inclined to view abortion restrictions through a lens of fundamental rights. Indeed, as the quotes from lawmakers discussed in this section reveal, it was not only judges but members of the Senate and Assembly as well who evinced a marked tendency to conceptualize abortion as a legal rather than political issue.

Perhaps due to what had become a less hospitable state Assembly and Senate following the Republican defeats in the early part of the 2000s, anti-abortion advocates again turned to litigation in their efforts to limit the practice in the Garden State. Specifically, pro-life activists sought to require doctors to provide what amounted to an anti-abortion message to patients seeking the procedure through a lawsuit against a Perth Amboy gynecologist. Interestingly, there does not seem to have been much in the way of a coordinated effort by pro-life interest groups behind the case, which was to be litigated over the course of several years, as no supporting briefs by these organizations were ever filed at any stage of the process. The case began in 1996 when Rosa Acuna, a Bound Brook mother of two, consulted with Dr. Sheldon Turkish regarding abdominal pain and headaches from which she was suffering and, following an ultrasound examination, Dr. Turkish informed Ms. Acuna that she was six to eight weeks pregnant (*Acuna v. Turkish* 2007). While accounts of the reason behind the decision differ between the plaintiff and the defendant, Acuna eventually elected to terminate the pregnancy after allegedly being informed by her doctor that a "seven-week pregnancy is not a living human being [but was] just tissue at this time" (*Acuna v. Turkish*). Several weeks later, Acuna was admitted to the hospital with vaginal bleeding and was diagnosed with an "incomplete abortion." After undergoing a dilation and curettage operation, Acuna asked a nurse what had happened and was informed that "the doctor had left parts of the baby inside of you" (*Acuna v. Turkish*). Following a long series of court battles with the case being juggled between the state's Chancery and Appellate Division courts, the New Jersey Supreme Court finally ruled against Acuna in a 2007 decision.

The *Acuna v. Turkish* case essentially sought to secure a ruling from the Court that would require doctors to inform women seeking abortions that the procedure would result in the termination of a "human life." Following what the plaintiff described as the realization that her fetus was in fact a living human being, Acuna brought a malpractice complaint against Dr. Turkish in the Law Division, Middlesex County, asserting a wrongful death claim on behalf of the estate of her "deceased infant," Andreas Acuna, as well as negligent infliction of emotional distress, negligence, and lack of informed consent claims on behalf of herself (*Acuna v. Turkish*). In terms of the second set of claims unrelated to the wrongful death assertion, Acuna specifically argued that the defendant failed to inform her that her unborn child was "a complete, separate, unique and irreplaceable human being," and that "Andreas" was capable of feeling pain; abortion involved the killing of an actual human being; she was at risk of suffering from "post-abortion stress syndrome"; and that she would suffer from the emotional trauma of the knowledge that she had "kill[ed] her own child" (*Acuna v. Turkish*).

Following a lengthy litigation process that saw the case heard several times at the trial and intermediate court levels, the New Jersey Supreme Court finally granted review in 2007. Specifically, the question ultimately considered by the Court was whether "defendant failed to provide [Ms. Acuna] with material medical information concerning the nature of the six- to eight-week-old embryo she was carrying and the consequences of her terminating her pregnancy" (423). The *Acuna* case is interesting for several reasons, including the fact that it was one of the few major decisions from the state's High Court that dealt with a tort claim rather than a challenge to a particular statute or injunction, though perhaps the most relevant point is the defendant's reliance on what seems to be a more "political" framing of the issue. Indeed, Justice Albin's opinion points out that "[d]efendant and *amici* argue that it would be bad public policy, and probably unconstitutional, under the banner of the law of informed consent, to compel obstetricians to voice plaintiff's non-medical and ideologically-driven viewpoint in the ongoing debate on abortion" (424, emphasis in original).

Despite this choice on the part of the respondents in the *Acuna* case, the Court continued, as it had in the previous *Byrne*, *Felicissimo*, and *Farmer* decisions, to frame its ruling again through a largely legal lens. Echoing the latter's focus on the relevant jurisprudential developments on the U.S. Supreme Court, Albin again made reference to *Casey*'s undue burden test, as well as citing a 2006 Eighth Circuit Court of Appeals decision (*Planned Parenthood Minn. v. Rounds*) that had issued an injunction against a South Dakota "informed consent" law as "violat[ing] both the First Amendment rights of physicians and the due process rights of women seeking abortion" (427). The Court also emphasized that both *Roe* and the much more recent *Gonzales v. Carhart* (2007) had "scrupulously avoid[ed] describing either a fetus or an embryo as an existing human being" (426). The majority of the opinion, however, was devoted to a discussion of the common law understanding of informed consent, concluding that "we do not find that the common law commands a physician to inform a pregnant patient that an embryo is an existing, living human being and that an abortion results in the killing of a family member" (428). Nevertheless, Albin did briefly invoke a more political tone when writing that "[w]e are not unmindful of the raging debate that has roiled the nation and of the sincerely and passionately held beliefs by those on opposite sides of the debate" (427).

As with the litigation surrounding abortion clinic protests which were the focus of the courts in the late 1980s and early 1990s, perhaps the most relevant conclusion that can be drawn from this case was also that the courts were the location of an attempt by a pro-life activist to mandate a pro-life message from doctors. Indeed, this mandate has been legislated in twenty-three states, which require "informed consent" from women before they undergo an abortion procedure, usually including an anti-abortion message, information about alternatives to the termination of pregnancy, fetal development, etc. (Gold and Nash 2007). In all twenty-three of these states, this requirement has been established by laws passed by the state legislature. Instead, it seems that Ms. Acuna sought to establish this requirement through a court ruling, though there was little formal involvement by pro-life activists or interest groups, as none of these were involved in the case, either as intervenors or through the submission of amicus briefs. The case was appealed to the U.S. Supreme Court, and at that point did attract the attention of the Christian Medical and Dental Association, the Catholic Medical Association, the Association of Pro-Life Obstetricians and Gynecologists, the Association of Pro-Life Physicians, and several local anti-abortion groups, all of which joined an amicus brief requesting review by the High Court (Brief for New Jersey Physicians Resource Council et al. as amicus curiae, *Acuna v. Turkish* 2008), though certiorari was denied. Nevertheless, the lack of organized support at the state level suggests that whatever efforts were underway at that point to require "informed consent" for women seeking abortions in New Jersey through the courts were half-hearted at best.

Attempts had been made prior to the *Acuna* case, however, to establish a version of "informed consent" via the legislature, most notably in 1979 when a package of abortion restrictions had been passed by the Senate and Assembly and vetoed by Governor Byrne. More recently, legislation had been tabled to establish a similar requirement, though neither bill was ever referred out of committee (see ASSEMBLY, No. 2275 [2000] and ASSEMBLY, No. 2016 [2002]). While the immediate causes of the failure of the informed consent bills in the legislature may be difficult to assess, it is worth nothing that both the Assembly and the Senate were controlled by Republican majorities at the time who, as demonstrated by the passage of the late-term abortion ban and parental notification law several years earlier, were not unwilling to legislate on the issue. Indeed, the makeup of the legislature in 2000 and 2002 was almost identical to what it had been in 1997 and 1999, making it all the more puzzling that the relatively minor abortion restriction represented by the informed consent law proposed in the Assembly was never brought to a floor vote, particularly when the much more sweeping late-term abortion and parental notification bills had passed by wide margins. Because political, or at least partisan, considerations seem insufficient in explaining the failure of the informed consent bill, there would seem to be evidence that what Page (2006) terms "negative externalities" were likely at work, which discouraged legislators from further efforts to enact abortion restrictions. Specifically, Page argues that, while path dependence approaches tend to focus on increasing returns, equally important is an understanding of negative externalities that occur when a particular path or institution consistently fails to yield meaningful policy outputs. Just as positive returns tend to help maintain a path once it has been established; these "negative returns" from alternative policy making venues will also reinforce the dominant institution. In the *Acuna* case, then, it would seem that by the early 2000s, the courts had even further entrenched themselves as the dominant policy making institution in the area of abortion. In this sense, the actual outcome of the case is not particularly important—though Acuna's claim was rejected in a unanimous decision by a Court consisting at the time of three Democrats, one Republican, and one Independent—but rather, the fact that an effort to establish an informed consent requirement through the judiciary itself is noteworthy and reflective of the overwhelming importance of the judicial path by 2007.

With the Democrats' hold on the state legislature and executive solidifying through most of the 2000s, efforts to curb abortion rights legislatively were largely moribund and the next major statutory move related to reproductive rights took the form of expanding women's access to contraception and the so-called "morning-after pill." Specifically, a bill requiring pharmacies to fill any legal prescription, including those for emergency or any other type of contraception, sponsored by Senators Fred H. Madden and Joseph F. Vitale, cleared the Senate by an overwhelming vote of 31–6 in June 2006 (New Jersey State Democrats 2006). A year later, the Assembly passed the same piece of legislation by a similarly wide margin of 56–18 (Women's Health Policy Report 2007), and the bill was signed into law by Governor Corzine in December of 2007. Despite the lack of significant opposition by lawmakers reflected by the substantial majorities with which the statute passed both houses, anti-abortion activists argued that the bill amounted to religious discrimination, with Marie Tasy of New Jersey Right to Life stating that the legislation "discriminate[d] against pharmacists. It says if you have religious beliefs, you need not apply" (Ertelt 2007). Opponents of the law took particular issue with language mandating that it was a "pharmacy's duty to fill prescriptions for in-stock drugs or devices without delay, notwithstanding sincerely held moral, philosophical or religious beliefs of pharmacist" (§1—C.45:14-67.1 2007). Nevertheless, there seems to be little evidence indeed that the pharmacy requirement was a particularly controversial piece of legislation outside of pro-life groups such as New Jersey Right to Life,[21] in contrast to the resistance that measures dealing with access to Plan B had faced in New York described in the following chapter.

Anti-abortion advocates were emboldened, however, by the election of Governor Chris Christie in 2009, arguably the most pro-life Governor of New Jersey in modern times.[22] While the Assembly and Senate remained in the hands of the Democrats following the 2009 election and state funding of abortion services through Medicaid has not yet faced any serious threats in New Jersey, Christie did issue a line-item veto of the state's 2010 budget that eliminated $7.5 million worth of funding for fifty-eight women's healthcare clinics. The Governor, echoing the case made by opponents of Medicaid funding for abortions during the battle over the issue in the mid-1970s, argued that he opposed taxpayer funding of abortions and, as these clinics offered this service, he believed they should not be eligible for state funds (Santi 2010). In a vote that in many ways illustrates the increasing polarization of partisan positions on the abortion issue over the past forty years, both in New Jersey as well as, arguably, the country as a whole, an attempted override of Christie's veto failed by a margin of 23–17 in the Senate, with every Democrat voting in support of the motion and every Republican voting in opposition (Santi 2010). As of this writing, there has been no litigation related to these cuts.

OVERVIEW

Considering then the extensive involvement of the courts in the development of abortion policy in New Jersey between 1970 and 2010, we see a clear and unmistakable contrast between the role of the judiciary in the policy making process in that state and its neighbor to the north. Specifically, three major trends are apparent in the analysis presented above, all of which are significant in understanding the relationship between the legislature and the courts in the state. The first of these is the timing of institutional involvement and the influence this had on how abortion was initially framed, and subsequently the role the courts would come to play in New Jersey. Again in contrast to the New York case, the first substantive change to abortion law in the Garden State took the form of the 1972 *Kugler* decision that struck down the state's 1849 law and was followed several months later by *Roe*, which of course precluded the state from maintaining its abortion ban. Going forward, the relationship between the courts and the elected branches was markedly different from that discussed in the following chapter, a fact reflected in the claim put forward in the second portion of the theoretical framework described in the introduction to this study. As Hacker (2002) notes, "the mechanisms creating path dependence involve the adaptation and response of individuals and organizations over time to a particular matrix of policies and institutions" (54). The interplay between the courts and the legislature can be plainly seen in the content of many of the opinions issued by the state Supreme Court, as well as some of the comments of elected officials. This was a dynamic relation where, as time went on, the scope of the rulings from the judiciary were increasingly assertive and repeatedly reinforced the framing of the abortion question as a legal one. The actions, or inactions, of the legislature were likely as important as those of the courts in establishing and maintaining the dominance of the judicial branch. Beginning with the *Kugler*, *Bridgeton*, and *Planned Parenthood of NYC* decisions in the 1970s, the courts stepped into the void created by the legislature's failure to create abortion policy and remained the primary location of decision throughout the 1980s, 1990s, and into the 2000s, despite the occasional, and arguably half-hearted, attempts by the elected branches to assert a more meaningful role.

The second major trend was the development of the Court's jurisprudence throughout the forty year period considered here. The importance of the *Byrne* decision in this sense cannot be overemphasized as it was both the first instance of the state Supreme Court directly overturning an act of the legislature and the case that would largely inform the subsequent reasoning in the clinic obstruction cases and the state *Farmer* ruling. As discussed in the preceding section, we see the Court consistently applying the balancing test first developed in that case, a view that differed markedly from that adopted by the U.S. Supreme Court in *Casey*, even after that decision was handed down. More importantly for the theoretical framework on offer here, the major opinions that followed the 1982 case all made mention of the issue conceptualization articulated in *Byrne*, though in a reduced form. Nevertheless, the seeds of that decision had clearly been planted five years earlier in Justice Pashman's partial concurrence in *Planned Parenthood of NYC*. The point, in any event, is that a very specific interpretive framework came to dominate the thinking of the justices of New Jersey's High Court, and indeed, all of the actors in the state's policy making community. Unlike in New York, this frame was one based on the language of legal discourse rather than political considerations such as the propriety of deferring to the choices of the elected branches or the expected results on the ground of restricting or expanding access to abortion.

Finally, the dialogue across cases and between successive courts reveals much about how the initial issue frameworks adopted by the justices of the New Jersey Supreme Court, as well as the relevant federal courts, informed both the way abortion was conceptualized as well as the proper role of the judiciary. Early decisions such as *Kugler*, *Bridgeton*, and *Planned Parenthood of NYC* were, somewhat paradoxically, both cautious in their limited scope, but did much to establish the court's future role as a robust actor in the development of policy in that issue area. While the courts became bolder in the 1990s and 2000s in their willingness to challenge laws passed by the legislature, and even initiate policy change on their own in the clinic access cases as well as *Acuna*, the rhetorical focus of their jurisprudence remained remarkably stable over time. The written opinions emanating from the major cases between 1972 and 2007 consistently stressed themes such as overbreadth, fundamental rights, and equal protection, as well as more specific concepts indigenous to legal discourse such as the undue burden test and the balancing approach developed in *Byrne*. While this may not seem particularly noteworthy in the sense that these concepts are often associated with any legal pronouncement, they nonetheless stand in contrast to the discursive frameworks that are found in the major abortion cases in New York. Again, given the similarities between the two states' High Courts in terms of ideological makeup and national reputation as legal innovators, it seems difficult to explain this difference apart from institutional first movement and the adoption of the ideas and norms inherent in the mandates of courts versus the elected branches.

It is also worth briefly addressing the role played by federal and state courts in New Jersey as they were somewhat different from the same interplay in New York. Indeed, with the exception of several cases in which district courts issued injunctions against clinic protesters, some of which were appealed to the Second Circuit and even to the U.S. Supreme Court, very little policy development took place in federal courts in the latter, and none of the laws passed by the Assembly and Senate were ever struck down.[23] While the vast majority of policy decisions within the judiciary took place in state courts in New Jersey, there is evidence that developments at the federal level had an important impact on the policy making community in that state. As mentioned above, it is assumed here that prior to the *Roe* decision, the field of potential frames through which the abortion question would be viewed was considerably wider than it was after that landmark ruling, both at the federal and state level, an idea reflected in the themes of the Crane Commission discussed in the previous section. Again in contrast to the New York experience, the first substantive change in abortion policy in New Jersey came when that state's law was struck down in *Kugler*, a case that was followed several months later by the landmark 1973 decision. The impact this had on the policy making community in the Garden State is evidenced by the language employed by members of the state Assembly and Senate as early as their deliberations surrounding the exclusion of Medicaid funding in 1974 and 1975. In addition, *Roe* was discussed extensively by the state Supreme Court in both the *Bridgeton* and *Planned Parenthood of NYC* cases with Justice Pashman quoting Justice Powell's opinion in his partial concurrence in support of his argument that the state Constitution might provide an added level of protection to the right to abortion than the federal document (see pg. 41, 42) in the latter case. The point here is that the New York Court of Appeals had issued its first decision treating this issue before

Roe, but following the passage of the liberalization law in 1970. The initial conceptualization of the question by that state's judicial branch, then, was one of deference to the elected branches, while in New Jersey, the court was considerably more likely to draw on the newly developing norm of abortion as a right subject to protection by the state and federal constitutions. So while the level of analysis in this study remains the policy making community at the state level, the external policy shock of *Roe* nevertheless had an important, and long-lasting, influence of how the actors in each branch would understand and conceptualize the issue, a development that was precluded in New York.

These three trends, as well as the influence of key events at the federal level, were significant in that they demonstrate both that the courts played a much more active role in the development of abortion policy in New Jersey than was the case in New York, as well as the multitude of approaches they employed throughout this process. Perhaps more importantly, however, is what these cases suggest about the relationship between the legislature and the courts, and the genesis of the interpretive framework that was to come to dominate in the former. Similarly, the actions of the courts over this period clearly demonstrate the importance of the initial location of decision as the involvement of the judiciary early in the process seems to have established a "niche" for the courts within this issue area that was subsequently reinforced over time and was finally solidified by the mid-2000s.

In terms of the actions of the legislature in the Garden State during the forty years of the present study, we find two themes that seemed to recur with some regularity. The first of these is that on a number of occasions, the members of the Assembly and Senate put forward considerable effort to avoid creating policy, particularly in the years leading up to and immediately following the U.S. Supreme Court's decision in *Roe*. This is important from the standpoint of the theoretical framework presented here as such avoidance, in contrast to the same institution's behavior in New York, left the narrative field open to defining abortion in legal terms. Indeed, this view was reflected in a number of the comments by lawmakers during the debates surrounding the conscience protection law and the Medicaid funding ban, suggesting that they had at least begun accepting the interpretive framework of the legal community. In addition, there does appear to be at least some evidence that the legislature may have at several points been engaging in something akin to the deferral behavior described by Lovell (2003), Graber (1993), and Whittington (2007). The case for this seems strongest in regards to the late-term abortion ban as a number of sources had indicated to lawmakers that the statute would almost certainly be struck down. Indeed, the Third Circuit's opinion in the federal *Farmer* case clearly hints at this when it pointed out that the drafters had been aware of modifications that would have made the law much more likely to pass constitutional muster. Rejection of the McGahn amendment proposed as part of the conscience protection bill also lends some support to the claim that this too was not meant as a serious attempt to create policy, though this appears less clear than the late-term measure. Nevertheless, the deferral theory does not explain all of the behavior of the legislature in New Jersey, particularly the parental notification requirement where lawmakers took considerable pains to include a judicial bypass and exceptions for rape and incest. Instead, the framing of the abortion issue in legal terms and the consequent jurisprudence that developed on the state's courts over time provide a more complete account of the lack of meaningful policy development emanating from the legislature.

Finally, the executive's actions over the course of the forty years considered in this study in many ways mirrored that of the legislature in its reluctance to engage the abortion issue. Specifically in the case of its inaction in dealing with the issue of limits on aggressive anti-abortion protests, in contrast to its counterpart in New York, the executive largely followed the example of the legislature and allowed the courts to deal exclusively with this issue. Similarly, Governor Byrne signed both the hospital requirement and Medicaid restriction bills, though he made it clear that he harbored serious reservations about the constitutionality of both, a position vindicated by the courts. In these cases, it would seem that the executive also accepted the predominance of the courts as the primary location of policy making around the abortion issue. While the Attorney General and the State Department of Human Services had issued guidelines regarding what would constitute a legal abortion in New Jersey following the *Kugler* and *Roe* decisions, this was only done reluctantly and after several unsuccessful attempts to prod the legislature into acting. The exception to the executive's seeming acceptance of the court's occupation of the abortion "niche" may be found during the tenure of Governor Whitman who twice seemed legitimately interested in crafting legislation, in cooperation with the Assembly and Senate, which would be sustained by the courts. This situation may have been unique, though, due to Whitman's status as the Republican governor of a largely socially liberal state and her possible presidential aspirations. Whitman was wary of challenging the conservative base of her party (Kocieniewski 1999a), despite her explicitly pro-choice position, and may have had political reasons for supporting some restrictions on abortion, particularly the parental notification requirement, which enjoyed high levels of support in public opinion polls. In any event, for the vast majority of the time between 1970 and 2010, the governor seemed to at least implicitly support the norm of judicial predominance within the abortion issue.

An examination of the role of the executive in the development of abortion policy in New Jersey reveals that the governor and members of other executive agencies in the state have been, as with other elected officials, largely reluctant to engage in the issue for the majority of the last forty years.

The most obvious exceptions to this have been the issuing of guidelines regulating abortion practices by the Attorney General and the State Department of Human Services when the legislature has been unwilling or unable to act. Additionally, a number of governors have been willing to exercise their veto powers in a number of instances, including the case of Governor Byrne's refusal to sign the 1979 package bill, which was not overridden, despite the super-majority by which the bill passed the Senate and Assembly—a phenomenon also seen in the New York case—as well as the use of this power as a negotiating tactic by Governor Whitman to shape legislation, which was more likely to survive judicial review. Interestingly, in both cases of a gubernatorial veto of abortion bills in New Jersey, the chief executives cited concerns about the constitutionality of the provisions, while stressing their own support of some restrictions in principle.

THE FEDERAL CONTEXT

A separate consideration of developments at the federal level in New Jersey is warranted here for two main reasons. The first of these is to highlight that the predominance of the legal frame in the Garden State was not completely an artifact of decisions by federal courts or that state's location in the Third Circuit Court of Appeals. Indeed, as the following chapter will demonstrate, the Second Circuit decisions dealing with the abortion question, both legal and political frames can be found in these appellate court rulings, suggesting that the predominance of the former in New Jersey was somewhat unique to that state. More broadly, because of the greater impact of federal court decisions on abortion policy making in New Jersey, most importantly in the *Kugler*, *Roe*, and *Farmer* decision striking down the state's late-term abortion ban, it is instructive to separate out the impact of federal and state judicial actions. Indeed, the vast majority of policy making in the courts did in fact take place in the latter jurisdiction, with the state's Supreme Court articulating a uniquely "New Jersey" set of jurisprudential developments; one that tended to challenge legislation on the basis of equal protection rather than substantive due process violations, as had the federal courts. Nevertheless, many of the frames adopted by the state's justices were first articulated by federal-level courts, and the first changes to New Jersey's abortion laws were the result of federal actions.

In terms of the theoretical framework proposed at the outset of this study, *Roe* was critically important as the decision was the first to alter the state's abortion laws since the nineteenth century.[24] Recall that the argument on offer here is that any issue will be considerably more open to a host of interpretive frameworks early in the process of policy development, but that once a substantive change to the status quo is made, the dialogue going forward will be largely informed by the norms and mandates of the sponsoring community. Indeed, as the opinions of the New Jersey Supreme Court, the statements of several members of the legislature, and the veto messages of the governors reveal, this is precisely what we find. While the courts in New York, as well as members of that state's executive, consistently conceptualized and discussed abortion in "policy" terms or, in the case of the former, as an issue best resolved by the elected branches, the idea of abortion as a "right" that enjoyed considerable constitutional protection was adopted early in New Jersey and persisted throughout the course of the forty years that followed the landmark decision. Despite the fact that the U.S. Supreme Court's pronouncement was exogenous to the policy making community in that state, it unquestionably tilted the dominant discursive framework toward an understanding of abortion as a rights issue, a concept that simply never took hold in New York in the same manner.

The federal *Farmer* decision, for its part, represents something of an aberration. As will become clear in the following discussion of other cases from the Third Circuit, there is little reason to believe that the conclusion the Appeals Court reached was based primarily on a tendency to conceptualize abortion in legal terms or as a question best left to elected officials. Instead, this decision appears to be better explained as a rare instance of legislative deferral as it is understood by Lovell (2003), Graber (1993), and Whittington (2007). Indeed, the preceding discussion makes clear that lawmakers had little reason to expect the law to withstand a constitutional challenge as the governor, their own legislative counsel, and ultimately the Court itself all pointed out that there had been numerous opportunities to remedy the law's defects that were stubbornly ignored by the members of the Assembly and Senate. While the political payoff of passing such an obviously flawed statute is not entirely clear, particularly absent a record of the floor debates leading to passage of the bill, few alternative explanations seem to account for this odd legislative decision. Given the refusal of lawmakers to make seemingly minor changes to the language of the law, it is unlikely that it represented a genuine attempt to enact a ban on late-term abortions. By the same token, it may have been the case that legislators felt compelled to pass a bill restricting abortion access in order to placate vocal pro-life activists, though again, this end could easily have been met by simply adding the changes suggested by Governor Whitman. In any event, regardless of the reason, it seems that lawmakers were intent on passing a law they knew would be struck down by the courts. This fact is made all the more puzzling given that two years later, legislators passed a parental notification law that showed little evidence of attempted deferral to the courts.

To illustrate the comparative absence of a predominantly "legal" frame in the relevant federal appeals court, a brief overview of some of the major cases dealing with abortion emanating from the Third Circuit Court of Appeals is also warranted here. To accomplish this, a LexisNexis search of the terms "abortion" and "Pennsylvania" or "Delaware" was examined, limiting the analysis to cases where a state law in either jurisdiction was challenged or an injunction against abortion protesters was issued, looking only at decisions from the appellate level.[25] This does not represent an exhaustive consideration of all of the relevant cases, though the major rulings from this Court serve to illustrate much the same point as was described in the preceding discussion of litigation from the Second Circuit. Specifically, opinions were identified that can reasonably be described as both "political" and "legal," suggesting again that the predominance of the latter frame in the New Jersey courts was a product of development in that state, with the exception of course of the *Roe* decision,[26] and not a trend inherent to the jurisprudence of the Third Circuit.

The overwhelming majority of litigation in the Third Circuit came, as might be expected, from Pennsylvania, with a number of statutes passed in that state being challenged at the federal level. The most well-known of these is of course *Planned Parenthood v. Casey*, the case that ultimately led to the adoption of the "undue burden" test when considering restrictions on abortion. It is not necessary at this point to reiterate the facts of that decision, though it bears mentioning that the Circuit Court ruling was itself quite similar to that offered by the U.S. Supreme Court the following year in its reliance on that standard first articulated by Justice O'Connor in her dissenting opinions in *Akron v. Akron Center for Reproductive Health Inc.* (1983), *Thornburgh v. American College of Obstetricians and Gynecologists* (1986), and her concurrence in *Hodgson v. Minnesota* (1990). In relying on this test, the Circuit Court decision in *Casey* may fairly be considered to be based on a "legal" interpretive framework as it made little reference to the propriety of deference to the elected branches or policy considerations related to the wisdom of restrictive or permissive abortion regulations. *American College of Obstetricians and Gynecologists v. Thornburgh* (1984) took a similar tone, though the ruling was of course overturned by the U.S. Supreme Court. That case involved a challenge to a number provisions of the Abortion Control Act of 1982, including an informed consent requirement, a twenty-four-hour waiting period, parental consent with judicial bypass, limits on private insurance coverage for abortions, a ban on the procedure post-viability, and a series of reporting requirements. All of these were struck down with the exception of the parental involvement portion of the law, though this was enjoined pending review by the Pennsylvania Supreme Court. Illustrating a decidedly legal understanding, the Court in that case wrote of the viability provision that "[w]e conclude that the language of section 3210(b) is not susceptible to a construction that does not require the mother to bear an increased medical risk in order to save her viable fetus" (300). In striking down the private insurance limits, Judge Sloviter argued that "[t]his requirement adds an additional barrier to a woman's access to an abortion that is unconstitutional" (303). Finally, in regards to the reporting requirements, the Court wrote that the "nature and complexity of the [provision] of the Pennsylvania Act have crossed the permissible threshold . . . 'related to the state's interest in protecting the health of its citizens'" (302).

Language that was somewhat less "legal" in tone was found in two of the clinic obstruction cases, *Roe v. Operation Rescue* (1990) and *Northeast Women's Center v. McMonagle* (1989). In the former case, the Court ruled that NARAL had standing to seek damages from the anti-abortion group, claiming that its "stated mission is to protect women's right to safe and legal abortions . . . [which is] clearly imperiled by Operation Rescue's efforts to deny women access to facilities that provide abortions" (866). A similarly ambiguous argument in terms of its "political" or "legal" nature can also be found in *Doe v. Beal* (1975), a case challenging a Department of Public Welfare directive banning financing of nontherapeutic abortions as violating Title XIX of the Social Security Act. In that case, the Court wrote that "once the state has decided to finance full-term delivery and therapeutic abortions as methods for the treatment of pregnancy, it cannot decline to finance nontherapeutic abortions without violating the requirements of Title XIX" (622). A similar challenge was brought against a Pennsylvania law requiring reporting and physician certification for publicly funded abortions in *Elizabeth Blackwell Health Center for Women v. Knoll* (1995) with the Court striking the statute down almost entirely on the basis of deference to the directives issued by the Secretary of Health and Human Services. Finally, in *Roe v. Casey* (1980), a Third Circuit panel struck down another Pennsylvania law limiting Medicaid financing to cases of life endangerment as inconsistent with the intent of the Hyde Amendment. The opinion in that ruling relied largely on a discussion of the legislative history of that amendment, writing that "we cannot help but note the drastic change in the nature of the discussion when the subject of abortion was introduced" (836) and arguing that "we are not free to substitute our speculation for the judgment of the duly constituted officials of the state" (838).

The point here, as with the analysis of some of the major Second Circuit rulings presented in the following chapter, is that both "political" and "legal" narratives can be found in the jurisprudence of the federal courts responsible for New Jersey. While the opinion in *Farmer* was replete with references to concerns such as overbreadth and the unconstitutionally vague nature of the late-term abortion ban, this was by no means an artifact of a consistent tendency among Third Circuit Court judges toward a highly "legal" interpretive framework. In addition, state Supreme Court justices did on several occasions take some cues from their federal counterparts, as discussed in the above case study. Concepts such as the undue burden test and time, place, and manner considerations featured prominently in many of the opinions of that institution. But these references did not prevent the New Jersey Supreme Court from developing its own line of case law that often relied on very different reasoning than that articulated by the U.S. Supreme Court. Indeed, the balancing test first described in *Byrne* would go on to inform several other decisions and used a decidedly different legal standard than parallel developments on the federal bench. So while there was undoubtedly some "crosstalk" between federal and state courts in New Jersey, the predominance of the judicial branch in the development of abortion policy does not seem to be explicable in terms of federal influence as the state's High Court was far from reluctant to follow its own legal path that frequently differed from that laid out by federal jurists.

It is however argued here that *Roe* had a highly relevant impact on the location of policy development in New Jersey by helping to frame the abortion question in legal terms before the legislature was able to act on the issue, as it did in New York. Recall that prior to the landmark U.S. Supreme Court ruling, the field of potential rhetorical frameworks was considerably more open than was the case following that decision. When the New York Court of Appeals issued its first major decisions treating the abortion question, the idea of reproductive rights as a primarily legal issue had not been firmly established, and indeed received scant attention from that state's judges. Instead, the main question before that Court was the proper institutional location of abortion decision making. *Roe*, then, had little impact in New York as abortion was already legal in the state, while in New Jersey, that same decision profoundly changed the legal status of the procedure. More importantly, however, is the fact that the courts in the former had begun developing their own set of jurisprudence from a very different point of departure; one where abortion as a political question had already become relatively well established. By contrast, all of the early state-level decision making in New Jersey, both in the courts as well as the elected branches, took place after the U.S. Supreme Court had clearly articulated abortion as a legal question. Indeed, further investigation of the narrative constructions that were adopted in states that had seen movement on this issue prior to the 1973 decision and those that had not has the potential to reveal the extent to which this argument is generalizable beyond the cases considered here.

CONCLUSION

New Jersey today is generally recognized to be one of the most pro-choice states in the nation and is well established among states with the most liberal abortion policies. Indeed, this reputation is well founded as the Garden State currently imposes few, if any, restrictions on abortion access and is among one of only a handful of states that provides Medicaid support for nontherapeutic termination of pregnancy. The state's policies related to abortion, though, while virtually identical to those of New York, exist in their current form almost entirely due to decisions reached by judges in state and federal courts. New Jersey lawmakers and judges struggled to develop policy dealing with abortion rights, including the perennial issues of parental notification, late-term abortion bans, clinic obstruction laws, the denial of Medicaid funds for abortion services, and the availability of the "morning-after pill," much as they had in New York, and indeed virtually every state in the country in the years since the U.S. Supreme Court's decision in *Roe*. Despite the Garden State's reputation for social liberalism, all of the restrictions mentioned above were enacted by the state legislature, usually by overwhelming majorities. Some examples of these unusually wide margins include the late-term abortion ban, which passed the Assembly 58–12 and the Senate 25–13; the parental notification bill, clearing the lower house by a vote of 59–17 and the upper chamber 31–8; the Medicaid restriction, which garnered 46 yeas to 18 nays in the Assembly and easily passed the Senate 22–14; and the 24-hour waiting period mandate, which was approved by the Assembly by a margin of 51–17 and the Senate by an equally wide 27–9. None, however, are currently part of New Jersey's legal code as all of the relevant laws were eventually struck down, either by federal or state courts.

While there is some evidence that legislators in the Garden State may have been attempting something similar to legislative deferral behavior, this approach does not account for much of the decision making that took place in the state over the forty years considered here. Indeed, in the case of the parental notification law passed in 1999 there is considerable evidence that both lawmakers and the governor were genuinely interested in passing a law that would survive in court as several alterations aimed at remedying constitutional deficiencies to the original bill were made at the request of Governor Whitman. The statute was, of course, nevertheless struck down by the state Supreme Court. In this sense, a more complete explanation of the role of the courts in formulating abortion policy in the Garden State may be found in the theoretical framework proposed in this work. Taking a broad view of the jurisprudential development of this issue over the forty years considered here, we see early intervention by the judiciary, coupled with reluctance on the part of the elected branches to produce meaningful policy, leading to a situation where by the early 2000s, few restrictions on abortion seemed likely to have survived review by the courts. An analysis of the discursive frames adopted by judges evinces that in the first decade of judicial intervention, a norm was established that understood this issue in terms of fundamental rights, equal protection, and a suspicion of overbroad statutory language. This is in stark contrast to the themes found in the major abortion cases in New York that were much more likely to speak in the language of proper institutional roles, albeit under the guise of constitutional requirements, that located the legislature as the appropriate venue for health care policy making.

Returning to the propositions articulated in the theoretical framework offered in the introductory chapter of this investigation, we see that in line with the argument presented here, the courts tended to consider the abortion question in New Jersey through the ideas inherent in their institutional mandate. More importantly, though, these particular issue frames came to be adopted by subsequent courts, as well as the other branches of state government, as reproductive rights came to be understood in "legal" terms. Finally, through a dynamic process of dialogue between the judicial and elected branches, the norm of abortion-as-rights was reinforced with each successive decision, to the point where it became very difficult for any other discursive framework to be adopted, and hence for any other institution to meaningfully alter the policy of the state. Courts continued to make reference to interpretive frameworks that had first been articulated in cases such as *Planned Parenthood of NYC* and *Byrne* in a reduced form, suggesting that they had become accepted as the appropriate lens through which to view abortion. At the same time, comments by elected officials in the legislative and executive branches clearly reflected the "knowledge claims" of the courts, describing their support, and even their opposition, to abortion in terms of "rights," "equal protection," and "privacy." These tendencies are all the more stark when considered in contrast to the same institutions in New York, where the "interpretive community" of the elected branches was the first to frame the discussion surrounding reproductive rights.

Of equal importance, of course, was the timing of institutional involvement, both at critical points by the federal judiciary as well as the state's own courts. As discussed in the previous section, no substantive change to New Jersey's abortion laws occurred prior to *Roe*, a fact it is argued here, that largely facilitated the adoption of abortion as a primarily legal question by the courts as well as officials in the elected branches. Indeed, the first major decision by the state Supreme Court treating this issue highlighted that the "federal constitutional right to an abortion during the first trimester is now well-settled" (*Bridgeton* at 647). The true critical moment in this process, however, would seem to be the landmark 1982 decision in *Right to Choose v. Byrne*, the foundations of which had been laid by Justice Pashman's partial concurrence in *Planned Parenthood of NYC*. Not only did that case further reinforce the predominance of the legal frame as the primary lens through which reproductive rights would be viewed going forward, but it began a jurisprudential line of reasoning that was distinct to the courts in New Jersey. A recognition that the state's Constitution set a higher standard than its federal counterpart for equal protection concerns as they related to abortion access reflected not only further development of the abortion-as-right discursive framework, but also represented the clearest and most enduring example of judicial preeminence in this area. While later decisions such *Felicissimo*, *Framer*, and *Acuna* are useful for demonstrating the continuation of the legal path of policy making, it was this decision striking down the state's Medicaid funding ban that seems most critical in accounting for the vastly different role of the courts in New Jersey.

The case of abortion policy making in the Garden State offers a fascinating juxtaposition to the story of the same issue in New York, discussed in the following chapter, both due to the many similarities between the two states on a number of measures as well as their virtually identical policy outcomes. What is different between the two, however, is that policy as it exists today is almost entirely the result of litigation in the Garden State, whether through the rejection of laws passed by the legislature or via actions initiated by private individuals, as in the case of "informed consent" and the injunctions issued against clinic protesters. Having examined a case where the courts had taken on the primary role of policy development on the abortion question, we turn now to a very different case where the court's role was largely overshadowed by the elected branches. Despite this very different route to policy change, though, the mechanism that drove judges to defer authority to the legislature was much the same as it was in New Jersey; the initial location of the issue in the state Assembly and Senate and the subsequent framing of abortion as a political question best resolved by elected officials.

NOTES

1. Though not uniformly so, particularly in the first decade considered in this chapter.
2. That being said, the extent to which *stare decisis* or other legal norms truly limits judicial discretion is a matter of some debate (see, for example, Maltzman et al. 2000; Segal and Spaeth 2002; Hathaway 2001; Graber 2006).
3. See *Madsen v. Women's Health Center, Inc.* (1994); *Schenck v. Pro-Choice Network of Western New York* (1997); *Hill v. Colorado* (2000); *inter alia*.
4. To be clear, the claim here is not that this early litigation had any meaningful impact on the role of the courts in the latter half of the twentieth century as these were followed by a lengthy period of inactivity, much as was the case in New York.
5. The exception being the relatively minor conscience protection statute that allows healthcare workers to refuse participation in abortion procedures.
6. Indeed, the focus of the 1967 case was a challenge to the constitutionality of the proscription on contraception that had been a part of the nineteenth-century Comstock Laws discussed above. Ultimately the Court overturned the ban, largely citing the recent U.S. Supreme Court holding in *Griswold v. Connecticut*.
7. While the New Jersey Supreme Court had recommended that the state reconsider its abortion law in *State v. Baird* in 1967, it did not strike the law down or even alter it in any meaningful way. Similarly, while the Attorney General had issued guidelines in 1971 restricting Medicaid funding for abortions performed in New York following that state's legalization of the procedure, this directive is perhaps better understood as an extension of existing state policy that already forbade financing for a procedure that was at the time still illegal in New Jersey.
8. Sixteen Catholic hospitals in the state already refused to perform abortions (Wechsler 1973).

9. The analogy is, admittedly, imperfect. The New Jersey Court did not overturn *Planned Parenthood of NYC* and Justice Pashman's earlier opinion was a concurrence in part while Justice Harlan's famous dissent was just that.

10. It is worth noting here that, following the U.S. Supreme Court's ruling in *Maher v. Roe* (1977), which found that the federal Constitution did not require states to finance nontherapeutic abortion through Medicaid, all of the challenges to New Jersey's ban on such funding were made in state courts. After this point, the only question of federal law that was presented by such plaintiffs concerned the definition of "medically necessary" contained in the Federal Medicaid Act (FMA).

11. This is in contrast to the veto message delivered by Governor Rockefeller in New York, issued a year before the *Roe* decision, discussed in the following chapter.

12. This is in contrast to the first major opinion treating abortion in New York where Judge Breitel refused in the majority opinion in *Byrn*, upholding a challenge to that state's 1970 liberalization law, to engage in what he considered a "moral" question best suited for political resolution.

13. This in and of itself is of course not particularly noteworthy as courts at all levels and in all jurisdictions commonly overturn statutes passed by legislatures. The particular relevance of *Byrne* is for the purposes of this study limited to the abortion question in particular, as well as the behavior of the courts in New Jersey as contrasted with those in New York.

14. Though the Court did instruct the Chancery Court to amend its injunction to allow for some protesters to operate on the sidewalk in front of the clinic, with the provision that these not interfere with access to the center.

15. See *Roe v. Operation Rescue* (1990), *Northeast Women's Center v. McMonagle* (1989), *inter alia*, discussed in greater detail below.

16. This is not to suggest that injunctions against protests had not been issued in other states and recognized as a legitimate legal function (see *Frisby v. Schultz* 487 U.S. 474 [1988]); simply that these New Jersey cases were the first of their kind in that state to treat this issue.

17. A fact, Barry writes, that "has not escaped our attention but on which we choose not to comment."

18. Contrast this with the fact that the same term was not found at all in the *Hope* case in New York, despite the fact that both decisions had been issued following the U.S. Supreme Court ruling in *Casey*.

19. Though of course much of the case also turned on the right to privacy found in the "penumbras and emanations" of that and other guarantees in the Bill of Rights.

20. The amending procedure of New Jersey's Constitution requires either a three-fifths majority vote in both houses of the legislature followed by a simple majority vote by the people, or passage by a simple majority in the Senate and Assembly in two separate legislative sessions followed by a similar simple majority vote by the people. Additionally, if a proposed amendment fails to secure at least a simple majority in either house, it cannot be proposed again until at least three general elections have been held.

21. Indeed, a LexisNexis search of terms related to the bill yielded only one result, an op-ed article praising the bill from the Princeton University student newspaper.

22. Christie has admitted to donating money to Planned Parenthood in 1994, however, claimed in a *Meet the Press* interview in 2011 that he opposed abortion except in cases of rape, incest, and to preserve the life of the mother (Phelps 2016).

23. Indeed, even these rare instances did not prevent the legislature in New York from passing its own version of the federal FACE law.

24. While *Kugler* had found the statute unconstitutionally vague the previous year, that decision was not upheld until 1974 by the Third Circuit Court of Appeals entirely on the basis of the *Roe* framework.

25. Though no cases originating in Delaware met this standard.

26. Determining whether *Roe* had a similar impact on the issue frames adopted in the other states in this Circuit is of course well beyond the scope of this study.

Chapter Three

The Development of Abortion Policy in New York State

Abortion in New York has been legal since 1970 with the state being one of only a handful to have liberalized its laws prior to the *Roe* decision in 1973. Since the passage of that landmark bill, though, the issue has been the source of a host of battles both in the legislature as well as in the state's courts as pro-life activists have sought to restrict access to the procedure while pro-choice interests have fought against these efforts and attempted to enact further protections for reproductive health such as FACE laws and over-the-counter sale of RU 486. More specifically, opposition to abortion rights in New York has been led primarily by the Catholic Church, with some Republicans and conservative-leaning lawmakers also seeking greater regulation of the procedure in the 1980s and 1990s. Similarly, Democrats and more liberally oriented lawmakers and activists have typically been strongly supportive of the pro-choice side, though the former were far from monolithically so in the first decade of the present study.

This chapter will first offer a discussion of the history of abortion laws in New York, with a particular focus on developments since the passage of the liberalization law in 1970, critical points in the policy making process, and the identification of the largely "political" frame that came to dominate discourse both on and off the court. As in the previous case study, a brief discussion will also be offered that aims to account for the influence of federal court decisions on the policy making process in New York and how this did or did not have implications for the predominance of the legislature in this issue area. Unlike the New Jersey case, federal court action had little impact in the Empire State in terms of altering policy, though for the sake of consistency as well as accounting for all possible variables, this section is nonetheless instructive. With this outline in mind, the case study that follows will help illustrate how the theoretical framework described in chapter 1 offers the most compelling explanation for why the courts played such a minor role in policy formulation treating the abortion issue in the Empire State compared to this same issue in New Jersey. Unlike the latter, the first changes to New York's abortion law were the result of the actions of the elected branches, a development that first framed the issue in political terms, both for the courts as well as the executive and legislature, resulting in a decreased role for the judiciary in the process of policy change.

Specifically, the laws, proposed bills, and court decisions discussed in the following chapter can be loosely categorized into seven substantive areas: (1) parental involvement requirements, (2) limits on funding for the procedure, whether through Medicaid or other sources, (3) injunctions against, or statutory restrictions on, the activities of abortion clinic protesters, (4) regulations regarding where abortions may be performed, whether enacted at the state or local level, (5) access to RU-486, or "Plan B," medication, (6) suits filed against so-called "crisis pregnancy centers," and (7) the legal status of abortion itself. Indeed, the last of these saw the passage of two laws and one landmark Court of Appeals decision in the span of just two years. It is also worth noting that all of these specific areas of lawmaking and litigation were also found in the New Jersey case, with the exception of the lawsuits filed by the state Attorney General against the crisis pregnancy centers.[1]

What emerges from the story of abortion policy making in New York is that the early involvement of the legislature in altering the state's abortion laws seems to have set in place a norm whereby policy making in this issue area was understood by those in the judicial branch to be the province of the legislature rather than the courts. What is also evident from the case presented below is that at most stages of the development of abortion law in New York, all three branches of government were involved in ways that affected the location of policy making, though often in a very complex interaction that offered all of these a number of opportunities to influence the agenda and the ultimate policy output. Nevertheless, "path switching"—in Pierson's (2000) terms—never took place, despite many opportunities for the court to assert a more robust role in policy making. These critical moments can be seen most clearly in the text of the numerous opinions offered by the New York Court of Appeals that time and again evinced an unwillingness to engage the abortion question, which it repeatedly insisted was a political question outside of its area of responsibility.

The most important factors in explaining why the courts played such a secondary role to the legislature in policy development in this issue area, then, were the early involvement of the latter body in setting the state's abortion laws and the resultant framing of the issue in political terms. In addition, this framing, which was not necessarily conscious, was reinforced by early court decisions that acknowledged the legislature's presumptive ownership of the abortion question and was reinforced by later ruling that maintained this understanding. Indeed, these factors become even more apparent when contrasted with the behavior of the same institution in New Jersey and its continued reluctance to wade into this politically volatile social area. That being said, we turn now to a discussion of what took place in Albany and elsewhere during the forty years from the first consideration of liberalizing the state's abortion law to the present situation in which New York is considered by many to be among the most liberal states in terms of abortion access. While the trajectory of this development was not always linear—indeed, abortion rights were at some points as likely to be curtailed by lawmakers as they were to be advanced, particularly in the 1970s—a trend toward fewer restrictions on the procedure is nonetheless unmistakable.

THE EARLY YEARS

At the time of the founding, none of the thirteen colonies maintained any abortion statutes, and the procedure was essentially unregulated until at least the beginning of the nineteenth century. New York was no different and, while an abortion case was litigated in Massachusetts in 1812—a case that was ultimately dismissed—efforts by state legislatures to pass laws limiting access to abortion did not begin until the 1820s. Connecticut was the first such jurisdiction, prohibiting the administration of abortifacients in 1821, followed by Missouri in 1825, Illinois in 1827, and finally New York in 1828. The apparent motivation behind these laws, however, was to combat the use of poisons administered to women with the goal of ending their pregnancy which quite often resulted in serious injury or death to both the mother and the fetus (Mohr 1979). Cyril Means, writing specifically of New York's statutory development between the seventeenth and nineteenth centuries, argues that "the preservation of the life and health of the pregnant woman" (1968, 452) was the primary purpose of the first laws to criminalize the procedure, though others (Dellapenna 2006; Gorski 2009) have disputed this claim. Nevertheless, this concern was reflected in the Connecticut and Illinois laws, which banned only the administration of abortifacient agents and only after "quickening," meaning the point at which fetal movement became perceptible (Mohr 1979). New York's law, which went into effect in 1830, differed significantly from those in other states at the time, however, in that it made abortion before quickening a misdemeanor punishable by up to one year in prison, while the procedure performed after this point was deemed to constitute manslaughter. Furthermore, the New York law included a provision allowing for the termination of pregnancy at any stage if it was deemed by two physicians to be necessary to preserve the health of the mother. Still, the 1830 law applied only to the individual performing the abortion, and it was not until an 1845 amendment that a woman submitting to an abortion was deemed guilty of a misdemeanor, with another amendment in 1881 elevating the crime to manslaughter (Abortion 2012).

The effectiveness of New York's early abortion laws in preventing the practice may have been somewhat questionable, however, as abortion providers continued to operate throughout most of the nineteenth (Mohr 1979) and twentieth centuries (Solinger 2017). Undoubtedly the most famous case of illegal abortions in New York was that of Madame Restell, who operated an abortion facility and provided abortifacients to mostly upper-class women for much of the middle of the nineteenth century. Restell, the alias of Ann Lohman, had begun selling "patent medicines" to women who wished to terminate their pregnancies in the late 1830s, several years after the legislature had passed its first law banning the practice, and faced a number of prosecutions throughout her career (Richardson 2011). The first of these occurred in 1839 when Restell was charged with assisting a woman in the procurement of an abortion, though after spending a night in jail, the charges were eventually dropped. In 1841, similar charges were brought and this time Restell was convicted, though her lawyers appealed the ruling and the presiding judge granted a new trial. This second hearing would not take place until 1844, however, and with the death of one of the prosecution's key witnesses, the charges against Lohman were again dropped (Richardson 2011). By the mid-1840s, Madame Restell had become a notorious figure in the New York City social and media scene and she was finally convicted of assisting Marie Bodine in procuring an abortion and sentenced to one year in prison. Upon her release, she immediately returned to her practice and managed to operate her abortion business with little police interference until the late 1870s (Richardson 2011). In 1875, the state had passed another law banning instruments designed to produce miscarriages or contraception and in the winter of 1878, Anthony Comstock, the namesake of the famous—or infamous—Comstock Laws targeting purported obscenity, discovered a stock of syringes, circulars, condoms, and other banned material in Madame Restell's facility and arrested her, later charging Restell under the newly enacted laws. Before she could be brought to trial, however, Madame Restell committed suicide, thereby ending one of the most well-known and publicized illegal abortion facilities in New York City for much of the nineteenth century (Richardson 2011). The point, in any event, is that despite a series of attempts to regulate and ban abortions in New York during much of the 1800s, the practice remained relatively common and, at least for those who could afford them, easy to obtain for many women in urban areas.

Abortion law in New York remained virtually unchanged after the 1881 amendment until the historic passage of legislation in 1970 that legalized the termination of pregnancy essentially at the discretion of the mother up to the twenty-fourth week, or, second trimester. Two years earlier, Governor Nelson Rockefeller had appointed an eleven-member commission to study the possibility of reforming the nineteenth-century statute consisting of lawyers, physicians, and other healthcare professionals. The result was a recommendation for the outright repeal of the state's current law and the introduction by Assemblywoman Constance E. Cook of the bill, which would eventually pass the Assembly by the slimmest of margins (Greenhouse and Siegal 2012). The new law was by all measures the most liberal such statute in the country, though New York was not the first state to loosen its limitations on access to abortion. In 1967, Colorado amended its penal code to allow for the termination of pregnancies resulting from rape or incest or if the life of the mother was threatened, with California, Oregon, and North Carolina following suit shortly afterward (Burns 2005). Just one month before New York's liberalization statute passed, a similarly broad bill was signed into law in Hawaii, which also allowed for the termination of pregnancy at the discretion of the mother, but also included a ninety-day residency requirement (Smyser 2000), bestowing upon New York the title, oft-repeated since, of the abortion capital of the United States.[2]

ESTABLISHING THE POLITICAL PATH

Figure 3.1 reveals both a markedly different ordering of institutional involvement in the abortion issue than the same illustration in New Jersey, as well as the location of important policy decisions. By far the most important event is the passage of the liberalization law in 1970, before both the *Roe* decision three years later and the first instance of judicial involvement by a state court in 1972. There are also fewer major rulings from the New York Court of Appeals than its counterpart in New Jersey. Indeed, over the forty-year period covered in this study, there were five substantive decisions from the former, three of which came in the same year, while the latter saw eight. Of perhaps greater significance, though, is the outcome of the New York cases, all of which upheld the challenged statutes or sustained the choices of executive branch officials; a very different pattern than the numerous laws struck down by the New Jersey Supreme Court. Also absent from the figure are protracted periods of legislative inactivity, again in contrast to the eighteen-year gap in action by lawmakers in the Garden State. In any event, the major point here is that the courts in New York never meaningfully altered the policy choices of the elected branches and, with the single exception of the federal *Schenck* decision, did not initiate any changes to abortion regulations whatsoever. The following section will discuss all of these in much greater detail and illustrate why the early involvement of the legislature, coupled with key actions by the executive, resulted in a highly diminished role for the judiciary as it related to the development of abortion policy in New York.

Perhaps surprisingly, the issue was not even present on the state's political radar screen a mere three years before Governor Rockefeller signed the bill into law. According to then-state senator John J. Marchi, "[a]bortion had barely entered into the public dialogue. I remember attending the [New York State] Constitutional Convention of 1967, and there wasn't a single bill on the subject, nor was there any advocacy" (Perez-Pena 2000). Similarly, Michael Long, then-Chairman of the New York State Conservative Party recalls that "[a]bortion was a nonissue up until then. The party wasn't even united on it then, because nobody had given it much thought. We first put a pro-life plank in the party platform in 1968, and we had a big internal fight about it. Nobody—and I mean nobody—expected this to become a reality" (Perez-Pena 2000). This is not to say that efforts to liberalize the 1830 abortion law had not been made up to that point; indeed in 1967, 1968, and 1969, Assemblyman Percy E. Sutton of Manhattan had introduced legislation that would have permitted abortion under very limited circumstances, though Senate Majority Leader Earl W. Brydges had on each occasion refused to allow a vote on the bill in the upper house (Perez-Pena 2000).

When Brydges finally allowed a vote in the Senate, he believed that a more liberal bill would certainly be defeated and thereby discouraged further pressure from pro-choice legislators in pressing the issue. Brydges, a Republican from Niagara Falls and a staunch Catholic, allowed a vote, which, to the surprise and shock of everyone in Albany, resulted in passage of the legislation by a vote of 31 to 26 (Perez-Pena 2000). The vote in the Assembly proved to be even more dramatic with a single legislator changing his vote at the last minute in order to break a tie and send the bill to the Governor's desk to be signed into law. There were, in fact, two votes in the lower house; the first, on March 30, resulted in 73 yeas to 70 nays, short of the 76 needed for passage, while the second, on April 9, ended in a dead-even 74–74 split. Before the vote was brought to a close, however, Assemblyman George M. Michaels, a conservative Democrat from Central New York, asked that his vote against the abortion bill be changed. Addressing the Assembly, Michaels articulated his reason for the last-minute decision:

> One of my sons just called me a whore for the vote I cast against this [while another had pleaded], Dad, for God's sake, don't let your vote be the vote that defeats this bill. I fully appreciate that this is the termination of my political career, but Mr. Speaker, I must have some peace in my family. And I therefore request you, Mr. Speaker, to change my negative vote to an affirmative vote.

What these two choices demonstrate is that, first, the fact that they were made early in the process had a disproportionate impact on where the issue would be located going forward, and second, that seemingly random or even trivial events can have a profound impact if they occur at early stages. As the

Year	Courts (State)	Courts (Federal)	Legislature	Executive
1970			Liberal. Law	
1971				
1972	Byrn, Robin, Wyman			Repeal Veto
1973		Roe v. Wade		
1974			Hospital Law	
1975				
1976				PC Veto
1977				
1978				
1979				
1980				
1981			Medicaid Law	
1982				
1983				
1984				
1985	RC Diocese of Alb.			
1986				
1987				
1988				
1989			PCAP Law	PCC Suit
1990				
1991				
1992				
1993				
1994	Hope v. Perales			
1995		Schenck		
1996				
1997				
1998				
1999			FACE Law	
2000				
2001				
2002				
2003				
2004				
2005				Plan B Veto
2006				
2007				
2007				
2008				
2009				
2010				

Figure 3.1. Major Developments by Branch in New York State

analyses of the major court decisions dealing with abortion that follow demonstrate, the early involvement of the elected branches had a highly significant impact on the way the Court of Appeals viewed this question. The passage of the 1970 liberalization bill is crucial as well simply by virtue of it being the first time a substantive change had occurred in New York's abortion policy since the nineteenth century. As Pierson suggests, "[e]arly draws in each trial, *which have a considerable random element*, have a powerful effect on which of the possible equilibria will actually emerge" (2000, 235 emphasis added). In this case, Brydges' decision to allow a vote on the liberalization bill seems to have been based on a simple error in judgment about the likelihood of its passage in the Senate, though this miscalculation had the very important result of helping to establish the norm of legislative predominance in this issue area early. Similarly, few could have predicted that George Michaels would have switched his vote at the very moment that the roll call was taking place in order to provide the necessary majority for passage. Indeed, the Assemblyman had twice voted against the same bill that year and was well aware that his decision to change his position would mean the end of his political career.

One difficulty associated with this understanding that has been put forward by critics of the path dependence approach is the problem of identifying a so-called "first cause" (see Mahoney 2000). If, as the argument goes, initial decisions related to the development of policy are largely determinative of its future trajectory, how far back in time must one go in order to locate this critical decision point? Is it, as Stephen Hawking (1988) once put it, "turtles all the way down?" While this critique is certainly valid, the development of abortion policy, both in New York and New Jersey and, arguably, the country as a whole, offers a particularly good example of an issue area where initial movement following a long period of inertia can clearly be identified.[3] Substantive policy change dealing with abortion in the modern era first occurred in the Empire State in 1970, a full eighty-nine years after the last statutory alteration, an amendment to the criminal code elevating the procedure from a misdemeanor to a felony in 1881. Indeed, no proposal to alter the law in this area legislatively, nor via the courts, was undertaken until Percy E. Sutton first tabled a liberalization bill in 1967, which was never brought to a vote in the full Senate or Assembly. Much the same type of inertia was present in New Jersey as well, where the issue did not find its way onto the legislative or legal agenda until the late 1960s. In this sense, the abortion question offers an excellent opportunity to identify a clear "decision point" where policy change treating an essentially dormant issue was initiated by a specific political institution, in this case, the state legislature.

The significance of the 1970 liberalization law for a path dependence understanding of abortion policy making in New York is also patently evident simply by virtue of the legislature's choice to act in this issue area, a decision that was far from inevitable, as the New Jersey case illustrates. By passing a statute legalizing abortion before any substantive action addressing this question had been taken in federal or state courts,[4] the legislature established itself as the state institution within which this policy issue would be resolved, an action that would have profound consequences for the proceeding forty years. Developments taking place early in any process tend to have disproportionate influence at later points in time and institutions that are established during these early points tend to endure. Conceptualizing the idea of the legislature as the "proper" location of abortion policy making as itself a type of institution, we see that this early movement significantly shaped both the role that other branches in the state saw for themselves as well as how the legislature itself viewed its role. Indeed, as the following discussion reveals, we do in fact see following the 1970 liberalization law a clear articulation within the judiciary of the idea that the Senate and Assembly were unquestionably the appropriate location for addressing this question, an understanding that persisted for the ensuing three decades.

While there may not have been a guarantee that this initial location would be maintained over the entire forty years that followed the 1970 bill, the actions of the other branches of government served to increase the likelihood that the legislative path would be sustained. This idea is articulated nicely as the path dependence assumption that "institutions and expectations a policy creates are of necessity densely interwoven with broader features of the economy or society, creating interlocking networks of complementary institutions" (Hacker 2002, 55). While economics are obviously of less concern for the development of policy surrounding abortion, the sentiment is valid in its emphasis on the ways that coexisting institutions react to each other's actions in a manner that makes those established early more likely to persist. In this case, the initial refusal of the courts to alter policies created by the elected branches in cases such as *Byrn*, *Robin*, and *Hope*, discussed in much greater detail below, left this responsibility implicitly, or even in some cases explicitly, to the legislature.

Beyond the fact that the legislature acted on the abortion question before any state or relevant federal court had weighed in on the matter, it is worth noting that New York's abortion law had been challenged in District Court in 1969, a year before the passage of the liberalization law. In *Abramowicz v. Lefkowitz*, four separate actions had been combined that sought to overturn the nineteenth-century law on the grounds that it amounted to a violation of the right to privacy (Greenhouse and Siegel 2012). The motion to convene a three-judge panel for the case, filed in the U.S. District Court for the Southern District of New York, was granted in November 1969 (*Abramowicz v. Lefkowitz* 305 F. Supp. 1030); however, the case was ultimately dismissed in 1972 as moot following the passage of the liberalization law. As it considered repealing its abortion statute in April 1970, though, the legislature was undoubtedly aware of this litigation.[5] In stark contrast to the choice of the New Jersey legislature, however, the Assembly and Senate in New York chose not to wait until the courts were able to rule on the matter and passed a repeal bill well before even the District Court had had a chance to create policy. While it may not be possible to demonstrate irrefutably that lawmakers were consciously attempting to ensure that they, rather than the courts, were the ones to create policy dealing with abortion, the *Abramowicz* case certainly suggests that a clear opportunity to defer policy making authority existed and that the state's Assemblymembers and Senators did not take it.

It would be instructive at this point to take a closer look at the specific wording of the statute that eventually passed the Senate and Assembly in 1970. The relevant section of Penal Law § 125.05 (1970) reads:

> An abortional act is justifiable when committed upon a female with her consent by a duly licensed physician acting (a) under a reasonable belief that such is necessary to preserve her life, or, (b) within twenty-four weeks from the commencement of her pregnancy. A pregnant female's commission of an abortional act upon herself is justifiable when she acts upon the advice of a duly licensed physician (1) that such act is necessary to preserve her life, or, (2) within twenty-four weeks from the commencement of her pregnancy. The submission by a female to an abortional act is justifiable when she believes that it is being committed by a duly licensed physician, acting under a reasonable belief that such act is necessary to preserve her life, or, within twenty-four weeks from the commencement of her pregnancy.

What is perhaps most striking about this statute is its brevity and the extent to which it imposes no restrictions whatsoever on a woman's ability to choose an abortion prior to the twenty-fourth week of pregnancy, particularly in contrast to other laws being proposed and passed at the time.[6] It is also notable for its remarkable simplicity and the explicit setting of an exact point before which abortions would be permitted. By setting the time at which a woman can obtain an abortion at such a specific date—again, something relatively unique within abortion law at the time—the legislature seems, at least in this area, to have left little room for interpretation by the courts. Comparing New York's statute again to Hawaii's, which was by most measures the second-most liberal law in the pre-*Roe* era, we see that the latter allowed for abortion only prior to "viability," a concept that was, and as demonstrated by many subsequent cases dealing with abortion still is, a relatively fluid definition. That being said, the use of terms such as "reasonable belief" and "necessary to preserve her life" are far from precise and leave ample room for further interpretation. Nonetheless, by setting a clear time frame of twenty-four weeks before which any abortion would be permissible, New York's law was comparatively specific, particularly in contrast to other liberalization laws at the time.

This fact of course did not prevent the 1970 statute from being challenged in court, the case that ultimately led to the *Byrn* decision. But the plaintiff in *Byrn*, discussed below, did not ask the Court for any type of statutory interpretation, as there was nothing in the law to interpret. Indeed, such a request was not at all out of the question, as this type of statutory interpretation was a major part of the plaintiff's argument in the New Jersey case of *Right to Choose v. Byrne*. Instead, the challenge was based entirely on the constitutionality of the law and the notion that allowing a woman to terminate her pregnancy amounted to a denial of the Due Process Clauses' guarantees of life in the New York State and U.S. Constitutions for the unborn fetus. This made the prospect of the Court of Appeals striking down the liberalization law considerably less likely as doing so would have involved the politically more costly decision of finding the entire law unconstitutional, rather than simply limiting it through statutory interpretation.

In contrast to the statements by lawmakers in New Jersey, which evinced a very legal understanding of the abortion question, particularly in the early to mid-1970s, Assemblymembers in New York framed the issue almost universally in political terms. Anthony Stella, a Bronx Democrat who switched his previous "yes" vote to one against the liberalization bill, explained that "[l]ast week I thought I cast a vote representing the people who live in my area—it is overwhelmingly Catholic—and I did so because I thought it was not my job to legislate my own morality. But I was wrong. My own parishioners expressed their surprise that I voted the way I did and made clear their feelings to me" (Kovach 1970c). Queens Republican John Gallagher stated more bluntly during the floor debate that "I point the finger at every member who votes for this bill and say 'you, sir, killed these innocent children'" (Kovach 1970c). Supporters of the bill in the Assembly also focused on political considerations such as proper public policy, with Constance Cook, who had been a prime sponsor of the legislation, arguing that "[i]t's just a matter of deciding that you can't sit here and decide who and when and how an abortion is to be performed—they are being performed now. My object is to get this whole question into the hands of a doctor and into the hospitals" (Kovach 1970c). Charles Rangel, then a Democratic Assemblyman from Manhattan who had voted in favor of the bill, also discussed the pressure he felt from the Catholic Church, though in this case highlighted that his parish had seen "fit to have my name called as one who acted improperly. And had it printed in the parish newspaper. But, I am hurt and disappointed that the clergy did not so act when we tried to stop the welfare cutbacks, or get decent housing, or get basic health care or hot water to our people" (Kovach 1970c).

The tone in the Senate was much the same, with Clinton Dominick, a Republican from Newburgh and one of the sponsors of the liberalization bill in the upper chamber, arguing that "[t]here is nothing worse than an unwilling mother and the unwanted child. It leads to divorce. It leads to broken homes. It leads to dropout. It leads to battered children—neglected children" (Kovach 1970b). Earl Brydges, the Senate majority leader who had previously blocked the bill from coming to a vote, closed the floor debate by lamenting that "I am terribly disturbed by this bill . . . I have a deep, real, abiding conviction that this is the wrong way for the state to go because we are a bellweather state and many other states will follow our lead" (Kovach 1970b). Finally, Waldaba Stewart, a Democrat from Brooklyn who cast the twenty-ninth and deciding vote in favor of liberalization, explained his decision as a choice "to help move the Empire State toward a new approach to a new society. We are venturing into new waters, toward a society in which we look honestly at ourselves and our relationships to our families" (Kovach 1970b). Conspicuously absent from both sides of the debate in New York, then, was any mention of abortion as a right or any other legal justification for removing the 1830 law from the criminal code, very much in contrast to the way the issue was framed by those in the elected branches in New Jersey. Instead, the focus in both the Assembly and Senate was on concerns regarding accurately reflecting the wishes of largely Catholic constituents, providing a safe medical environment for abortions, the perceived negative social consequences of unwanted children, and even the impact of liberalization on the policies of other states.

The next major action on the abortion issue was to repeal the 1970 liberalization law in 1972, a bill that was vetoed by Governor Rockefeller. This was almost certainly a result of the intervening elections, which had seen several pro-choice members of the Assembly and Senate lose their seats, as well as the founding of the New York State Right to Life Party in 1970 and their lobbying efforts within the state capitol, though unfortunately campaign donation records prior to 1980 are not available and therefore the actual impact of the Right to Life Party on legislative races in 1970 is difficult to assess. Several Senators and Assemblymembers did, however, change their previous votes from the liberalization law two years earlier, though this occurred on both sides of the issue. In the weeks leading up to the vote in Albany, however, Governor Rockefeller had made it widely known that he would veto the bill and it therefore seems likely that its passage was not meant as a serious effort to make policy, but rather as a political act in response to intense pro-life lobbying efforts (Narvaez 1972b). Because the repeal bill never became law, it is impossible to know how the courts would have responded, and in any case, the *Roe* decision in 1973 precluded the outright ban on abortion that would have resulted without the Governor's veto.

The failure of the repeal bill by virtue of the Governor's veto does nonetheless afford an opportunity to once again consider a counterfactual to the path dependent trajectory of abortion policy making that actually took place. In terms of timing, the 1972 vote took place before the Court of Appeals had handed down its opinion in *Byrn*, meaning the only state court decision that had yet been offered up to that point had been *Matter of City of New York v. Wyman*, upholding an executive directive denying state funding for abortions that were not deemed medically necessary. In addition, if the Court can be taken at its word in *Byrn*, it would have potentially sustained the repeal law as it had made explicit its deference to the legislature in setting the state's abortion policy in that decision. In that sense, the successful passage of the 1972 bill may well have made little difference in the court's reluctance to create abortion policy, particularly as the reinstatement of the 1830 law would have in any event been voided a mere nine months later by the U.S. Supreme Court in *Roe*. Extending the hypothetical even further, the next major Court of Appeals decisions dealing with abortion were the Suffolk County Medicaid ban, which the Court upheld in 1978, and the *Hope* decision, which also sustained a restriction on the procedure. It would seem reasonable then to suspect that even if the repeal bill had been signed into law, the path of legislative dominance in this issue area, and the courts' consequent refusal to create policy treating abortion, had been established to some extent as early as the 1970 liberalization bill.

In terms of the rhetorical frame that had begun to take root in the elected branches when the repeal bill was passed, the Governor's veto message is instructive. By way of example, Rockefeller wrote that "I can see no justification now for repealing this reform and thus condemning hundreds of thousands of women to the dark age once again." Striking a similar tone, the Governor also argued that "[t]he truth is that a safe abortion would remain the optional choice of the well-to-do woman, while the poor would again be seeking abortions at a grave risk to life in back-room abortion mills." Finally, Rockefeller made perhaps the most clearly "political" case for his rejection of the bill in claiming that "the extremes of personal vilification and political coercion brought to bear on members of the Legislature raise serious doubts that the vote to repeal the reform represented the will of a majority of the people of New York State" (quoted in Greenhouse and Siegel 2012, 159).

The language and rhetorical frames that informed the thinking of Assemblymembers and Senators during the debate before passage of the repeal bill was very similar to what was apparent two years earlier and was also notable for its lack of any mention of abortion as a legal question. The prime sponsor of the legislation, Republican Senator James Donovan of Chadwicks, for example, characterized abortion as the "barbaric slaughter of innocents" and that "we are exterminating one human life every three minutes, round the clock" (Narvaez 1972a). Roy Goodman, a Republican Senator from Manhattan who opposed the 1972 bill, by contrast, argued that "[t]his is not a human being . . . It is a series of organisms which may eventually become a human being" (Narvaez 1972a). Fellow Manhattan Senator Manfred Ohrenstein, a Democrat, focused for his part on the impropriety of religious influence on policy making, stating legislators "have no right to come to the floor of this body and ask us to enact into law church doctrine. The church is seeking a confrontation here" (Narvaez 1972a). On the Assembly side, Constance Cook expressed palpable frustration with the repeal effort, claiming that "we are now engaged in a purely political activity in the midst of the primary season and I'm absolutely sure the public is way smarter" (Farrell 1972a). Another opponent of the bill, Democratic Assemblyman Albert Blumenthal of Manhattan, asked "[w]hy does this Legislature keep entering my bedroom and the bedroom of every couple in this state? Why can't you stay out of people's personal business?" (Farrell 1972a). Neil Kelleher, a Republican from Troy, displayed a fetus in a jar to the Assembly and stated that "[it] feels heat, feels cold, feels pain—don't kid me, you know life is there" (Farrell 1972a). Bronx Democrat G. Oliver Koppell even decried a letter from Richard Nixon supporting the repeal bill, arguing that the President had "put into jeopardy the lives of every citizen of the world by his actions in Vietnam [and] cannot come and talk to me of life" (Farrell 1972a).

Also in 1972, the Court of Appeals upheld a directive from State Social Services Commissioner George Wyman banning the use of Medicaid funds for elective abortions in *City of New York v. Wyman* (30 N.Y.2d 537). In response to this decision, abortion rights groups for the first time since the 1970 liberalization law sought federal intervention, appealing the ruling to the Second Circuit. After hearing the case in August, a three-judge panel unanimously voted to overturn the Court of Appeals decision, finding that the government's refusal to fund abortions for women who could not otherwise afford them amounted to discrimination. Specifically, Judge J. Edward Lumbard, who authored the opinion in *Klein v. Nassau County Medical Center*, argued that the policy violated the Equal Protection clause as poor women "alone are subjected to state coercion to bear children which they do not want to bear" (501). This case was significant for several reasons, though the most salient of these are that it represented the first time that a state-level court handed down a decision related to abortion, although the Court did not issue a written opinion, as well as the first instance of federal intervention on this particular issue. In addition, it demonstrated that the courts in the state were not simply institutions staffed by pro-choice judges who were happy to support the liberalization laws emanating from the other branches but were more accurately characterized as unwilling to circumvent decisions made by the executive or the legislature. Finally, the Court of Appeals decision once again represented an example of a state-level court serving to legitimize the choices of the elected branch, in this case the executive, though this decision was ultimately overturned at the federal level. The Second Circuit decision was appealed to the United States Supreme Court, though certiorari was denied, almost certainly due to the High Court's upcoming ruling in what would be its *Roe v. Wade* decision in 1973 (*New York Times* 1976).

The first major instance of judicial involvement in the abortion issue came several months after the failure of the repeal bill with the Court of Appeals decision in *Byrn v. New York City Health & Hospitals Corporation*. The argument put forward by Byrn, the lead counsel in the case, was that the court ought to recognize embryos as human and therefore protected by the 14th Amendment guarantee of life found in the Due Process Clause, as well as asking that he be appointed the legal guardian of all unborn children in New York. The court ruled against Byrn in a 5–2 decision with Judge Charles D. Breitel stating that "the Constitution does not confer or require legal personality for the unborn; the legislature may, or it may do something less, as it did in the abortion statute, and provide some protection far short of providing legal personality" (890). The real question, according to the Court, however, was whether the fetus was a person, which, according to New York law, it was not. Referring again to the prerogative of the legislature, the court wrote that "[t]he issues [of the personhood of unborn fetuses] are outside the law unless the legislature should provide otherwise" (890). In this sense, the Court was not making policy but was simply affirming the policy created by the legislature. Note here that the court explicitly states not only that the legislature's choices in addressing the abortion issue ought to be controlling in determining what may and may not be imposed in terms of restricting abortion policy, but that it offers extremely wide latitude to this branch in either direction. Indeed, the Court stated that while it found no constitutional justification for granting personhood to unborn fetuses, the "legislature may, or it may do something less, as it did in the abortion statute," suggesting not only that it recognized and supported the legislature's decision in passing the 1970 law, but that it would be equally deferential to this institution had it chosen a radically more restrictive policy direction. In this sense, not only did the Court refuse to interfere in the lawmaking authority of the legislature, but it preemptively set the precedent that if the legislature chose to reverse itself, that too would be considered by the judiciary as a legitimate and constitutionally permissible act.

Significantly, the Court also refused to rule on whether or not a woman had a constitutional right to terminate her pregnancy, despite the fact that the respondent in *Byrn*, the Health and Hospitals Corporation, had explicitly asked the judges to weigh in on this very question during oral argument (Price and Keck 2014). In this sense, the New York State Court of Appeals had refused to do what the U.S. Supreme Court would do a year later in *Roe*, namely, establish a constitutional right to abortion, based either on the U.S. or state constitutions. This decision is important particularly in light of the fact that the legislature did indeed vote to repeal the 1970 liberalization law two years later. In other words, the Court very well could have asserted a policy making role, which would have entrenched the right to abortion in the state regardless of what the legislature subsequently chose to do, but opted again to leave this decision up to the Assembly and Senate. This choice is made all the more relevant when considering that the *Byrn* decision came in 1972, two years after the election that had seen George Michaels and other pro-choice legislators lose their seats, largely on the basis of their "yes" votes on the liberalization law. In any case, the Court had demonstrated at least a passing policy preference in support of abortion rights by rejecting the argument put forward by Byrn, and so the question becomes, why did the Court not choose to exercise its influence and further establish this right in the face of possible legislative action against it? This question has several possible answers and will be addressed later in this work.

Returning to the theoretical framework on offer here, the *Byrn* decision also demonstrates well how the language and understanding inherent in a given institution's mandate can influence how other branches view certain policy questions. The Court's majority opinion can be broken up into two main sections: the first of these consists of a cursory overview of historical views of abortion, which Judge Breitel concludes is of little importance to the present case; while the second considers Byrn's claim regarding the legal personhood of unborn fetuses. Much like Justice Blackmun's majority opinion in *Roe*, Breitel stresses the difficulty of resolving the question of when life begins, though the resolution of this issue is based on considerably different reasoning in *Byrn*. While Blackmun stresses that the constitutional understanding of personhood under the Due Process Clause has never included the unborn, Breitel writes that "[w]hether the law should accord legal personality is a policy question which in most instances devolves on the Legislature" (201) and that "[t]here are, then, real issues in this litigation, but they are not legal or justiciable" (203). Judge Jasen's concurring opinion echoes this view in claiming that legal personhood "is a value judgment not committed to the discretion of judges, but reposing instead in the representative branch of government" (205). It is abundantly clear from the above quotations that the judges of the Court of Appeals were not basing their ruling in *Byrn* on a "legal" understanding of the question in the sense of rights, precedent, or common law, but rather on what might better be termed "judicial restraint" in the tradition of legal scholars such as Felix Frankfurter and Oliver Wendell Holmes. Unlike Holmes and Frankfurter, though, this deference to the legislature was not consistent, as some of the landmark cases discussed in chapter 1 demonstrate, and therefore seem to be explicable more in terms of the initial occupation of this issue area by the legislature. In other words, the deference to the legislature demonstrated in Judge Breitel's opinion was not based on a doctrinal commitment to judicial restraint, but rather was a product of both the initial framing of abortion in political terms related to the institutional first movement by the elected branches and the adoption of that view by the Court of Appeals.

Indeed, even the dissenting opinions offered in *Byrn* were notable for the lack of "legal" language when critiquing Breitel's ruling. Judge Burke, whose colorful dissent was joined by Judge Cipleppi, wrote that "[t]he proponents of abortion take refuge in concocted distinctions as to what living human beings are persons and what living human beings are not persons—to justify the massacre of the innocents" (209, 210). In addition to this focus on the argument regarding when a fetus ought to be considered a person, Burke made frequent references to the Holocaust, Nazi Germany, and Soviet atrocities. The seven-and-a-half page dissent went on to argue that the Declaration of Independence required the Court to invalidate the law—going so far as to invoke the spirit of Thomas Jefferson—and that the existence and availability of contraception and adoption as alternatives to abortion made the law unnecessary. In many ways, Burke's dissent had more in common with a passionate speech on the floor of Congress than a legal opinion, though it shared the theme of Breitel's majority decision in the use of language that was decidedly political in nature. In this sense, the early rulings of the Court had clearly adopted an issue frame that more closely resembled what would be expected from the elected branches, regardless of the direction of the argument.

Viewing *Byrn* through the lens of a knowledge claim, we find clear evidence both of "constrained meaning" and the influence of a particular knowledge community, in this case the legislature. Here again a comparison with Justice Blackmun's opinion in *Roe* the following year reveals that the question of whether or not a fetus was to be considered a legal "person" was addressed in both decisions, though it was viewed quite differently by the two courts. In deciding this issue, it seems reasonable to suppose that the "competing knowledge claims" could have been derived from two sources; the common law or constitutional definition of personhood or the authority of the elected branches to make this determination. It was of course the former that was adopted by the majority opinion in *Roe*, but the latter course was followed by the New York Court of Appeals in *Byrn*. Indeed, references to the common law as they related to the question of abortion were made primarily with respect to whether or not the procedure had historically been viewed as a crime in English and New York law,[7] while the rejection of Byrn's claim regarding the protected status of unborn fetuses under the Due Process Clause was based almost entirely on the legislature's refusal to make this determination. In answering the same question, however, Justice Blackmun looks to the "Fifth, Twelfth, and Twenty-second Amendments, as well as in §§ 2 and 3 of the Fourteenth Amendment" arguing that "in nearly all these instances, the use of the word is such that it has application only postnatally. None indicates, with any assurance, that it has any possible pre-natal application" (*Roe* at 157). The underlying interpretive framework that took root in *Byrn*, then, would seem to have its origin in the actions of the legislature that preceded that decision. This alone is not necessarily sufficient to demonstrate that the "political" frame had been fully adopted by the judiciary in New York when treating the abortion question, though as subsequent decisions reveal, this frame, or "knowledge claim" to use Brandwein's (2011) terminology, seems to have "won" as the principle interpretive lens adopted by the courts, resulting in the continued location of policy making within the elected branches.

The same year it handed down the *Byrn* decision, the Court of Appeals also heard a case challenging a law passed at the local level that touched on abortion rights. In 1971, the town of Hempstead passed an ordinance requiring that all abortions be performed only in Hempstead General Hospital. At the time, Bill Baird—who had previously gained national attention as the respondent in the landmark case of *Eisenstadt v. Baird* (1970)—had been offering low-cost abortions at his Parent's Aid Society clinic in the town and challenged the constitutionality of the law. In *Robin v. Hempstead*, the Court of Appeals ruled in favor of Baird, declaring that the state had reserved for itself sole discretion in deciding where abortions could be performed, and that the only limitation it had chosen to enact was that the procedure be performed by a physician. This ruling was a crucial victory for abortion rights in New York as several other municipalities had enacted, or had been debating, similar restrictions on access to abortion services but were now forbidden to do so unless the state legislature chose to act (Bower 1996). As in *Byrn*, then, the Court again played the role of legitimizing the choices of the elected branches by choosing not to alter the status of abortion policy that had been established by the legislature.

In *Robin* we see again a Court signaling its unwillingness to circumvent the choices of the legislature, though in this case, the question before the Court dealt with the ability of localities, specifically the Village of Hempstead on Long Island, to legislate in matters that allegedly fell under the jurisdiction of the state government. Echoing a theme from *Byrn*, *Robin* explicitly declared that the state had "reserved to itself regulation of the practice of medicine in general and of the performance of abortions in particular" (350), making clear, as early as 1972, that it was inclined to allow the legislature broad latitude in this policy area. Interestingly, the Court also pointed out that amendments to the Public Health Law had been offered that would have clarified where abortions could be performed, the question that was at the heart of this case, though it had chosen not to include these. The opinion in *Robin* went on to argue that this omission was in fact an implicit statement by lawmakers that they did not wish to limit the procedure to hospitals alone because they were clearly aware that such an option was available to them but chose not to pursue it. Applying Lovell's (2003) standard, then, it would seem on the surface that the legislature may in fact have been engaging in a sort of deferral because it had refused to include an amendment that would have clarified its intention. That being said, the Court also pointed out that "following amendment of the Penal Law dealing with abortions, the State Department of Health amended the State Hospital Code, pursuant to section 2803 of the Public Health Law, in order to authorize and regulate the performance of abortions in both 'hospitals' and 'independent out-of-hospital health facilit[ies]'" (350). In other words, the amendments proposed to the Public Health Law, which would have clarified the facilities in which abortions could be performed, would have been superfluous as this clarification had already been made by the executive following passage of the 1970 liberalization bill. This is significant in light of the theoretical approach proposed in this work regarding the interrelationship between the branches of government and their role in influencing the extent of court involvement. While the *Byrn* ruling had made it clear that the legislature was to have broad latitude in terms what would or would not be permissible regarding abortion, *Robin* suggests that this deference was to extend to the executive as well. Further illustrating the importance of interpretive communities, the Court in the latter decision again emphasized that it was taking its cues largely from the elected branches rather than its own authority as derived from the Constitution or its status as a separate institution.

In some respects, the *Robin* decision could also be understood as an example of judicial policy making in line with Lovell's (2003) description of deferral in the sense that the Court established a rule prohibiting localities from restricting the types of facilities within which abortions could be performed. Referring again to Judge Fuld's opinion in the case, however, it seems clear that the executive, through the State Department of Health's amendment to the Hospital Code, had already established the policy that abortions were to be permissible both in hospitals and independent out-of-hospital facilities. In this sense, the Court did not create a policy that had not previously existed, but rather reaffirmed one that had already been articulated by the executive branch. Indeed, it seems difficult to suspect that the Department of Health's directive was meant only to apply to *some* facilities in the state, arguably leaving the Court with little choice but to either overturn the executive's policy, which certainly would have represented an example of judicial policy making, or to sustain the choice made by the Health Department, the path it ultimately chose.

A closer examination of the opinion offered in *Robin* will help illustrate the way in which this case clearly demonstrated the view the Court was to take in regards to the abortion question in the decades that followed. Specifically, Judge Fuld writes that "[t]here can be no doubt that the State has reserved to itself regulation of the practice of medicine in general and of the performance of abortions in particular" (350). This idea is indeed quite similar to that expressed by Judge Breitel in *Byrn* with its explicit reliance on the prerogative of the legislature as the dominant interpretive community dealing with the regulation of abortion. Further elaborating on this point, the Court went on to claim that the "State's purpose and design [is] to pre-empt the subject of abortion legislation and occupy the entire field so as to prohibit additional regulation by local authorities in the same area" (350). Finally, in reference to the ability of localities to enact abortion restrictions, Fuld wrote that:

> prior to amending the statute, the Legislature had before it two bills which expressly provided that an "abortional act is not criminal, and thus is legally justifiable, when performed in a hospital which has been certified" under provisions of the Public Health Law (see 1970 Assembly Int. No. 8; Senate Int. No. 3500). Neither of these bills became law. Thus, although the Legislature was aware of the additional restrictions that were urged and could have been placed in the abortion law . . . it nevertheless enacted a statute without the restrictions sought to be imposed by the village (351, 352).

Taken together, these portions of the Court's opinion in *Robin* again illustrate the initiation of a line of decisions that would highlight its view of the abortion issue as political, if only by virtue of its continued insistence that the elected branches had clearly intended for themselves to be the principle policy making institutions responsible for the development of policy in this area. Indeed, Fuld refers specifically to the liberalization law in striking down the Village's ordinance as justification for adopting this "political" narrative.

Beyond articulating how the Court was to view the abortion question in New York going forward in legal and constitutional terms, *Robin* and *Byrn* had the critical effect of emphasizing the importance of these early decisions, as well as in relation to the legislature's institutional first movement. Viewing norms and legal understandings as institutions, *Robin* set the rhetorical and precedential stage for the courts to adopt a view of abortion not in terms of rights but as a question for the political branches. By the same token, Judge Breitel's famous quotation in *Byrn* regarding the ability of the legislature to choose among a host of options related to abortion restrictions, or the lack thereof, began the process of foreclosing the courts as a viable institution for the development of policy in this area. This of course does not mean that future litigation on this question was not to take place, it obviously was, but *Byrn* was the first case that truly began the establishment of the norm of judicial nonintervention in New York. As Hathaway (2001) puts it, "[t]he nonergodicity of the common law system makes early cases on a legal issue dramatically important. Because the path of the common law is locked in at an early stage, early decisions are crucial to the direction of the law" (130).

Byrn and *Robin* are also crucially important cases from a path dependence standpoint as they can both be understood as "critical moments." Indeed, the latter was the first case handed down in New York that dealt with the abortion question at all and, as discussed above, was rather explicit in its insistence that this issue area was to remain within the province of the legislature. Perhaps more importantly, though, was the Court's choice in that decision to adopt the legislature-as-controlling frame reflected in Judge Breitel's opinion. *Robin*, however, dealt only somewhat peripherally with the question of abortion and was more important for the precedent that it set of firmly refusing to second-guess the choices of the Senate and Assembly. *Byrn*, for its part, served to effectively cut off the judicial route as a plausible avenue for policy change regarding the legality of abortion itself in the state. By dismissing the plaintiff's claim in a terse five-page opinion, as well as concluding its decision with the above-mentioned quote regarding the legislature's role as the sole policy making institution tasked with the development of abortion policy, the *Byrn* ruling may reasonably be viewed as one of two critical moments within the judiciary's participation in the path dependent development of this issue in New York. To clarify, then, *Byrn* may be understood as an unequivocal declaration of the Court's refusal to act as a viable path for abortion policy making, while *Robin*'s status can best be conceptualized as an articulation of the constitutional justification for the legislative path, as well as an elaboration of the institutional role the Court saw for itself. In this sense, both of these 1972 cases—indeed, the decisions for both were handed down a mere month apart, with *Robin* being decided in early June of that year while *Byrn* was announced in early July—appear to fulfill the role of critical moments in the development of New York's abortion policy as they each served to demonstrate exactly what role the judiciary would play in relation to the legislative branch.[8]

MAINTAINING THE POLITICAL PATH

Abortion opponents, seemingly stalled in the courts following the 1972 decision, soon shifted their efforts to repeal the 1970 law again to the legislature. Despite the failure of a repeal bill in 1972, the Assembly and Senate had seen the arrival of no fewer than fifty new members for the 1973 session, and groups such as the New York State Right to Life Committee saw the potential for passing a similar bill that year with the support of a veto-proof majority (Buckley 1973). At the same time, anti-abortion groups were also actively targeting Governor Rockefeller, who was repeatedly heckled at a series of town hall meetings because of his position on abortion, and against whom the Right to Life Committee had committed significant resources in an effort to defeat in the next election. Indeed, the legislative session that began in January of 1973 was disrupted several times by anti-abortion protesters, some of whom went so far as to occupy the Assembly chamber, refusing to leave until a repeal bill was brought to a vote (Buckley 1973). But while the intensity of the abortion debate in New York may have reached a crescendo in 1973, the chance of outright repeal was significantly curtailed that same year with the announcement of the *Roe* decision.

If the years from 1970 to 1973 had seen a flood of activity around the abortion issue in New York, both from supporters and opponents of liberalized laws, then 1974 and 1975 were conspicuous in the absence of a comparable level of movement. This was certainly not the case around the country, however, or for that matter, the region, as both New Jersey and Pennsylvania lawmakers had spent much of 1974 and 1975 attempting to amend their abortion statutes in order to circumvent *Roe* (Waggoner 1974; *New York Times* 1975). Some limits were placed on abortion by the legislature in 1974 when a bill was passed by the Assembly and Senate, and signed into law by Governor Wilson, which required that abortions performed after the twelfth week of pregnancy be carried out in a hospital and that a second physician be present during abortions occurring after the twentieth week in order "to take control of and provide immediate medical care for any live birth that is the result of the abortion" (Narvaez 1974). Opponents of the bill claimed that it was intended only as an election-year publicity tool and that it was unnecessary, if not unconstitutional, though the New York statute was never challenged in court (Clines 1974).[9] The bill did represent the first statewide legislative victory for the pro-life side since the 1970 liberalization law, though the practical effect of the law on abortions throughout the state may have been negligible.

Still under tremendous pressure from pro-life groups, the legislature passed a parental consent bill in 1976 by a vote of 94 to 43 in the Assembly and 35 to 22 in the Senate, with Governor Carey vetoing the bill only hours before it was set to come into law. The influence of these lobbying efforts can be seen in the fact that many believed that a number of legislators in both houses who had had personal reservations about voting for the parental consent bill did so only with the understanding that it would in fact be vetoed by the governor, though wanted the ability to have gone on the record as having supported the pro-life measure (Greenhouse 1976). More telling, however, was the fact that virtually no effort was made to override the veto, despite the fact that only five legislators would have been required in the Senate and six in the Assembly in order to achieve the override,[10] something that may have been possible through alterations to wording of the legislation. Indeed, the Governor's staff had made it clear to Democratic members of both the Assembly and Senate that he would veto the parental consent bill if it were to make it to his desk before the final vote was held in either chamber (Petersen 1976). In this sense, a kind of deferral did seem to have taken place in as much as a number of legislators appear to have consciously voted against their policy preferences for political reasons, though with the understanding that the bill would fail to receive the governor's signature. Deferral in this context is similar to the phenomenon described by Lovell (2003) and Graber

(1993) in that it represents a way to pass decision making from the hands of lawmakers to another political actor, though in this case, the "target" of the deferral is not the courts but rather the executive. Such a strategy might be advantageous to legislators seeking a policy outcome that they prefer, but for which they would like to avoid a public, roll call vote record. Unlike in the theories proposed by Lovell (2003), Whittington (2007), and Graber (1993), however, the executive branch is not, as are the courts, unelected.

The parental consent bill can also be understood in the context of the wider national debate on this particular abortion restriction. Indeed, a number of states had begun passing parental notification and consent laws in the mid-1970s in an effort to test the boundaries of the *Roe* decision, though these efforts were initially derailed by the U.S. Supreme Court's decision in *Planned Parenthood of Central Missouri v. Danforth* (1976). Taking issue both with the Missouri statute's regulation of abortion in the first trimester in contravention of the *Roe* framework as well as the overbroad nature of the law, the Court found that requiring a minor to obtain written parental consent was an unconstitutional abridgement of the right to privacy. Similarly in 1979, the High Court struck down Massachusetts' parental consent law in *Bellotti v. Baird*, despite the inclusion of a judicial bypass provision. The first such statute to be upheld did not come into effect until 1981 when the Court sustained Utah's considerably less restrictive law, which required only that a physician notify a minor's parent or guardian of her abortion, in *H.L. v. Matheson*. Two years later, a parental consent law was upheld for the first time in *Planned Parenthood of Kansas City, Mo. v. Ashcroft* (1983) while a series of subsequent cases further affirmed the ability of states to require either parental notification or parental consent. Indeed, since the mid-1970s, a majority of states have enacted such laws, suggesting that the attempt to pass a similar statute in New York was part of a national strategy to implement these types of requirements (Gaylord 1994). The proposed New York law would have required the permission of the parents or legal guardians of women under the age of 18 in order to terminate their pregnancy, with exceptions for women who had previously given birth or were married. Unlike the New Jersey and Pennsylvania laws, however, it has been suggested that the New York bill was less of a concerted effort by committed pro-life legislators to undermine abortion rights and more of an attempt to placate anti-abortion constituencies (Dullea 1976). Indeed, a virtually identical version of the 1976 bill has been introduced in the Assembly and Senate in every subsequent legislative session though it has never made its way out of committee.

As with Rockefeller's message in 1972, Carey's statement accompanying his veto of the parental consent bill is also instructive in terms of the largely political frame it took. The Governor's 1976 veto took place under somewhat different circumstances, with Carey waiting until the last minute before rejecting the measure, though his message echoed many of the same themes as Rockefeller's had four years earlier. Specifically, the Governor wrote of the bill that it was: "illusory [and would] not accomplish its stated purpose. On the contrary, it is an attempt to substitute symbolism for a substantial and legally sound treatment of a serious issue" (Carey 1976, 456). In addition, Carey discussed "the significance of the family structure," his refusal to sign the bill on the basis of making a "strong moral statement" and his commitment to not imposing his own objections to abortion on the citizens of New York. Finally, the Governor wrote that "[r]egrettably, a higher proportion of early teenage pregnancies are among those who lack a secure home. It is with respect to these children that the bill's defects are most glaring, since it would impose upon them a cruel and intolerable burden" (Carey 1976, 456). While a single paragraph of the Governor's veto message was devoted to the questionable constitutionality of the bill, the main thrust of Carey's argument was based on concerns regarding the propriety of the proposed legislation rather than its legal implications.

Unfortunately, news reports from the time offer considerably fewer examples of lawmakers' statements regarding the parental consent bill than had been the case for the liberalization and repeal measures, making an analysis of the frames through which legislators saw this action more difficult. Nevertheless, several quotes regarding the proposed law suggest that Carey's political view of the question was apparent in the legislature as well. Herbert Miller, a Democratic Assemblyman from Queens, for example, expressed frustration with the proposed consent requirement, arguing that "[t]he leadership was completely intimidated by members who wanted this bill so as to enhance their chances for re-election. This didn't take the ordinary course of bills in this House and the leadership took unprecedented steps to advance passage of this unfortunate bill" (*New York Times* 1976). Although it never came to a vote, Democratic Senator Karen Burnstein of Woodmere, Long Island, had proposed an amendment to the measure that would have required parents refusing consent to an abortion to bear financial responsibility for the child. Defending this addition, Burnstein stated that a parent preventing access to the procedure was imposing "his or her moral judgment on their child [and] ought to be liable for the financial consequences" (Smothers 1976). The point here being that lawmakers in the mid-1970s were still conceptualizing abortion in terms such as "moral judgment" and considerations related to re-election, something that is particularly noteworthy following the *Byrn* and *Roe* decisions.

The failure of the parental consent bill may also have prevented path switching as it seems that there was good reason at the time to suspect that such a law would not have survived judicial scrutiny. As mentioned above, several similar laws had been struck down by federal courts in the mid-1970s, and New York's proposed legislation, requiring not just parental notification but also consent, would almost certainly have been found unconstitutional either in federal or state court. At this early stage in the development of abortion policy making in New York, a significant decision by the courts, such as striking down the parental consent bill, might have had important repercussions for the role the courts were to play later on in the process.[11] Involvement by the courts in striking down any of the failed legislative restrictions from the early to mid-1970s may have seriously challenged the then-emerging norm of a relatively uninvolved court. In addition, the parental consent bill vetoed by Governor Carey is an unambiguous example of a critical juncture where path switching could very well have taken place. As Capoccia and Kelemen (2007) write, "contingency [is] the key element of critical junctures. During critical junctures change is substantially less constrained than it is during the phases of path dependence that precede and follow them. In critical junctures contingency is enhanced, as the structural constraints imposed on actors during the path-dependent phase are substantially relaxed" (368). With the "contingency," or counterfactual, in this case being Carey's failure to veto the parental consent bill, 1976 represents a crucial year for the role of the courts by virtue of what they *did not* do. This is not to suggest that the Governor or the legislature consciously recognized that enactment of the law might have resulted in a changing norm of increased judicial involvement in abortion policy and acted to avoid this; simply that the development itself, the result of its own set of political and strategic choices, likely had the effect of decreasing the chances that the courts would play a significant policy making role in this issue going forward.

No sooner had the parental consent bill been proposed, passed, and vetoed, that the battle over abortion rights in New York State again switched its focus and venue. In 1978, the Suffolk County legislature passed an ordinance barring the use of state Medicaid funds for abortions, overriding the veto of County Executive John Klein (Cerra 1978). What is perhaps most interesting about this action, however, is that it represented another attempt by anti-abortion interest groups to shift the policy debate from the state to the local level, having previously secured similar ordinances in Niagara and Seneca counties (Cerra 1978). The order was challenged in court almost immediately following its passage and was upheld in a ruling by Justice Frank DeLuca, who claimed that the county legislature did in fact have the power to refuse to devote its share of Medicaid expenses to abortion coverage, a figure amounting to approximately one-third of the total cost.

The battle over state financing of abortion soon did move to the state and local levels, though, and became a crucial part of the 1978 and 1979 budget battles in Albany with lawmakers finding themselves in a stalemate over the issue. A year earlier, both the Republican and Democratic leadership in the Assembly and Senate, as well as the Governor, had all pledged their support for government funding of abortion before an audience of family planning advocates in the wake of the Hyde Amendment and the ending of federal money for abortion services (Rule 1978). This commitment among the leadership, however, was not able to prevent a deadlock over passage of the 1978 budget as Senate Republicans refused to accept the governor's bill without the inclusion of their own amendment banning state aid for abortion. While they were able to delay passage of the budget for several days, the GOP eventually relented and allowed the question to be presented as a separate bill that passed the Senate but was defeated by a 78 to 66 vote in the Assembly (Meislin 1978). Almost the same scenario played out during the 1979 budget debate with the Republican-controlled Senate initially refusing to pass the bill with the Medicaid funding intact. After a conference in which Senate Majority Leader Warren Anderson pleaded with his colleagues to approve the Assembly version of the budget, though, the bill was approved in a 33 to 23 vote. Unlike in 1978, however, there was to be no separate bill amounting to a New York State version of the Hyde Amendment, though the reasons for this remain somewhat unclear (Dionne 1979b).

While 1980 saw no similar drama around the passage of a budget that included state funding for abortion as had been the case in 1978 and 1979, the issue again rose to prominence in 1981 with the bill this time being delayed by nearly a month and a half over the issue. Like the 1978 debate, the impasse was eventually resolved by removing the budget amendment banning state aid for abortions and allowing the issue to be voted on separately, though this time the new bill was defeated in both the Senate and Assembly (Herman 1981a). The previous month, seven Assembly Republicans who had normally supported Medicaid funding for abortions had dramatically walked out of the Assembly chambers in protest of what they called a charade during floor debates on a budget amendment banning Medicaid funding of abortion as they claimed that the issue was nothing more than a symbolic act as the measure had no chance of being passed after four years of similar attempts by pro-life legislators had failed (Herman 1981b). Ironically, the protest was not meant as an objection to the bill itself, which they themselves supported, but of the fact that floor debate time was being used for an issue that everyone present knew was a nonstarter when the Republicans felt that the focus ought to have been on the Senate version of the budget, which the Democrat-controlled Assembly opposed. A mere seven hours later, however, the Speaker reconvened the session and brought the bill to a vote, essentially forcing the members to return and oppose it, with the amendment being predictably defeated in a 77 to 68 vote. The 1981 battle over the funding of abortions through Medicaid was the last of its kind, however, a fact conceded by Senator James Donovan, the sponsor of the bills in the late 1970s and early 1980s, in a 1985 interview in which he admitted that "we simply didn't have the votes" (*New York Times* 1985).

The tendency of lawmakers in New York to frame the abortion question in political terms was again apparent during the funding battles of the late 1970s and early 1980s. Donovan, who had been one of the strongest proponents of the repeal bill vetoed by Governor Rockefeller, asked during the 1979 debate if "this government [will] go on financing the killing of its future citizens? It's as simple as that. God help us if we don't turn this around soon, because the anti-life people have conquered the nursery and perhaps the next step is the geriatric ward" (Dionne 1979a). Senator Roy Goodman, who had been outspoken in his opposition to the 1972 repeal effort, responded with a similarly rhetorical question, inquiring, "is it their right to foist upon those of us who disagree with their doctrine of what is and what isn't life? Let us rise at this time and defeat this vicious amendment [which amounts to] cruel and inhuman punishment for poor women" (Dionne 1979a). Jon Fossel, a Republican Assemblyman from Ossining who had led the walkout protesting Medicaid funding in 1981, stated that "[t]his process is a charade. But I can tell you we are strongly 100 percent and forever behind treating people fairly when it comes to having an abortion or not having an abortion" (Herman 1981b). Also speaking of the walkout, Assemblywoman Elizabeth Connelly, D-Staten Island, commented that "I think it was poor judgment to do, to cut us off in the middle of debate with my mouth open. Obviously, they knew they didn't have the votes. This is supposed to be a fair and open system" (Herman 1981b). Again in contrast to New Jersey, legislators in New York—after a decade of battles over abortion—continued to avoid discussing the issue with reference to any type of legal argument, still preferring to focus on questions of proper procedure, the consequences of restrictions to the lives of poor women, and existential musings regarding when life began.

One of the most interesting aspects of the abortion funding debate in New York can be seen when it is contrasted with the same issue as it played out at the national level. A similar compromise to the one that eventually broke the stalemate in Albany had been proposed in the Senate version of the Hyde amendment—the removal of any specific funding restrictions for abortion from the appropriations bill and a separate vote on the matter being held subsequently—though this was rejected by a substantial margin in the House of Representatives. Why then were lawmakers in New York able to secure this particular compromise, while Congress would settle only for a version that allowed exceptions for the life of the mother? It is worth noting that the partisan distribution in Congress during passage of the Hyde amendment and that in Albany during the budget battles of the late 1970s were somewhat different. In the case of the former, both Houses were controlled by large Democratic majorities, while the latter was composed of a firmly Democratic Assembly and a Republican-controlled Senate. Indeed, the establishment of the GOP as the anti-abortion party seems to have advanced more quickly in

New York as the vote on the Medicaid funding ban broke down along much clearer partisan lines in the Assembly and Senate than was the case in Washington, where large numbers of Democrats had supported the Hyde amendment.

More relevant to the present study, however, is that the legislature in New York seemed to go very much out of its way to ensure that it remained the venue developing abortion policy, consciously or not. While it is impossible to know definitively what lawmakers in Congress expected the result of the inevitable litigation that followed passage of the Hyde amendment to be, it seems at least plausible that some may have voted in favor of the measure with the expectation that it would be struck down by the courts. Indeed, Lovell (2003) claims that members of Congress will take into consideration their beliefs regarding the ideological makeup of the Court when engaging in deferral behavior, and lawmakers certainly had at least a reasonable expectation that the Hyde amendment might be struck down following the *Roe* and *Doe* decisions three years earlier, as well as *Bigelow v. Virginia* (1975) and *Planned Parenthood of Central Missouri v. Danforth* (1976), which had also struck down abortion restrictions.[12] New York, however, seemed to take more care to ensure that its decision regarding Medicaid funding of abortion would not be challenged in court by severing the funding bill itself from the restriction on the use of these funds for elective abortions; the separate bill to that end of course ultimately failing to pass the Assembly. In the language of path dependence, this choice again served as a self-reinforcing sequence that helped keep this issue firmly within this institutional realm.

The debate over Medicaid funding for abortions also represents another critical moment during which the courts could have begun to play a more assertive role in this issue area, as they had in a number of other states, including New Jersey. Had the judiciary, as it did in the Garden State, instead been the "first movers" in this issue area, it is entirely likely that lawmakers in the Assembly and Senate would have been content to leave it there for many of the same reasons articulated by Lovell (2003), Graber (1993), and Whittington (2007). Up to that point, the courts had a somewhat mixed record on the constitutionality of bans on abortion funding, with the Court of Appeals ruling in *Wyman* that the government had no obligation to provide such payments, though the Second Circuit Court of Appeals had overturned that judgment. The outcome of a case challenging a ban on Medicaid funding for abortions was therefore very much an open question, suggesting that lawmakers on either side of the issue did not necessarily have any reason to expect that their policy preferences would be vindicated in the courts. As with the parental consent and 1972 repeal bill, though, there would be no opportunity for the judicial branch to weigh in on the matter as the funding ban was defeated in the Assembly. Also seeming to repeat the scenario that had played out in the early and mid-1970s, political and strategic decisions had conspired to avoid a path switching event and a consequent change in the dominant political narrative that might have resulted in a more significant role for the courts. As discussed above, in order to ensure that a budget would be passed, a separate vote on the Medicaid ban was allowed and defeated, providing no opportunity for a court challenge. The period of the late 1970s and early 1980s, then, can be understood as another "critical juncture." This also suggests that ten years after the liberalization bill had been passed, there remained opportunities for greater court involvement. As Jones-Correa notes, "multiple alternatives may result from any single juncture, and that discarded alternatives remain as challengers to institutions" (2000–2001, 543). In other words, the courts may still at this point have potentially been a viable institutional location for the creation of abortion policy, but once again the actions of the legislature precluded this switch. Just as Governor Carey's veto of the parental consent bill demonstrates the importance of considering the policy making community as a whole in understanding the role of the courts, this shift in the level of analysis is again critical here as developments within the legislature had a potentially crucial impact on what the court would have the opportunity to do, and therefore its future behavior.

Following the renewed activity by anti-abortion activists that had characterized the late 1970s and early 1980s, the years between 1981 and 1985 again saw little to no movement on the issue in New York State, with not a single bill on the matter being submitted for any floor action. By the middle of the decade, however, pro-life forces were again wading into the legal and legislative fray, though, as had been the case after previous periods of inactivity, the location and venue had again changed. The focus this time was on attempts to limit the number of abortion clinics that were to be opened or, similarly, types of medical facilities in which abortions could be performed. In 1985, the Westchester Right to Life Committee brought a suit against the Westchester Women's Health Organization Clinic in White Plains for operating without a license, which it in fact was, though it had previously been allowed to continue operation by the state pending the approval of its application (Melvin 1985). The case was dismissed by Judge Louis Palella, who wrote that "the cogent issue of jurisdiction had not been met," and suggested that the issue would be moot in the near future in any case as Planned Parenthood had already agreed to take over the clinic. That same year, the legality of two abortion clinics in Albany and Hudson had been challenged by the Roman Catholic Diocese of Albany on the grounds that the state had not properly inspected the facilities before issuing them licenses. This time the trial judge agreed with the church, as did the intermediate appellate court; however, these rulings were later overturned by the New York State Court of Appeals (Carroll 1985).

In *Matter of Roman Catholic Diocese of Albany v. New York State Dep't of Health* (1985), the plaintiffs argued that the Department of Health (DOH) had impermissibly relied on a numerical policy, the so-called "50 percent rule," which stated that a need for an abortion clinic existed when less than half of "all abortion services were available on an out-of-hospital basis" (142), which was not found in statutory law. While the Supreme and Intermediate Appellate courts had ruled in favor of the Diocese, the Court of Appeals reversed, relying almost entirely on the reasoning of the dissenting judge in the lower court's decision. Illustrative of the Court's view was Judge Levine's declaration that "[n]either [previously discussed case law] nor the State Constitution's regulation-filing requirement (NY Const., art. IV, § 8) were intended to overturn the general principle of administrative law that an agency is free to evolve standards, if consistent with the statutory framework, on a case-by-case basis and to apply them to the individual proceeding at hand" (148). In other words, administrative agencies were free, according to the Court, to apply standards that were not necessarily provided for in state law in order to meet the requirements that might arise under specific circumstances. While this decision had the practical effect of allowing the Planned Parenthood clinics at issue to open in Albany and Hudson, what is most significant about this case is that the Court again demonstrated a substantial willingness to offer wide latitude to other branches of government to operate and set policy as they saw fit. On a broader level, this decision may also be understood as an example of reinforcement, in the path dependent sense, of the role that the Court saw for itself not as an appropriate route to policy change, but rather as a legitimizing force sustaining the legislature's primacy in this area.

Indeed, Judge Levine's dissent was replete with references to the propriety of allowing the executive broad discretion in setting policy as it related to the regulation of abortion clinics. For example, Levine stressed the importance of allowing "agencies [to] announce or evolve guidelines to aid in making ad hoc decisions in performing their adjudicative function" (146) and that "[s]ince, in its January 11, 1985 decision, DOH employed the 50 percent rule as nothing more than a nonconclusive, nonbinding guideline to be weighted along with other factors on the public need issue in adjudicating individual cases, there was no need to file it as a regulation" (148). Finally, the dissenting judge concluded by emphasizing that "a weighing of factual data and balancing of competing factors [was] within the sole province of the administrative agency" (148). Recall again that the Court of Appeals relied heavily on Levine's reasoning, suggesting that it too shared the view that executive branch actors, in this case the Department of Health, enjoyed considerable latitude in developing policy generally, and standards for abortion services in particular. In this sense, the Court was behaving in a manner somewhat similar to the regime maintenance described by Whittington

(2007), a practice that was almost entirely absent from the major decisions handed down by the Supreme Court in New Jersey.

Beyond the fact that this case further reinforced the norm then developing within New York's judicial branch regarding the free hand that was to be given to the elected branches in developing abortion policy, a clear reliance on a "political" interpretive framework is evident in the opinion offered in *Matter of Roman Catholic Diocese of Albany*. For example, the Court wrote that a need for the clinics existed due to:

> the policy (reflected in the State's formal health and medical facility plans) in favor of development of alternatives to institutional health care, a projected needs analysis based upon current use ratios showing an over-all deficit in abortion services by 1990, a trend, particularly in Albany County, of steadily increasing out-migration of county residents to seek abortion services in other localities, [and] a ratio of such out-migration to total abortions obtained by Albany County residents which was at least twice as high and as much as 25 times higher than that found in other major upstate population centers (146).

Besides evincing a reliance on considerations such as the benefits of establishing the clinics in their proposed locations, rather than the legal authority of the executive to set standards for such facilities, the Court again here seems to be adopting the "knowledge claim" indigenous to the elected branches. This is not to suggest that considerations such as the likely results on the ground of particular rulings are not to be found within the dialogue of courts. It is nevertheless noteworthy that, coupled with its ultimate decision to defer to the authority of the executive, much of the opinion offered in *Matter of Roman Catholic Diocese of Albany* was concerned with what might be considered "political" issues such as population movement and anticipated healthcare needs.

Grassroots activism at the level of actual abortion clinics was not limited to those on the pro-life side of the issue during this period either. In 1987, the State Attorney General's Office brought a suit in state Supreme Court against the AAA Pregnancy Problem Center in Brooklyn claiming that the center was engaging in deceptive advertising. Specifically, the organization, and others like it throughout the state, were presenting themselves as "clinics" for pregnant women when they were in fact operated by pro-life groups, were not licensed or able to perform any medical services, and instead provided only "counseling" aimed at discouraging pregnant women from seeking abortions (Gross 1987). The court ruled that the "clinics" could no longer advertise themselves as medical facilities, place ads under "abortion services" in the Yellow Pages, and that they must inform women immediately that they did not offer abortion or contraceptive services. In 1989, similar action was taken by then–Attorney General Robert Abrams against a crisis pregnancy center on Long Island, ordering the facility to abide by the same regulations that had been imposed on the Brooklyn establishment (Kasindorf 1989).

It bears mentioning at this point that the Court in the "crisis pregnancy" cases did indeed appear to be engaging in policy making as it had limited the operations of a pro-life group and had influenced to some extent what types of establishments could be considered involved in abortion-related activities. That being said, these decisions did not alter abortion policy in the state in any meaningful way as the "clinics" in question were not performing the procedure and access to reproductive services was neither increased nor decreased. Additionally, the push to restrict the activities of the centers had been initiated by the executive branch through the Attorney General's Office, suggesting that the institutional first mover there too had been one of the elected branches.[13] Indeed, in most similar cases from that period, the party initiating the suit had been private entities challenging such centers as violating state advertising laws or claiming damages for emotional distress.[14] Nevertheless, a case can certainly be made that the crisis pregnancy center cases from the mid-1980s represented a rare instance of active policy making on the part of the courts in New York.

CONSOLIDATING THE POLITICAL PATH

One of the few instances where the pro-life side of the abortion issue saw success in the legislature was when the state decided not to provide Parental Care and Assistance Program (PCAP) funding to eligible women at the end of the 1980s. The issue arose following a 1986 federal law authorizing funds for state PCAPs provided the states followed federal guidelines regarding the use of the funds for abortion services and the legislature had been deadlocked for the next three years over debate about whether to expand state Medicaid funding to cover abortions for PCAP eligible women. Finally in 1989, the Assembly passed the Senate version of the bill, which denied the funds to families whose income was below 185 percent of the national poverty level, something seen as a victory for the more pro-life leaning Senate. Ultimately, the passage of the bill was likely the result of necessity as pediatricians and other healthcare professionals had begun making it clear to lawmakers that delays in approving the PCAP program was resulting in serious health concerns for prenatal care, with New York's infant mortality rate having become one of the highest in the nation as the two sides battled over the issue (Gutis 1989). This sentiment was expressed by then-Speaker Mel Miller when he claimed that "[a]lthough most of my conference would favor that abortions be paid for under this program, they feel the program is so important that it must be approved" (Gutis 1989).

It is unclear as to why exactly the Assembly leadership eventually became the one to capitulate on the issue, and the reaction from abortion-rights activists such as the Family Planning Advocates of New York State was swift. Executive director of the group Shirley Gordon was quoted as saying regarding the bill that "[p]regnancies are never risk-free [and that] a physician needs to have the full resources available to provide care. He may feel he needs to terminate a pregnancy" (Gutis 1989). While it is possible that this may in fact have been a rare instance of legislative deferral as described by Lovell (2003)—a group of lawmakers faced with a necessity to compromise with political opponents passes a piece of legislation that it believes will be struck down in the courts—it seems unlikely that many in the Assembly maintained such expectations as the court had offered few indications that it was likely to do so. Indeed, a decade earlier the Court of Appeals had ruled that Medicaid funding of abortions was not mandated by the state constitution and had firmly established that it would almost certainly uphold whatever decision the legislature chose to make in this area, which is exactly what happened in the *Hope* case, discussed below. What seems more likely, albeit perhaps counterintuitive to more cynical observers, is that the Democratic members of the Assembly had been sufficiently convinced of the necessity of at least allowing PCAP funding to become available to those that were in need that they simply agreed to the Senate version at the expense of their policy preferences regarding abortion.

The case of the exclusion of PCAP funding for abortion services serves well to illustrate the development and self-reinforcement of the passive role taken by the courts and is well in line with the predictions of the path dependence approach. In *Hope v. Perales*, the plaintiffs argued that PCAP's denial of funding for abortion was unconstitutional—specifically, "by reason of underinclusiveness, for its failure to include medically necessary abortions in a prenatal care public funding scheme for women with incomes up to 85 percent over the Federal poverty level" (571)—with the Court of Appeals upholding the law and denying the rights claim. An examination of the Court of Appeals decision in *Hope* reveals an explicit and repeated attitude among the judges of deferral to the legislature. Specifically, Chief Judge Kaye wrote in *Hope* that "[i]t is not the role of the courts to pass upon the wisdom of the Legislature's policy choice, even though there may be differences of views about the decision to exclude a medically necessary service from an otherwise comprehensive prenatal care program" (578). This point is noteworthy for its emphasis on two important themes. The first is the Chief Judge's explicit claim that she did not see the role of the Court as one of "second-guessing" the choices of the elected branches, a statement that was conspicuously absent from the language employed by the courts in New Jersey. The second is that Kaye seems to suggest that she herself does not appear to support that choice when she described the procedure at issue as "medically necessary" and the PCAP program as "an otherwise comprehensive prenatal care program." Nevertheless, the Chief Judge chose to uphold the law, a decision that would seem important both as a simple refusal to alter the policy decisions of the legislature, as well as a signal to lawmakers that the Court was likely to continue this norm of accepting the policy outputs of the elected branches. Further reinforcing this idea is the frequency with which the Court explicitly mentions that it sees its role as almost subservient to that of the legislature. In the brief seven page opinion in *Hope*, the Chief Judge mentions her view that the legislature ought to have the final word in determining what, if any, restrictions it chooses to impose on abortion access or funding four separate times. Therefore, we see here again an attitude within the judiciary not of eagerly seeking out, or even accepting, opportunities to make policy regarding a controversial issue, but rather a conscious refusal to take on that role.

This same notion of reinforcement and legitimization can also be seen quite explicitly in the *Hope* opinion when Chief Judge Kaye writes that "[w]e cannot say beyond a reasonable doubt that, by not including abortion funding in PCAP, the Legislature has transgressed its powers" (578). Here again we see a Court declining to alter the choices of the legislature, or, in the terminology of path dependence, to "switch" from the legislative to the judicial path. Adding another layer to the legitimization of the legislature's role, the Court also emphasizes that "both [the Aid to the Needy and Public Health Clauses of the New York State constitution] expressly accord to the Legislature discretion to promote the State's interest in aiding the needy and promoting public health 'in such manner, and by such means as the legislature may from time to time determine' (NY Const, art XVII, §§ 1, 3)" (578). This portion of Judge Kaye's opinion is significant not only for the deference it demonstrates to the legislature, but also in the sense that it offers constitutional reasoning and justification for that branch's primacy in the development of abortion policy. As in the *Robin* case, this pronouncement may be reasonably viewed as a form of policy making inasmuch as it further establishes the state's position of not providing PCAP funding for abortions, though again we see no substantive alteration of existing policy, but rather the legitimization of the legislature's choices. Perhaps more significantly, the *Hope* decision represented an opportunity for the abortion issue to "switch paths," which was not taken. Instead, by upholding, what was in this case a limitation on abortion access, the Court kept this issue within the legislative stream, maintaining the choice that the elected branch had made twenty-four years earlier when the liberalization law was first enacted.

The failure of the Court to "switch paths" in *Hope* seems also to be based on the jurisprudence it had established in earlier cases. Indeed, Michael P. Tierney, the attorney representing New York in the case, argued that the State Constitution did not establish a fundamental right to funding for abortion on the basis of two important earlier precedents, *Byrn* and *Matter of City of New York v. Wyman*. The Court's opinion, while acknowledging that the federal Constitution established a fundamental right to reproductive choice, emphasized that this right did not extend to a requirement that the state finance abortions, relying on the U.S. Supreme Court's opinion in *Harris v. McRae*. Consequently, the Court wrote that "[o]nly the State Constitution is in issue [and that] every enactment of a coequal branch of government . . . is entitled to a strong presumption of constitutionality, and that plaintiffs bear the heavy burden of establishing the contrary beyond a reasonable doubt" (*Hope v. Perales* at 574, 575). This burden, Judge Kaye argued, had not been met and that "PCAP does not penalize the exercise of the right of choice, as it does not deny eligibility for any benefit to which participants choosing to abort would otherwise be entitled" (577). The continuity of the Court's abortion jurisprudence therefore remained unbroken as it again refused to find a right in the State Constitution that had not been acknowledged by the legislature. This unwillingness again is particularly striking given that the Court of Appeals had on many other occasions been far from hesitant to find rights in the state document that had not been found in the federal Constitution in issue areas such as sexual privacy (*People v. Onofre* [1980]), religious liberty (*People v. Acme Markets, Inc.* [1975]), freedom of expression (*People v. Ferber* [1981]), or other cases discussed in chapter 1. The difference in the abortion case, it would seem, was the prior establishment of the norm of legislative predominance found in *Byrn* and *Robin*.

As in *Byrn*, much of the language employed by Judge Kaye in *Hope* emphasizes considerations that more closely resemble those that might be considered "political," or at least policy-focused, in nature rather than "legal." In discussing the importance of sustaining the PCAP law, the Chief Judge wrote that "[s]tudies have documented the correlation between infant mortality and neurological abnormalities on the one hand, and low birthweight and premature birth on the other—conditions ameliorated by proper care throughout pregnancy, which can be costly . . . PCAP unquestionably is highly effective in meeting its objective" (572). In response to the plaintiffs' claim that the failure of the program to fund abortion services represented a burden on women choosing to terminate their pregnancies, Kaye further argues that:

> [a]s defendants point out, PCAP may even make abortion more affordable for these women as—irrespective of pregnancy outcome—the statute offers free testing for fetal abnormalities that may early in pregnancy indicate the need for (and thereby reduce the cost of) an abortion, mental health and social services, family planning and 60-day postpartum care (575).

In line with the theoretical framework proposed here, *Hope* then clearly sustains the earlier framing choices the Court had made in adopting, implicitly or explicitly, a view of the abortion issue not just as one belonging to the elected branches, but also as understood through a lens much more in line with the mandate of those same branches.

Finally, *Hope* is instructive inasmuch as the opinion of the Court in many ways reflected adherence to the interpretive framework established in *Byrn* and *Robin* in a somewhat reduced form. As mentioned in chapter 1, one method for establishing that a particular narrative has in fact taken root and been established as the "accepted" rhetorical frame according to Brandwein (2006) is that the "winning" view will be referenced by subsequent players in a reduced form. This is precisely what we find in Judge Kaye's opinion. In addition to her statement regarding the Court's reluctance to second-guess the choices of the legislature discussed above, the Chief Judge also writes that "we are bound to accept the legislative determination that PCAP-eligible women are not indigent or in need of public assistance to meet their medical needs" (577). While Judge Breitel had spent considerable time articulating the reasoning behind his claim that the legislature was the proper venue for the resolution of abortion policy questions, the *Hope* Court seems largely to take this understanding for granted. Indeed, the thrust of the opinion in that case focused more on explaining the history and legislative intent behind the PCAP law than offering a justification, constitutional or otherwise, for why the elected branches ought to enjoy wide latitude in creating policy in this area. In this sense, the third criteria for the identification of accepted frames described earlier in this work is well supported by the Court's opinion in *Hope*.

As with the abortion legislation passed by the Senate and Assembly in the 1970s and 1980s discussed above, the PCAP controversy can also be understood through the theoretical framework proposed here in the sense that both the judicial and legislative branches were faced with an opportunity to change the route of policy development from the latter to the former. Indeed, as mentioned above, this may very well have been the hope of lawmakers in the Assembly who wished to see the inclusion of abortion funding in the PCAP program, though such a determination is impossible to establish with any certainty. In any event, the ultimate decision regarding whether this particular juncture would see a change in the location of abortion policy making from the elected branches to the judiciary was made by the latter, which in *Hope* chose not to deviate from the now twenty-year-old norm that this policy area was the exclusive domain of the legislature. What may be somewhat unique about the PCAP issue, though, is that it represented the first point at which lawmakers made abortion policy essentially by omission. Unlike the 1970 liberalization law, the 1972 repeal, and the explicit inclusion of abortion funding in Medicaid, the Public Health Law signed by Governor

Cuomo in 1989 made no reference to abortion at all, though it was unquestionably this exclusion that generated the intense controversy that accompanied this legislation. By refusing to require the inclusion of public financing for the termination of pregnancy in the program, the Court effectively added another dimension to the previously articulated norm of noninterference with legislative choices. While *Byrn*, *Robin*, and *Matter of Roman Catholic Diocese of Albany* had all refused to strike down affirmative choices made by the elected branches regarding abortion, the PCAP issue further expanded what was to be considered within the purview of the legislature, in this case, the denial of financial support for abortion access.

Indeed, the PCAP legislation may in fact be understood as the final word on the legislature's institutional dominance of the abortion question for two reasons. Most importantly, this law represented the first time that the legislature had passed a measure limiting reproductive rights since the parental consent bill in 1976, though the latter was never reviewed by the courts owing to Governor Carey's veto. In this sense, the PCAP law offered the most important opportunity for path-switching yet as the Court could have continued its theretofore almost uninterrupted tradition of ruling in favor of abortion rights, with the 1972 *Wyman* decision being the only exception. Instead, the policy chosen by the legislature was again the final word on the matter and remains the state's policy up to the present. In other words, prior to the PCAP bill, the "path" of policy making related to abortion may have been an ideological one that was focused on maintenance of the pro-choice position by various interests in the state. Following the 1994 law, though, it becomes increasingly clear that the path was an institutional one where the courts had accepted legislative preeminence regardless of ideological content. While it would seem that by this point the secondary role of the judiciary in the development of abortion policy had been well established—indeed, as suggested above, a reasonable case can be made that such a point had been reached by the early 1980s—the *Hope* decision that resulted from passage of the PCAP law serves as arguably the final "critical moment" for the courts. Secondarily, the story of the passage of the PCAP measure was somewhat unique as a rare victory for the then largely pro-life Republicans. As suggested by the Shirley Gordon quote above, the outcome of the fight over PCAP was apparently best seen as a capitulation—albeit a relatively minor one—by the pro-choice Democrats who, to put it bluntly, "blinked first." This relative aberration then offers support for the theory on offer here inasmuch as the courts accepted not just the policy preferences of the legislature, but its language and understanding as well, particularly as articulated by Judge Kaye.

Apart from being perhaps the final opportunity for the courts to take on a more assertive role in abortion policy making represented by the PCAP law, this decision point is particularly noteworthy as it was not the actions of the legislature that prevented path switching in 1994, but the Court of Appeals decision in *Hope*. Indeed, this particular policy decision is a unique example of a critical juncture as it does not require the consideration of a counterfactual, as had been the case with the failed Medicaid ban and parental consent law. Indeed, PCAP's exclusion of funding for abortions represented a very real opportunity for the Court of Appeals to create policy in this area, something, as noted above, that Assembly Democrats may well have anticipated or at least hoped for. Indeed, Greif (1994) stresses "the theoretical and historical importance of culture in determining societal organizations, in leading to [the] path dependence of institutional frameworks" (914). If norms can be taken, in this context, to be analogous to culture, it would seem that through the relationship established between the courts and the elected branches over the preceding twenty-five years leading up to *Hope*, the noninterventionist position of the courts on the abortion issue had been well established indeed by the middle of the 1990s, a claim that is also supported by the opinion offered by Judge Kaye in that case discussed above.

Despite the success anti-abortion activists had seen in the final version of the PCAP law passed by the state legislature, no serious legislative or legal efforts were made in the early 1990s to limit either access or funding for abortions in New York State inasmuch as the issue was absent from the Assembly and Senate's agenda and there were no court decisions akin to *Hope*, *Byrn*, or *Robin* in the previous decades. Instead, as they had a decade earlier, activists again turned their attention to individual abortion clinics, staging a number of high-profile protests, often involving serious intimidation and occasionally violence, particularly at centers in Buffalo and Rochester. Led by Randall Terry's Operation Rescue group, protests had become increasingly volatile in the early 1990s with over 500 people being arrested in one 1992 incident in Buffalo (Myers 1993). This led the Assembly in 1993 to pass a bill that would define the blocking of a health facility as aggravated harassment, a misdemeanor punishable by up to one year in prison, and allow for up to four years of prison for repeat offenders. Similar laws had been passed in California, Maryland, Kansas, Nevada, Oregon, and Wisconsin and were at the time being considered by 12 other states (Myers 1993). That same year a bill was passed by the New York City council that allowed the victims of abortion clinic harassment to sue their harassers for triple damages in an effort to combat violence at city clinics (Bennett 1993). The Assembly bill never came to a vote in the Senate, however, though it is unlikely that such a measure would have passed the upper house, which was dominated by upstate Republicans as well as several pro-life Democrats (Bennett 1993). In any case, the issue would become moot the following year when Congress passed similar legislation making it a crime to obstruct access to abortion clinics or to harass women attempting to use the facilities.

Further restricting the aggressive protesting that had become common in the early and mid-1990s by groups such as Operation Rescue, the Second Circuit Court of Appeals in 1995 upheld a District Court injunction against the group in *New York v. Terry*, rejecting the defendant's claim of a First Amendment violation, though on the grounds that Terry had failed to raise this claim at the trial level.[15] Five years earlier Richard Arcara, a federal District Court judge, had issued an injunction against a coalition of pro-life groups collectively referred to as Project Rescue requiring, among other limitations, protesters to maintain a fifteen-foot "buffer zone" around clinic entrances, driveways, and patients seeking access to the facilities, while allowing two "sidewalk counselors" to enter the zone and speak to women entering the clinic until such time as they were asked to stop. This injunction was challenged, however, following the U.S. Supreme Court's ruling in *Bray v. Alexandria* (1993), which had rejected a Washington, DC abortion clinic's claim that aggressive protesters had violated their patients' right to abortion access and interstate travel. Upon rehearing, the District Court sustained the injunction and Project Rescue appealed to the Second Circuit Court of Appeals. In a divided opinion, a three-judge panel upheld the majority of the injunction, with the exception of the fifteen-foot buffer zone and the cease and desist provision directed at the "sidewalk counselors." The case was reviewed en banc and in *Pro-Choice Network of Western New York v. Project Rescue* (1995), the full Court, relying on much the same logic as it had that same year in *New York v. Terry*, reversed the panel decision and sustained the original injunction. The case was eventually appealed to the U.S. Supreme Court, and in *Schenck v. Pro-Choice Network of Western New York* (1997), the Court upheld the fixed buffer zone around the clinic's property, but struck down the "floating bubble" provision that required protesters to remain fifteen feet away from patients attempting to enter the clinic as an unconstitutional infringement of the Free Speech Clause of the First Amendment. Specifically, the majority opinion argued that the speech restriction established by the "bubble" was broader than necessary to protect the government's interest in maintaining access to medical facilities.

The rest of the 1990s were characterized mostly by the introduction of competing pieces of legislation passed by the Senate and Assembly, with the former focusing on obtaining a ban on late-term abortions and the latter proposing stronger penalties against the obstruction of access to abortion clinics by pro-life activists. Neither bill was able to obtain the necessary votes in the other chamber, however, until the Freedom of Access to Clinic Entrance law was finally approved by the Senate in 1999. While a similar piece of legislation had been enacted by Congress several years earlier, enforcement of the statute had been questionable and the state law was intended to allow state troopers and local police officials to arrest individuals blocking access to abortion facilities. Passage of the bill, as with Medicare funding legislation in previous decades, was the result of the common practice in Albany of tying disparate pieces of legislation together by refusing to pass the priority bills of one house without a similar concession from the leadership in the other (Levy 1999). Also in line with most previous legislative action around the issue, virtually all of the negotiation that resulted in the FACE law was conducted between the Senate Majority Leader, Assembly Speaker, and the governor and involved legislation related to expansion of the state's DNA database and the construction of several new power plants (Levy 1999). It seems likely that Governor Pataki, the first Republican to hold the office of chief executive in twenty years, agreed to sign the bill in order to maintain his position as a social moderate in a state that was becoming increasingly supportive of abortion rights, if the lack of intensity of the debate within the legislature or the number of bills limiting abortion rights brought to the floor during this period are to be considered a reliable proxy for the public's sentiments on the issue. With this fact in mind, Senate Majority Leader Joe Bruno's decision to prod his conference into supporting the FACE law, despite his own opposition, can best be understood as one of political expediency aimed at securing his own legislative priorities, the fact that a somewhat less stringent Senate version of the bill was passed, and the increasing political unpopularity of the pro-life position (Levy 1999).

What we do not see, though, is any reason to suspect that Bruno expected the courts to intervene and ultimately vindicate his own policy preferences. In 1994 the U.S. Supreme Court had upheld the federal version of the FACE law in *Gregg v. U.S.*, offering the Majority Leader no reason to believe that the law could be found unconstitutional on Freedom of Expression grounds, as opponents had argued. Additionally, while portions of the District Court's injunction against Project Rescue had been struck down by the U.S. Supreme Court in *Schenck*, the "buffer zones" around the clinics themselves, which were codified by the New York State FACE law, were nonetheless upheld in 1997. A challenge in state court was, if anything, even less likely to succeed, though one did take place with a Utica district court upholding the conviction of a family of protesters under the law in 2001 (McKinley 2001). The point here again, in any case, is that legislators seem to have reached a compromise with each other and, despite the comparatively long time frames over which these compromises were negotiated, there is no reason to believe that either side expected any other institution to involve itself in the process or the ultimate outcome. Indeed, the courts had by the late 1990s effectively removed themselves from the abortion debate altogether, suggesting that the dominance of the legislative path within this issue area had by this point become almost universally accepted.

On the other side of the issue, efforts to introduce some of the limits to abortion access that had been permitted by the U.S. Supreme Court's ruling in *Planned Parenthood v. Casey* in 1992 were again being introduced in the

New York legislature in the mid-1990s. While not specifically dealt with in the *Casey* decision, Senate Republicans in 1996 introduced and passed legislation that would have banned late-term abortions in the state, though this was largely a symbolic act as the bill had virtually no chance of being approved by the Assembly (Levy 1996). Indeed, despite the fact that the bill would never reach his desk, Governor Pataki was a vocal proponent of the legislation, a move that was almost certainly calculated to appeal to conservative supporters who had been disenchanted with the Republican following his signing of a bill offering workplace protection for gays and lesbians earlier that year (Levy 1996). Similarly, the Governor could safely avoid evoking the ire of the state's pro-choice voters as he was almost certainly aware of the fact that the legislation would have no chance of passing in the lower house. Eventually, though, Assembly Speaker Sheldon Silver did allow the bill to come to a vote on the floor where, to no one's surprise, it was defeated along a largely partisan vote (Purnick 1996).

The issue of late-term abortions surfaced again in 1998 when Silver announced that he would be open to allowing a vote on a substantially less restrictive version of the bill passed by the Senate two years earlier. The legislation proposed by the Speaker would have banned the "dilation and extraction" procedure after the twenty-fourth week of pregnancy, a provision that would in practice have essentially no impact on abortions in New York as the termination of a pregnancy at this stage was already banned outright as per the 1970 law (Goodnough 1998). In the end, however, Silver decided against bringing the bill up for a vote as support for the measure among conservative, upstate Democrats had eroded in the weeks after it was proposed, and the bill would have had little chance of passing the Senate, which favored a much more restrictive version (Goodnough 1998). This proved to be the last time the late-term abortion ban issue was raised in the legislature and it was not until the next decade and passage of the federal ban on the procedure that the laws in New York were altered in this area.

Despite the fact that the bill was never brought up for a vote in the Assembly, the statements from Senators debating the measure in the upper chamber nevertheless provides yet another opportunity to consider the rhetorical frames through which lawmakers were viewing the abortion question after nearly thirty years since passage of the liberalization law. Serphin Maltese, a Queens Republican who had been the prime sponsor of the late-term ban, for instance, stated that "I believe this is akin to infanticide. I think this is a reprehensible, absolutely barbaric practice" (Perez-Pena 1999). Rochester Democrat Richard Dollinger reportedly shouted in response "[d]on't you dare be in the maternity room with me, my daughter, my wife" (Perez-Pena 1999). Echoing the "infanticide" characterization, Democratic Assemblyman Eric Vitaliano of Staten Island, who had been pegged by Speaker Silver to introduce the bill before deciding against a floor vote, argued that "[gi]ven the procedure itself, that might be enough to convince some legislators, regardless of what they think about abortion, that this is closer to infanticide . . . I certainly think it is infanticide" (Hernandez 1996). This is again in contrast to the dominant narrative surrounding the same issue in New Jersey where both Governor Whitman and several lawmakers in the Senate and Assembly had focused almost exclusively on the constitutional and other legal deficiencies in the late-term abortion law in that state.

The legislature's political reasoning surrounding its passage of the bill allowing for over-the-counter sale of the "morning-after pill" may once again present an example of legislative deferral to the executive, similar to that seen in the parental notification and repeal bills in the 1970s. The subsequent veto of the bill can likely be explained as a purely political move aimed at strengthening Pataki's pro-life credentials in anticipation of a possible presidential run in 2008, especially given the Governor's previous, although tepid, support of abortion rights in previous years, a suggestion made by some commentators at the time (Hernandez and Baker 2005). While the Senate had rejected the bill in 2003, it is likely that increased pressure from abortion rights groups between 2002 and 2004 led at least some in the Senate to reconsider their previous negative votes. Indeed, contributions to state races by NARAL and Emily's List, which had totaled $14,700 for the 2002 campaign, almost doubled to $25,568 for the 2004 election.[16] In this sense, legislators may very well have felt pressure to support the Plan B bill, though been confident that it would not become law as the governor had publicly stated that he would in fact veto the legislation. So as with the parental consent bill that Governor Carey had refused to sign in 1976, there would seem to be some evidence that a form of legislative deferral to the executive was taking place around the "morning-after pill" legislation, though in this case it may have been pro-life leaning lawmakers who were persuaded to support a piece of legislation that did not square with their policy preferences in order to insulate the Senate from being seen as obstructionist.

Interestingly, in 2001 the Center for Reproductive Rights had filed a Citizen Petition to the FDA requesting that the Administration allow over-the-counter access to Plan B for anyone over the age of seventeen. This request was met with years of delay, eventually prompting the group to bring suit against the FDA and in the case of *Tummino v. Von Eschenbach* (2006) a U.S. District Court for the Eastern District of New York ordered the Administration to answer the petition. Following this ruling, the FDA approved over-the-counter sale of Plan B to women over the age of eighteen, though requiring that the medication be held behind the counter and that women present photo identification before they could receive the drug. This decision prompted another lawsuit, and in 2009, the same District Court ruled in *Tummino v. Hamburg (NY)* that the Administration had "acted in bad faith and in response to political pressure" and that its refusal to allow unrestricted access to Plan B "lacks all credibility," and was founded in "fanciful and wholly unsubstantiated 'enforcement' concerns." The FDA complied with this order and that same year allowed the medication to be sold to minors seventeen years of age and older without providing photo identification at pharmacies. A further petition was submitted in 2011 by the Center for Reproductive Rights requesting that Plan B be made available to anyone regardless of age, a change that the Commissioner of the Administration agreed to implement. Before the directive could take effect, however, Secretary of Health and Human Services Kathleen Sebelius indicated that she was unconvinced that the age restrictions could be eliminated, and on December 12, 2012, the FDA once again denied the petition. In response, the Center once again brought a suit against the Administration and, in an April 4, 2013, ruling, District Court Judge Edward Korman ordered the FDA to allow the sale of the medication over-the-counter to all women regardless of age (*Tummino v. Hamburg* No. 12-CV-763 (ERK) (VVP)). On appeal, the Second Circuit Court of Appeals sustained the District Court's ruling (*Tummino v. Hamburg*, ___ F. Supp. 2d ___, 2013) and the Obama administration has declined to pursue the case (Mears 2013).

The ultimate outcome of the Plan B controversy in New York is interesting as it seems to be a rare instance of policy making taking place in the courts, contrary to the vast majority of previous decisions discussed above. It is worth noting that the policy the ruling struck down was a federal directive rather than a state law or executive department policy. It is also unclear as to why the challenge to the FDA's denial of over-the-counter sale of Plan B medication was initiated in New York, though the group that led the effort, the Center for Reproductive Rights, is headquartered in New York City. Nevertheless, a court decision treating an issue related, if only peripherally, to abortion emanating from a New York court in 2013 is certainly noteworthy and may signal a new focus on litigation as a strategy either for the pro-choice or pro-life side of the debate. That being said, 2013 also saw a protracted battle in the legislature over a provision in the Women's Equality Act, strongly supported by Governor Andrew Cuomo, which would codify the U.S. Supreme Court's *Roe* decision should that ruling ever be overturned, though the legislation remains stalemated in the Senate (Mosher 2013). In any event, the importance of federal action for abortion policy making in New York is discussed in greater detail below, though in terms of the theoretical framework on offer here, in particular its emphasis on the policy making community at the state level, these recent developments may have little impact on the role of the courts going forward.

New York State today is almost universally recognized as one of the most pro-choice states in America, though a close examination of how this title was earned reveals that it was by no means a certainty at many stages over the course of the past forty years. Far from emerging out of consensus, the legalization of abortion in the Empire State was more a product of the specific timing of institutional involvement and issue framing by the courts and the elected branches. While the tide seemed always to move in the direction of greater reproductive freedom, opponents of abortion rights quickly organized themselves into a formidable political and social force and came very near on several occasions to rolling back the gains that had been achieved both legislatively and through the courts. With this in mind, the following section will present a brief overview of some of the main themes from the New York case, particularly as they relate to the theoretical framework on offer here. As in the previous chapter, a discussion of the federal context as it relates to abortion litigation in the Second Circuit Court of Appeals will also be offered.

OVERVIEW

The preceding case study clearly reveals that the courts in New York played a largely secondary role to the elected branches in the development of abortion policy, very much in contrast to the active role the judiciary took in New Jersey. Nevertheless, the mechanism that led to this divergent role, it is argued here, was quite similar, specifically, the location of initial policy change and the subsequent framing of reproductive rights in terms most closely associated with the branch that played the role of first mover. Just as *Roe* and *Byrne* represented the critical moments in New Jersey by articulating the abortion question in legal terms at a time when the dominant narrative had yet to be firmly established in that state, the importance of the 1970 liberalization bill in New York cannot be overstated. Indeed, this legislative action both led to the first major litigation of the issue in the *Byrn* decision and largely informed the view the majority in that case was to take, a fact reflected in Judge Breitel's frequent reference to the prerogative of the legislature in determining what limits may or may not be placed on abortion access. Furthermore, this jurisprudential emphasis on noninterference in the choices of the elected branches was never altered in subsequent decisions and seems to have informed the reasoning of virtually all of the cases that followed.

In terms of the field of potential narrative approaches that might have come to prominence in New York or New Jersey, there is evidence that both states were actually quite similarly situated. Recall from the previous chapter that the Crane Commission, which had recommended revisions to New Jersey's abortion statute, invoked a number of rationales for liberalization focusing variously on legal as well as political concerns. The Froessel Commission report, which was published in 1968 and significantly influenced the shape of the liberalization bill, was remarkably similar in stressing the need for reform for legal as well as more policy-oriented concerns. For example, the report cited New York City Medical Examiner Dr. Milton Helpern who argued that the "current law places an unfair discrimination on the poor," while also arguing that "[u]ntil our law is liberalized [the] so-called abortion racket will continue unrestrained operated by doctors who have no regard whatsoever for the law—and sometimes by what have been called untrained butchers using coat-hangers" (Clarity 1968). The commission's dissenting report also employed the language of rights as well as politics, claiming that legalization would violate the "fundamental rights of the human child" as well as "compound our social problems in the State of New York if we attempt to solve them by legalizing the destruction of innocent, albeit burdensome, individuals" (Clarity 1968). Similarly, a memorandum circulated by Assemblywoman Constance Cook, discussed briefly in the preceding section, also made both legal as well as policy arguments in favor of legalization. On the one hand, Cook wrote that "[s]tatistics on illegal abortions in the United States indicate that the effort to make an immoral act illegal has failed. On the other hand, great personal tragedies have resulted from attempts to end unwanted pregnancies" and that if the "bill is adopted, abortion would be subject only to the concerned conscience of the individual and the best medical advice of her physician" (quoted in Greenhouse and Siegel 2012, 148, 149). At the same time, the memorandum made several references to the recent California Supreme Court ruling striking down an "abortion statute which was similar to the present New York law . . . on the grounds of being vague, an invasion of privacy, a limitation of the civil rights of women, and obsolete" (quoted in Greenhouse and Siegel 2012, 148, 149).

The point here is that in terms of rhetorical frames, the abortion debate in New York began in very much the same place as it did in New Jersey, with political and legal justifications for legalization being prominent, and even invoked by opponents of reform. It was only after meaningful change took place that one came to dominate the understandings of all three branches of state government rather than the other. This change, of course, was located in the legislature in New York and the courts in New Jersey. In the case of the former, these critical moments—the liberalization bill that was legitimized by the Court of Appeals in 1972—were followed by a number of instances that precluded path switching and reinforced the understanding of abortion as a political question. Specifically, the vetoes of Governors Rockefeller and Carey served to reinforce the political path by foreclosing important opportunities for the courts to play a more meaningful role by preventing the Court from striking down New York's revived statutes in *Roe* and potentially voiding the parental consent law. The legislature too played an important part in keeping the issue of Medicaid funding bans off of the Court's agenda by separating the provision from the wider spending bill. Nevertheless, the most important events for the purposes of this study are the *Byrn*, *Robin*, *Matter of Roman Catholic Dioceses of Albany*, and *Hope* decisions, all of which repeatedly framed the abortion controversy as a political question and refused to alter the choices of the elected branches even, arguably, when those choices ran counter to the policy preferences of the judges on the Court of Appeals.

All of these cases, which represent the most important opportunities for the judicial branch in New York to formulate policy related to abortion between 1970 and 1995, have essentially the same themes. Specifically, a willingness among the judges of the Court of Appeals not only to grant broad discretion to the elected branches in making decisions on everything from the legality of abortions themselves to funding of the procedure to the regulation of clinics where abortions may be performed, but also to highlight a "political" frame, understood here as this issue falling properly within the purview of the legislature and executive agencies. In other words, we find a judiciary that consistently reinforced the legislature's legitimacy as the proper path for policy change, as well as critical moments where the courts chose not to change paths themselves nor facilitate outside interests in doing so. In addition, an analysis of the opinions themselves reveal that the judges on the state's High Court adopted an issue frame very similar to that which might be expected from the elected branches early on in the sequence of decision making—a choice which was sustained and reinforced in subsequent rulings. By the same token, the statements from lawmakers in New York were almost universal in their focus on political concerns ranging from the negative social impacts of abortion restrictions to accusations of election-year posturing to emotionally laden claims about the destruction of fetal life.

Finally, it is worth emphasizing one of the crucial differences between traditional path dependence approaches and this phenomenon as it is understood in the present study. Rather than maintaining the developmental path established early in the process on the basis of tangible, material benefits that accrue from these early gains, the elected branches continued to be the primary institutional location of change in New York, at the expense of the courts, because the frame of abortion as a political question continued to "win." Indeed, it was largely within the courts themselves that evidence of this "victory" of the legislature as the proper venue for policy development in this issue can be found. In this sense, increasing returns as they are understood by Pierson (2000) and others were not truly present in the case described above. Instead, judges in New York continued to adhere to the concept of abortion as an issue belonging to the legislature because "justices, working in legal institutions . . . share assumptions and beliefs" (Brandwein 2006, 241). It is these shared beliefs that are responsive to path dependent pressures as they continue to be supported by successive decisions dealing with a specific issue, assumptions that can be traced back to early rulings that initiated a given path. In other words, it is the embedding of frames within institutions, and more specifically the individual actors that collectively guide them, and not the location of decisions in a particular venue itself that is the source of this reinforcement.

THE FEDERAL CONTEXT

With the exception of the *Abramowicz* case and several of the of the clinic obstruction injunctions, most notably the U.S. Supreme Court's decision in *Schenck* that struck down part of the lower court's ruling that barred protests at a number of locations in the state, the vast majority of judicial involvement in the abortion policy making process in New York took place in state courts. This is particularly noteworthy when contrasted with the New Jersey case where several critically important developments were located in the Third Circuit Court of Appeals. Nevertheless, it is at this point instructive to briefly discuss the federal judicial context within which policy development took place. As mentioned in the introduction to this work, the level of analysis of this study remains the policy making community within New York, however, for the purposes of the foregoing discussion, decisions regarding cases emanating from other states in the Second Circuit Court of Appeals will also be considered to the extent that they inform the theoretical framework on offer here.

A thorough consideration of the entire body of federal court jurisprudence related to abortion, even one limited to the Second Circuit, is of course well beyond the scope of the present study; however, some of the themes that emerge from an overview of the most relevant decisions from that Court are significant as they relate to the argument at the heart of this work. As in the previous chapter, a LexisNexis search was conducted of all appellate court decisions from the Second Circuit that included the term "abortion," "Connecticut," and "Vermont." These results were then narrowed to examine only those involving challenges to state laws or injunctions issued against abortion protesters. The majority of these involved cases originating in New York and dealt for the most part with various claims against Randall Terry and the anti-abortion group Operation Rescue. The remainder of the relevant litigation came from Connecticut and took the form of several challenges to executive directives from the executive agencies of that state with one case involving the application of a Vermont campaign finance law to a pro-life activist committee. What an examination of the opinions issued in these decisions reveals is that the "legal" frame, as described in the introduction to this work, seems to have been as common as the "political" one.

All of the New York State federal cases, as mentioned above, involved injunctions against aggressive anti-abortion protesters, both before and after passage of the FACE law discussed in the preceding overview section. Perhaps the most important of these was *Pro-Choice Network v. Schenck* (1995), the clinic obstruction case that was partially overturned by the U.S. Supreme Court. The main thrust of the opinion delivered by Judge Oakes centered on addressing concerns related to the possible overbreadth of the district court's injunction, its content neutrality, and adherence to the Madsen test. For example, in describing the Court's level of scrutiny, Oakes writes that "while not amounting to [what we] have applied to content-based restrictions of speech, [it] is more rigorous than the test that has traditionally been applied to content-neutral regulations of the time, place, and manner of expression" (386). By contrast, the Court's opinions in *New York v. Terry* (1989) and *New York v. Operation Rescue* (2007), the former also dealing with a district court injunction and the latter with the anti-abortion group's alleged violation of the federal and state FACE laws, both focused to a much greater extent on what might be considered more political considerations involving whether or not the protesters had been "threatening" or "abusive" in their actions against women seeking access to abortion clinics. While this may not be surprising in the case of the *Operation Rescue* decision given that it did not involve a challenge to the constitutionality of the statute, this difference in focus in *Terry* is interesting as the facts of the case are not markedly dissimilar than those in *Schenck*. Indeed, considered in temporal sequence, the Second Circuit decisions seem to alternate between a focus on the contested facts of the case—whether or not an injunction was the appropriate response to the actions of anti-abortion protesters—and constitutional issues such as the free speech considerations raised by the relevant laws and court orders. If a "political" frame may be identified, at least to some extent, as one concerned with policy responses to perceived real-world problems and a legal frame as more focused on principles such as those articulated in the First Amendment or stare decisis, the relevant Second Circuit decisions can be said to reflect both.

Turning to the cases from Connecticut and Vermont, these too evince a focus on both "political" as well as "legal" frames. Echoing much the same sentiment as the New York Court of Appeals in *Byrn*, the Second Circuit's decision in *Roe v. Norton* (1975), which involved a challenge to a Connecticut Welfare Department regulation defining what constituted a "medically necessary" abortion, was largely deferential to the choices of the executive in that state. In his opinion for the Court, Judge Bryan wrote that "[b]eyond the minimal requirements for qualification, the states have wide latitude to determine the scope of coverage and to institute wide-ranging and comprehensive medical programs under their medical assistance plans" (933). In *West Hartford v. Operation Rescue* (1989), a case involving a city ordinance aimed at limiting aggressive abortion clinic protesters, however, the Court seemed more concerned with balancing the free speech rights of anti-abortion activists against those of women seeking the procedure. In that ruling, Judge Dorsey wrote that "the right to medical services, including abortion, and the right to emergency police, fire and ambulance services are rights common to all members of the general public" (381). The Second Circuit also heard a case challenging the constitutionality of Connecticut's abortion ban in *Abele v. Markle* (1971) as well as a Department of Income Maintenance directive limiting Medicaid funding to abortions necessary to preserve the life of the mother in *Women's Health Services v. Maher* (1980). Both of these were rejected on procedural grounds, though, and returned to the lower courts.[17] Finally, in *Vermont Right to Life Committee v. Sorrell* (2000), two provisions of a state campaign finance law—requiring reporting and imposing expenditure limits—were ruled partially unconstitutional as applied. This case too emphasized a "legal" solution to the issue, with the Court writing that the "question, then, is whether a narrowing construction can be applied to either set of provisions to rescue it from facial invalidity on the First Amendment grounds raised by VRLC" (386), a question it proceeded to answer in the affirmative.

These cases, while far from exhaustive, suggest that a pattern similar to the one found on the New York State Court of Appeals was not apparent at the federal level as both types of frames seemed to be present in many of the cases decided by the Second Circuit during the period considered in this study. What this means is not entirely clear, though it should be emphasized that the argument on offer here is based on the level of analysis being the policy making community in New York, meaning the three branches of government discussed above. From the standpoint of the theoretical framework proposed in this work, though, it bears mentioning that in the one area where federal courts weighed in on the same issue as elected officials, limits on the protest activities of anti-abortion activists, judicial involvement did not appear to supplant an active legislature. Indeed, several federal court decisions in the late 1980s and 1990s issuing injunctions against pro-life groups were followed by passage of the state FACE law in 1999, which was itself upheld in district court in *New York v. Kraeger* (2001). In this sense, federal rulings in this area did not result in legislative surrender of the issue but rather the development of two parallel streams of policy making—one at the federal level and one in the state house. The point, in any event, is that, at least as it relates to this rather specific example of policy making, federal judicial involvement was not sufficient to alter the behavior of the legislature and dissuade it from continuing its active role in developing abortion policy. More importantly to the question at the heart of this study regarding the secondary role of the courts under certain circumstances, however, it is worth noting that virtually all of the cases dealing with injunctions against clinic protesters were located in federal court. This is in contrast to the same issue in New Jersey where several important rulings limiting the activities of pro-life groups were issued by state judges. In terms of this specific area of abortion policy, it seems possible that at least one item was kept off of the agenda of state-level courts by federal involvement.

CONCLUSION

The theoretical framework on offer here is that early developments related to abortion policy, both within the elected branches as well as on the Court, helped frame the issue in political terms, an understanding that was subsequently reinforced as that development progressed. The isolation of this interpretive framework is most evident in the landmark cases of the Court of Appeals in cases such as *Byrn*, *Robin*, and *Hope*, though this narrative seemed to predominate in the legislative and executive branches as well. Indeed, far from inviting intervention on the part of the courts, lawmakers in the Assembly and Senate seemed determined to resolve disputes and determine policy around this issue themselves, in many cases bearing the political costs of doing so, including ending their own political careers. Furthermore, this willingness to deal with abortion policy does not seem to be explicable on the basis of some form of consensus around the issue that facilitated agreement within a legislature that was overwhelmingly populated by pro-choice Assembly members and Senators. Despite New York's reputation as one of the most culturally liberal states in the country, opposition to abortion rights has often been intense, particularly from the influential Catholic Church, which led almost all of the early lobbying efforts against liberalization. In addition, if the location of local-level restrictions on abortion access is to be taken as a proxy for public opinion on the issue in different regions, there would seem also to be a meaningful divide regarding abortion rights between much of upstate New York and Long Island and the more urban areas in and around New York City. Finally, the repeal of the liberalization law in 1972, the hospital restriction bill of 1974, the passage of parental consent legislation, and the elimination of PCAP funding for abortion procedures all indicate that not only were pro-life legislators numerous and influential for much of the last forty years, but that they too were able to formulate and implement policy in line with their political goals through the legislative process. Finally, the policy outputs from the Court also do not seem to support the idea that development in this issue area was led principally by the ideological commitments of largely pro-choice judges as, despite a stable partisan makeup that was heavily Democratic, the period between 1970 and 2010 saw decisions supportive of restrictions as well as expansions of abortion access.

The purpose of this chapter has not been to analyze why abortion policy was formulated as it was in New York State, but rather why the development of this policy took place almost exclusively in the legislature rather than the courts, as has been the case at the federal level as well as a number of states. In terms of specific events, the process of policy making fits well with many of the characteristics regarding path dependence described by Pierson (2000; 2004), Mahoney (2000), and others who emphasize the importance of the "first mover" in setting specific issues along a particular institutional path. In this case, George Michaels' abrupt and unpredictable vote-switching as well as Senate Majority leader Earl Brydges' miscalculation regarding the likelihood of passage of the liberalization bill in 1970 were the catalysts, which, while they may have appeared relatively insignificant at the time, had a profound impact on future developments. Governor Rockefeller's veto of the repeal bill two years later was also critical in maintaining legislative dominance as it foreclosed any chance of a *Roe*-type decision by the New York Court of Appeals, which may have led to a form of path-switching, particularly at that early stage. Of similar importance to the initial legislative involvement in the abortion issue were the series of court decisions such as *Byrn*, *Hope*, and *Robin*, whereby the judiciary repeatedly refused to alter the policy choices of the legislature. These "reactive sequences" (Mahoney 2000) served to entrench the path that had been earlier established by the decisions of the legislature. Even when the elected branches chose to restrict reproductive rights, the Court maintained its deference to the choices of lawmakers by upholding the removal of abortion funding from the PCAP bill in the early 1990s, which was not an insignificant move by a Court of Appeals that has rarely been shy of wading into political territory.[18]

The second component to the theoretical approach described in this study emphasizes that ideas and institutions are not only inseparable, but that there exists an ongoing dialogue between branches of government that informs the understandings courts will have of particular policy questions. The former in particular highlights the social construction process that leads judges to accept or reject ways of conceptualizing legal issues on the basis of the frameworks adopted by the wider interpretive community. In the case of abortion policy development in New York, it is clear that the terms of the debate within the legislative and executive branches were defined almost exclusively by the ideas that are traditionally associated with these institutions—concerns such as reflection of the public will, feasibility of implementation, and a focus on the anticipated results of policy choices. In turn, the courts too adopted this construction, as was plainly evident in the opinions issued in the key cases throughout the forty years considered here. The end result, then, was not simply that judges thought and wrote about the issue in terms similar to those more typically associated with the elected branches, but that they consistently refused to alter the choices of those same institutions.

Bringing these two concepts together reveals that when policy is created by a particular institution first, following a long period of inaction, the norms and issue frames that constitute that institution will tend to be adopted by the courts when they rule on the relevant policy question. What the preceding chapter suggests is the mechanism through which this process occurs. When the Court of Appeals first weighed in on the abortion question in 1972, there existed little legal precedent upon which to frame its conceptualization of the issue or base its ruling, either from previous courts, or indeed from courts in other states. What did exist, however, was a nascent body of language and frameworks that had emanated from the elected branches and it was this understanding from which the courts took their cues. As a result, the judiciary came to view abortion in "political" terms and therefore saw the issue as one properly resolved by the elected branches.

Policy making surrounding abortion in New York provides much important insight into how controversial issues are dealt with by lawmakers, particularly in a state with such considerable geographic and demographic diversity. Despite facing tremendous pressure from interest groups and potential electoral consequences regardless of the position they took on the issue, lawmakers do not seem to have made any serious attempt at deferring their policy making authority to the courts. The judiciary, for its part, embraced this legislative predominance throughout the course of the forty years considered here and never seriously altered the choices of the elected branches. As mentioned in the introductory chapter to this work, absent a clearly defined narrative at the point in time when the Court first issued an opinion in this issue area, the field of potential "candidates" was considerably wider than it may have been later in the process, allowing the judges on the state's High Court to look to a host of sources in treating the abortion question. Because little extant case law existed in the country in 1972, and none in New York, it seems reasonable that the Court chose to offer a wide latitude to the elected branches.

NOTES

1. The reason for this single difference is not entirely clear, though the fact remains that no evidence was found regarding either litigation against these centers by the state or individual parties or laws that addressed them.

2. Indeed, the abortion rate in New York has consistently been well above the national average, standing at 44.2 per 1,000 women between the ages of 15 and 44 compared to the national average of 26.3 in 1991 and 37.6 versus 19.6 nationally in 2008 (Guttmacher 2012). Additionally, in 1972, the year before *Roe*, New York was the only state permitting abortions that did not have a residency requirement.

3. Indeed, arguably the first serious attempt to propose changes to prevailing abortion law in the United States in the twentieth century came in 1962 with the American Law Institute's publication of the model penal code, which included, among other changes, a recommendation to amend existing laws to include certain exceptions related to the health of the mother (Greenhouse and Siegel 2012).

4. At least to the extent that they would have applied in New York. Indeed, the Supreme Court of California had struck down that state's abortion statute as unconstitutionally vague in

1969 (*People v. Belous*), and a number of legal actions had begun throughout the country, though none had been decided by early 1970.

5. Indeed, Assemblywoman Constance E. Cook had published a memo in the New York State Legislative Annual in 1970 that made several references to the pending case (Greenhouse and Siegel 2012).

6. By contrast, Hawaii's law allowed abortion only prior to "viability," provided for conscience objection protections, and stipulated a fine if these restrictions were violated (Haw. Rev. Stat. § 453-16); Washington state's law, passed by referendum, included parental or spousal consent provisions as well as a ninety-day residency requirement (Matern 1996); Alaska's abortion law also required parental consent, a thirty-day residency requirement, and conscience protections for persons refusing to perform an abortion (AK ST § 18.16.010).

7. Breitel writes, for example, that "abortion of a quick child was a high crime at common law . . . although one commentator has argued persuasively that, in fact, it was not; that abortion was a purely ecclesiastical offense punishable only by spiritual penalties" (318).

8. Recall that critical moments are defined throughout this analysis as points in time when the actions of judges or lawmakers have important repercussions for institutional roles going forward. To consider a counterfactual here, had the Court sided with Byrn in that case and relied on the Equal Protection claim the law professor had put forward, this could have had profound implications for how the judiciary understood abortion in subsequent cases and, by extension, their own role in creating policy.

9. Though a similar law in Ohio was eventually struck down in 1983 by the U.S. Supreme Court in *City of Akron v. Akron Center for Reproductive Health*, which was itself overturned in *Planned Parenthood v. Casey* in 1992.

10. Note that the margins by which the repeal bill had passed four years earlier were much closer, with the vote in the Assembly being 79 to 68 and the Senate voting 30 to 27 in favor of repeal. In this sense, an override of the governor's veto would have been considerably more difficult in 1972 than in 1976.

11. Such a challenge was all but a certainty, as Planned Parenthood officials had already drafted a request for an injunction of the law should the governor have failed to veto the bill (Dullea 1976).

12. Graber (1999) makes this very point specifically in reference to the Hyde amendment.

13. Admittedly, all litigation is of course initiated by a party outside of the court.

14. See, for example, *Planned Parenthood v. Kempiners* 200 F.2d 1115 (1983), *Fargo Women's Health Org. v. Larson* 381 N.W 2d 177 (1986), *Stoner v. Williams* 46 Cal. App. 4th 986 (1996), *Boes v. Deschu* 768 S.W. 2d 205 (1989), *Enary v. Pennsylvania Public Utility Comm.* 78 Pa Commw. 636 (1983), *Planned Parenthood v. Problem Pregnancy of Worcester* 418 N.E. 2d 1044 (1986), *Mother of Unborn Baby Care of N. Texas v. Doe* 6895. W. 2d 336 (1985), *Roe v. San Diego Pregnancy Servs. Inc.* No.657592 (1994).

15. Indeed, Operation Rescue and other groups affiliated with Randall Terry had spent much of the late 1980s and 1990s engaged in litigation in New York—among other states—though they enjoyed little success as the courts consistently rejected their claims in cases such as *New York State NOW v. Terry* (1989), *Town of West Hartford v. Operation Rescue* (1993), and *US v. Randall Terry* (1994).

16. These numbers include only donations to individuals or their campaign organizations competing for Assembly or Senate seats or the New York State Democratic Committee and not contributions to national races that might be affected by the presidential race in 2004.

17. Specifically, in *Abele*, the Court ruled that some of the plaintiffs lacked standing to challenge the law while in *Maher* the case was returned without a decision on the merits with a recommendation that the legislature consider passing a statute in line with the recently upheld Hyde Amendment.

18. See chapter 1 for examples of the New York Court of Appeals repeated willingness to engage in this type of "judicial policy making."

Chapter Four

Different Issues, Different States

Any work relying on a case study approach will, of course, run the risk of sacrificing generalizability for a deeper analysis of the specific events behind larger political and legal processes. In a more specific sense, any reader of the preceding chapters would be correct in pointing out that there exist a number of cases where policy change was initiated by the courts or a legislature, though final resolution of the issue was ultimately located in the other branch of government. It would therefore be beneficial to examine how policy developed in just such a circumstance, particularly involving another polarizing social issue. The goal here is not, then, to demonstrate that the theory described in this work operates in exactly the same way under all circumstances—indeed, the following discussion illustrates that it does not—but rather to identify what other salient factors influence the institutional location of decision making and hopefully identify promising routes for further research. Nevertheless, much of what has been identified in the abortion cases discussed thus far as playing an important role in this location can also be seen in the following cases.

In order to offer some further illustration of the theoretical framework presented in this study, the following chapter will offer a discussion of the development of another issue in New York and New Jersey: changes to those states' laws regarding capital punishment following the U.S. Supreme Court's decision in *Furman v. Georgia* (1972). As with abortion, the death penalty is a controversial social issue that often cut across party lines, particularly in the late 1960s and 1970s, and saw considerable involvement by both the courts and the elected branches. Considerable pressure was also brought to bear on lawmakers by groups both supporting and opposing capital punishment during the forty years following the Supreme Court's landmark ruling, including the Catholic church, which strongly advocated for abolition.

There were, however, also a number of important differences between the development of abortion and capital punishment policy in New York and New Jersey, most importantly as they relate to the states vis-à-vis the federal government. Unlike the *Roe* case, *Furman* did not represent the establishment of a strict pronouncement regarding the constitutionality of the death penalty and states were left with a number of statutory options to remedy the deficiencies the Court had identified. Indeed, a mere four years later, seven of the Justices would vote to uphold several states' revised capital punishment laws in *Gregg v. Georgia* (1976).

In addition to the death penalty case in New York and New Jersey, this chapter will also present an analysis of the development of abortion policy in two other, though also quite similar states, Minnesota and Wisconsin. Like New Jersey, both of these states saw the first major change to their abortion statutes come after *Roe v. Wade*, though each ended up with markedly different policies on this issue, with Wisconsin maintaining some of the nation's most restrictive laws while Minnesota remains a comparatively liberal state in terms of abortion access. It is not my purpose here to explain why these two states reached rather different policy ends on this issue, however, but instead to consider how the theory proposed in this book applies to other states and political circumstances. As in New York and New Jersey, we find in these two Midwestern states a notable difference in the level of involvement of the courts and the legislature, with Minnesota's judiciary taking a considerably more active role in policy development than its counterpart in Wisconsin. Perhaps more importantly, though, are the rhetorical frames around abortion found in the two states, with lawmakers in both using a combination of political and legal language, though this often depended on the position of the speaker on abortion rights as well as the particular issue being discussed.

In terms of methodology for the case studies presented in this chapter, much the same approach is used here as the preceding chapters discussing New York and New Jersey. Specifically, a search on LexisNexis was performed for all court cases containing the phrases "death penalty" or "capital punishment" and "New York" or "New Jersey" from the two state court systems as well as federal district courts and the Second and Third Circuit Courts of Appeal. The same phrases were also searched between the years 1970 and 2010 within the ProQuest Historical Newspapers database for the *New York Times*, examining all public statements by lawmakers made during this period dealing with the death penalty. For the Minnesota and Wisconsin cases, a similar search was performed using LexisNexis and the term "abortion" for all state courts, federal district courts, and the Seventh and Eighth Circuit Courts of Appeal. For statements from lawmakers, an archival search was performed using two state newspapers, the *Star Tribune* of Minneapolis and the *St. Paul Pioneer Press* in the case of Minnesota and the Wisconsin

State Journal and *Sheboygan Press* for Wisconsin using the search term "abortion." Finally, gubernatorial veto messages and signing statements were analyzed in cases where these were present.

This chapter will offer a brief analysis of the state of the law leading up to the Supreme Court's *Furman* and *Gregg* decisions, as well as the responses from courts and lawmakers in New York and New Jersey. Consideration of this issue reveals a number of similarities to the development of abortion policy discussed in the preceding chapters, particularly as it relates to the discourse between the courts, the executive, and the legislature. These cases, however, illustrate a number of important differences as well. Unlike in the abortion cases, the courts in both states, while remaining highly involved in the policy making process, never issued a firm declaration regarding the constitutionality of capital punishment. Beyond this, the first changes to New York's death penalty statute came from the elected branches, though the issue seems to have ultimately been resolved by the Court of Appeals. The first substantive change to New Jersey's law, however, came via the Supreme Court's decision in *Furman*, though abolition was eventually accomplished legislatively. How then does this issue fit with the cases presented in the preceding two chapters? What the following discussion reveals is that the frame adopted by the institution first responsible for policy change was still highly influential for the location of decision making. Unlike the abortion cases, however, the courts never firmly adopted a primarily "political" *or* "legal" view of the issue and were therefore less constraining of how lawmakers thought about and discussed capital punishment. Following this, the cases of abortion policy development in Minnesota and Wisconsin will be considered, with a focus on the differing frames employed by judges and lawmakers in these states and their likely impact on the location of policy making there. Finally, some discussion will be presented regarding how these particular case studies inform the theoretical framework proposed in this book and how it might be further refined in light of the addition of these cases.

THE *FURMAN* AND *GREGG* DECISIONS

On June 29, 1972, the U.S. Supreme Court handed down its decision in *Furman v. Georgia*, vacating the death sentences of two defendants in Georgia and one in Texas,[1] and imposing a *de facto* moratorium on capital punishment across the country. A one-paragraph per curium opinion curtly stated that "[t]he Court holds that the imposition and carrying out of the death penalty in these cases constitute cruel and unusual punishment in violation of the Eighth and Fourteenth Amendments" (239, 240). This brief ruling, however, was followed by nine separate opinions, five concurring with the decision and four offering dissents. Justices Brennan and Marshall, as they continued to do over the rest of their tenure on the Court, argued that capital punishment was unconstitutional under all circumstances. Justice Douglas rested the majority of his opinion on the disproportionate imposition of the death penalty on the poor and racial minorities, writing that "[i]t would seem to be incontestable that the death penalty inflicted on one defendant is 'unusual' if it discriminates against him by reason of his race, religion, wealth, social position, or class" (*Furman* at 242). Justice Stewart, rejecting as unproven the notion that capital punishment was imposed disproportionately on African Americans or the indigent, nonetheless pointed to the "capricious" way in which death sentences were handed down, a similar point to that made by Justice White. The dissents, authored by Chief Justice Burger and Justices Powell, Blackmun, and Rehnquist, took issue primarily with what they saw as judicial usurpation of the legislative and popular will, as well as making arguments relying on stare decisis and the historical use of capital punishment.

Following the *Furman* decision, thirty-five states passed new death penalty statutes that sought to remedy the constitutional deficiencies the Court had identified (Blomberg and Lucken 2000). This led the Supreme Court to again take up the issue in 1976, this time ruling in *Gregg v. Georgia*, in a 7–2 vote, that capital punishment itself did not violate the Eighth Amendment's prohibition on cruel and unusual punishment and that the Georgia law at issue had adequately addressed the concerns regarding capricious application of the penalty identified in *Furman*. Specifically, Justice Stewart's opinion for the Court focused on four major arguments regarding the constitutionality of the death penalty, including the value of deference to the legislature, historical acceptance of capital punishment, the lack of opposition among the American people, and retribution and deterrence as reasonable legislative ends. Stewart also highlighted aspects of the new Georgia statute that remedied earlier concerns the Court had identified, the most important of these being the bifurcation of trials into guilt and penalty phases, with the consideration of aggravating and mitigating circumstances in the second portion, and the inclusion of a proportionality review system designed to compare a particular death sentence to other capital cases in order to identify potential bias. As they had in *Furman* four years earlier, Justices Brennan and Marshall authored dissenting opinions in which they reiterated their position that capital punishment amounted to cruel and unusual punishment in all circumstances.

How then do the Court's opinions in *Furman* and *Gregg* fit into the "legal" or "political" frames described in the previous chapters? Recall that emphasis on concepts such as "rights," "equal protection," "overbroad language," and other similar terms are associated with what might be referred to as a more legal conceptualization of policy questions. On the other hand, more emotive and politically charged language such as "imposing morality," "value judgment," or "the will of the people" may be more characteristic of a political frame. An analysis of the Court's opinions treating capital punishment in the early- to mid-1970s reveals that the Justices seemed to be thinking about the issue in both more highly political, as well as legal, terms than had been the case with some of the major abortion decisions such as *Roe* and *Casey*. For example, Justice Douglas writes in his *Furman* opinion that "these discretionary statutes are unconstitutional in their operation. They are pregnant with discrimination and discrimination is an ingredient not compatible with the idea of equal protection of the laws that is implicit in the ban on 'cruel and unusual' punishments" (257,257), evincing a concern for decidedly legal issues. Justice Brennan's concurring opinion, however, argues that "[a]t bottom, then, the Cruel and Unusual Punishments Clause prohibits the infliction of uncivilized and inhuman punishments. The State, even as it punishes, must treat its members with respect for their intrinsic worth as human beings. A punishment is 'cruel and unusual,' therefore, if it does not comport with human dignity" (270).

Both frames can also be seen in *Gregg*, though Justice Stewart's opinion for the Court seemed to take a decidedly more political tone. While concerns about judicial interference in the legislative process are not uncommon, particularly when choosing to uphold a challenged statute, Stewart makes the point rather forcefully, writing that "in assessing a punishment selected by a democratically elected legislature against the constitutional measure, we presume its validity. We may not require the legislature to select the least severe penalty possible so long as the penalty selected is not cruelly inhumane or disproportionate to the crime involved. And a heavy burden rests on those who would attack the judgment of the representatives of the people" (175). In terms of the value of retribution as a legitimate legislative objective, Stewart argues that "the decision that capital punishment may be the appropriate sanction in extreme cases is an expression of the community's belief that certain crimes are themselves so grievous an affront to humanity that the only adequate response may be the penalty of death" (184). Finally, in addressing the Georgia statute at issue specifically, the majority opinion takes a somewhat more legal tone, claiming "[t]he provision for appellate review in the Georgia capital sentencing system serves as a check against the random or arbitrary imposition of the death penalty. In particular, the proportionality review substantially eliminates the possibility that a person will be sentenced to die by the action of an aberrant jury" (206). That the Court would emphasize both legal and political frames would have important implications for how lawmakers and judges in New York and New Jersey would consider the question of capital punishment, particularly in contrast to the abortion issue.

CAPITAL PUNISHMENT IN NEW YORK

In March 1965, the Temporary Commission on Revision of the Penal Law and Code of Criminal Procedure, a bipartisan report that had been requested by the legislature and Governor Rockefeller, issued a strong recommendation that New York's death penalty be abolished. Among the participants on the commission were state district attorneys, members of the Assembly and Senate, and law school faculty members, including Herbert Wechsler of Columbia University and head of the American Law Institute. While recapping many of the common arguments in support and opposition to capital punishment, the authors of the report emphasized that "[t]he social need for the grievous condemnation of the gravest crimes can be met, as it is met in abolition states, without resort to barbarism of this kind" (Sullivan 1965). Two months later, on May 19, the Assembly approved, in a narrow 78–67 vote, a Senate bill amending the state's death penalty law to limit its applicability only to those convicted of killing a law enforcement officer or who committed murder while serving a life sentence (Robinson 1965). Governor Rockefeller signed the bill into law shortly afterward while also commuting the sentences of the twenty inmates then on death row to life imprisonment (Apple 1965a).

Supporters and opponents of the measure spoke almost entirely in terms of political considerations. One of the primary sponsors of the bill, Richard Bartlett, a Republican member of the Assembly from upstate New York, commented that "[t]his is an opportunity for New York State to lead in an advance to a more humane and civilized treatment of offenders in our courts" (Robinson 1965). Democratic Senator Manfred Ohrenstein of Manhattan similarly argued that "the death penalty has not acted as a deterrent for murder. It has acted only for the most primitive desires for revenge. Tragically, it has also been used with greater frequency in cases affecting members of minority groups" (Apple 1965b). Opponents of the revised death penalty law also spoke in highly charged, emotional terms, with the minority view of the 1965 Commission writing that "[t]he nature and complex make-up of our population, the ugly moods and attitudes which now appear to prevail among varying ethnic and social groups in this state, the boldness with which atrocious crimes are committed, with less and less effort at concealment, the frequently appalling lack of regard for the rights and sensitivities of others make it entirely possible that movement toward abolition of capital punishment in the state at this time may be taken by the lawless masses as a signal for even further outbreaks of lawlessness" (Sullivan 1965). Others opposed to the measure invoked a more democratic appeal, proposing an amendment to the bill that would require an advisory referendum on repeal of the state's capital punishment statute (Robinson 1965).

During the remainder of the 1960s and into the early 1970s several relatively minor additions were made to New York's death penalty statute, once in 1967 allowing for the imposition of capital punishment for those convicted of murder while serving a fifteen year to life sentence in prison and again in 1971 for individuals found guilty of killing a corrections officer during the performance of their duties (Lentol, Weinstein, and Aubry 2005). The following year, the U.S. Supreme Court handed down its *Furman* decision, effectively banning the death penalty in all fifty states, including New York. The state's capital punishment statute was officially ruled unconstitutional in 1973 with the Court of Appeals decision in *People v. Fitzpatrick*, finding that allowing essentially unregulated jury discretion in imposing the death sentence amounted to cruel and unusual punishment. Judge Fuld's opinion in the case offers little insight into the view the Court was inclined to take in regards to capital punishment, with the Chief Judge revealing little of how the Judges of the state's High Court were likely to conceptualize the question.

> [s]ince, then, the New York statute here challenged (Penal Law, § 125.35, subd. 5) leaves infliction of the death penalty solely to the discretion of the jury, we conclude, in light of the Supreme Court's reading of the Eighth Amendment in *Furman* [*v Georgia*] (408 U.S. 238, supra), that we have no alternative but to hold that that penalty constitutes cruel and unusual punishment within the sense of that provision (30).

A year after the *Fitzpatrick* ruling the legislature passed, and Governor Wilson signed, a law restoring capital punishment in cases involving the murder of a police or corrections officer or committed by someone serving a life sentence. Statements by lawmakers in both the Assembly and Senate concerning the 1974 bill reflected primarily political concerns centered on the alleged deterrent effect of the death penalty and the public support it enjoyed. Assemblyman Burton G. Hecht (D), for instance, said of the bill that "[t]his may be the most crucial issue coming out of the Legislature this year. I firmly believe that the people of the State of New York overwhelmingly support restoration of the death penalty" (Narvaez 1974). Sen. Thomas McGowan (R) for his part argued that the measure would "deter the killing of every human being on the face of this earth . . . the prime purpose of the bill is to protect the life of the police officer as the lowest symbol of authority" (Andelman 1974). Finally, in criticizing the bill, Assemblyman Stanley Kink (D) sounded a somewhat more legal note, stating that "[w]hat the Supreme Court said was there had to be criteria judges and juries could believe with consistency. But consistency is what is missing from this bill" (*New York Times* 1974).

Following the U.S. Supreme Court's decision in *Gregg* to essentially reauthorize the death penalty as an option for states, the Senate and Assembly passed a bill allowing for death sentences in cases of premeditated murder or when killing during the commission of another violent crime, though the bill was vetoed by Governor Carey. In debating the measure, lawmakers evinced a tone similar to what they had taken three years earlier during debate of the police and corrections officers' bill, speaking in heated, political terms, both in support as well as opposition to the proposal. Sen. Jeremiah Bloom (D) stated that "[t]he fear of burning is a deterrent" and accused the NYCLU, who opposed the death penalty, of "hav[ing] bleeding hearts for every criminal but not one word of compassion for the victim." Sen. Manfred Ohrenstein (D), an opponent of the bill, asked "[w]hat purpose is accomplished by taking another life? Something bad is accomplished. We do harm to ourselves as a society, demeaning the belief in life, destroying a life when it serves no purpose" (Bird 1977a). In vetoing the expanded death penalty bill, Governor Carey said that "all of us, in frustration and righteous anger . . . fall back on the solution of capital punishment, even though we know it to be illusory. [The death penalty] is no proven deterrent to crime and never has been in an open society; it leaves no room for human fallibility; it lowers all of us who abide by the law and the Judeo-Christian tradition of preserving and perfecting human life and dignity" (Bird 1977b).

Ultimately, Carey's veto would be the first in a long process of the legislature passing reinstatement bills only to be vetoed by a succession of governors. Indeed, a death penalty bill was passed in every year following *Gregg* until finally being signed by Governor Pataki in 1995. More importantly to the present study, though, is the apparent preponderance of a political frame, at least among elected officials. Indeed, the claimed deterrent effect of the death penalty featured prominently in the arguments of both opponents and supporters, a position that can reasonably be understood as "political" inasmuch as it is focused on the expected outcome of policy on a particular measure—in this case, the number of murders. Beyond this, the most common frames seem to have been ones regarding the impropriety of the state's taking of life and the democratic will of the people. These too seem as more political concerns as they deal in the realm of emotion and values, rather than legally articulated requirements. Remember that the Supreme Court in both *Furman* and *Gregg* had offered a number of potential legal frames that lawmakers could have adopted, including Eighth Amendment concerns regarding cruel and unusual punishment as well as Due Process or Equal Protection arguments, much as they had in New Jersey's abortion debate. As we will see, though, both lawmakers and the courts continued to frame capital punishment in New York in political terms, with the notable exception of the latter when dealing with what it understood as federal mandates.

Indeed, the police and corrections officers' death penalty statute passed in 1974 was ultimately struck down by the Court of Appeals in its 1977 decision in *People v. Davis* on the basis that similar laws had recently been struck down by the U.S. Supreme Court. Writing for the Court in this case, Judge Cooke stated that "since New York's statute provides neither for the furnishing of information, without which there cannot be consideration of the individual offender and the circumstances of a particular offense, nor standards to guide the sentencing authority in the use of that information had it been furnished, unconstitutionality is certainly indicated. Indeed, since the statute requires by its terms a mandatory death penalty for the enumerated crimes, it is indistinguishable from those death penalty statutes found unconstitutional in *Woodson v North Carolina* and *Roberts (Stanislaus) v Louisiana*" (32). Further demonstrating the Court's reluctance to wade into the broader question of the death penalty's continued use in New York, Cooke's opinion begins by emphasizing that "we are called upon to determine the constitutionality of New York's death penalty statute—a legal issue—not to express our views as to whether such a statute, granted that it is constitutional, is wise or advisable—a legislative concern" (23).

Nevertheless, seven years later the Court of Appeals would strike down the remaining provision of New York's capital punishment statute allowing for a death sentence in cases where the defendant was serving a life sentence at the time of the murder in *People v. Smith* (1984). Here again the Court based its ruling on *Woodson v. North Carolina*, rather than the state Constitution or even a broader understanding of federal limits. This reluctance is evident in Judge Kaye's opinion for the Court in which she states that "New York's mandatory death penalty is constitutionally infirm as applied to this defendant because of its failure to provide for the consideration of individual circumstances, one of the three deficiencies of a mandatory death penalty articulated in the plurality opinion in *Woodson*. In view of our conclusion that New York's statute contravenes the Federal Constitution, we do not reach the issue of the State Constitution's similar prohibition of cruel and unusual punishments (art I, § 5), or defendant's additional arguments that a mandatory death penalty for life-term inmates suffers from the other two deficiencies of a mandatory death statute identified in *Woodson*" (79, 80). That being said, the Court in *Smith* did echo some of the major themes that had been prevalent during the legislative debates of the 1970s, arguing that "a discretionary death penalty, which allows for the consideration of the character as well as the record of the individual offender and the circumstances of the particular offense, differs little in terms of deterrence from a mandatory death penalty and does not in fact detract from the value of capital punishment as a deterrent" (77).

Lawmakers too continued to discuss the death penalty, whether in support or opposition, in terms of its potential deterrent effect throughout the 1980s. Some examples of this include Sen. Carol Berman (D), who used a recent vacation to argue that "I was in Florida, the leading death penalty state, and what did I find? A murder every morning on the front page of my newspaper, with my grapefruit" (Purnick 1980). Assemblyman G. Oliver Koppell (D) sounded a similar note about "enormous frustration in people in New York. People are searching for an answer. Politicians don't have easy answers, so they love to talk about the death penalty. It becomes a code word for being tough on crime" (Kolbert 1989). Finally, Assemblyman Vincent Graber (D) spoke in more emotional terms, suggesting that "[w]e have a death penalty. We have a death penalty that was imposed in this state some 2,000 times. Who were the people that this illegal death penalty was imposed on? They were law-abiding citizens" (Gargan 1983). Besides the continued absence of what might be considered a legal rhetorical frame, what is also notable here is a lack of reference to any of the Court of Appeals decisions or, indeed, even the Court itself. Certainly the notion of an "activist" Court undermining the democratic will of the majority was a well-worn theme during the Reagan 1980s, though there seems to have been very little, if any, evidence that similar arguments were being put forward by lawmakers discussing the death penalty. This may be because there was in fact little in the Court's opinions to attack. While the state's judges had indeed struck down parts, and eventually the entirely, of New York's capital punishment statutes, they had also been emphatic that the legislature could pass a constitutionally sound law if they chose to do so. This attitude within the Court is similar to what had taken place during the abortion debate discussed earlier, though in the case of capital punishment, the judiciary would continue to play a more active role in practice, if not necessarily in word.

With the election of George Pataki as governor in 1994, supporters of the death penalty finally had a chief executive who would be willing to sign a restoration bill into law. The first Republican governor in twenty years had made a "tough on crime" plank a major part of his campaign against Mario Cuomo and made good on his promise to restore capital punishment in New York less than three months into his first term. Among the death-eligible crimes in the new law were murder of a police or corrections officer or judge, murderers involving torture, and murder committed during the commission of another serious crime such as robbery, kidnapping, or rape. In signing the reinstatement bill, Pataki claimed that "[w]hat demeans society is when too many police officers respond to a call risking their lives to protect us and we as a society can't do everything in our power to protect them and save their lives. This bill is going to save lives" (Dao 1995a). Marking a similar tone, Sen. Dale Volker (R) argued in support of the law after its passage in the Senate, saying "[t]here are people who are dead today who would be alive if we had a death penalty." Sen. Martine Luster (D) opposed the measure, saying "[t]his chamber has a long and honorable history. What we are about to do here tonight is to taint that history with fraud—a fraud upon the people of this state. It is a fraud to tell the people that they will be safer as a result of this legislation" (Dao 1995b). Just as it had been for most of the past twenty-five years, then, the dominant narrative among lawmakers in New York upon finally passing a capital punishment statute was once again one of the deterrent potential of the death penalty.

In December 1998, the New York State Court of Appeals, in *Hynes v. Tomei*, invalidated two plea provisions of the capital punishment statute that allowed criminal defendants charged with first degree murder to forgo a jury trial, plead guilty, and thus avoid the possibility of a death sentence. The Court of Appeals, tracking the U.S. Supreme Court's decision in *United States v. Jackson*, declared sections 220.10(5)(e) and 220.30(3)(b)(vii) of the New York Criminal Procedure law unconstitutional, as they "'needlessly' encourage[d] guilty pleas in violation of *Jackson*." This time writing in much more "legal" terms, Chief Judge Kaye reasoned that "like the invalidated Federal Kidnaping Act provision, New York's death penalty statute explicitly provides for the imposition of the death penalty only upon a jury verdict. As a result, under the New York statute, only those defendants who exercise the Fifth Amendment right against self-incrimination and Sixth Amendment right to a jury trial put themselves at risk of death. Nevertheless, respondents argue that the New York statute is distinguishable from the Federal Kidnaping Act in several ways. We conclude that the distinctions are without a constitutionally cognizable difference" (623). Putting the issue more bluntly, the Court also claimed that "a procedure which offers an individual a reward for waiving a fundamental constitutional right, or imposes a harsher penalty for asserting it, may not be sustained" (621, 622). Four years later, the Court of Appeals affirmed a reversal of a death sentence on the same grounds as *Hynes* in *People v. Harris* (2002). The court here was asked to pass on the constitutionality of New York's death penalty law, but declined to do so, arguing that the "decision to authorize capital punishment for classes of crimes is one best left to the Legislature unless clearly wrong. We recognize that the Legislature can determine among the sins of society those that require a criminal sanction, and prescribe the appropriate punishment" (476).

New York's capital punishment statute was finally rendered inoperative with the Court of Appeals' ruling in *People v. LaValle* (2004), finding the "deadlock" provision of New York's death penalty law unconstitutional. The provision instructed jurors that if they could not reach a unanimous decision on either death or life without parole, the judge would sentence the defendant to life with the possibility of parole after twenty to twenty-five years. Judge Smith's majority opinion elaborated on the Court's reasoning, writing that "New York's deadlock provision is unique in that the sentence required after a deadlock is less severe than the sentences the jury is allowed to consider. No other death penalty scheme in the country requires judges to instruct jurors that if they cannot unanimously agree between two choices, the judge will sentence defendant to a third, more lenient, choice" (116, 117). This,

Smith argued, "gives rise to an unconstitutionally palpable risk that one or more jurors who cannot bear the thought that a defendant may walk the streets again after serving 20 to 25 years will join jurors favoring death in order to avoid the deadlock sentence" (118). As it had in a number of earlier cases, however, the Court continued to highlight its view that the ultimate decision regarding the death penalty in New York lay with the legislature. To emphasize this point, Smith wrote that "[w]e cannot, however, ourselves craft a new instruction, because to do so would usurp legislative prerogative. We have the power to eliminate an unconstitutional sentencing procedure, but we do not have the power to fill the void with a different procedure, particularly one that potentially imposes a greater sentence than the possible deadlock sentence that has been prescribed. As the Court noted in *People v Gersewitz* (294 NY 163, 169 [1945]), we have 'no power to supply even an inadvertent omission of the Legislature'" (131).

While *LaValle* proved to be the last word on capital punishment in New York,[2] a bill to amend the statute struck down by the Court of Appeals did pass the Senate in 2004, though it was never brought to a vote in the Assembly. During debate of this measure, lawmakers seemed to focus less on a deterrent argument than they had for most of the previous forty years, with supporters making a case based largely on what might be termed retributive justice and opponents highlighting the possibility of a wrongful execution. Sen. Dale Volker (R), for example, said following the Court of Appeals decision in *LaValle* that "[e]very time we pass the death penalty the murders go down, and then after they go down, people say, 'Well I don't know if we need the death penalty,' and then we get rid of the death penalty, and the numbers go up dramatically." Assemblyman Mark Weprin (D), also after the *LaValle* decision, expressed concern over the possibility of executing and innocent person, saying "I just don't know how you explain that to a mother whose child is completely innocent and who is murdered by the state for something they didn't do." Assemblyman David Townsend (R) responded that "I would say to you, Mark, and everybody here, what do we say to the innocent wife, mother, son, daughter, husband of the innocent police officer, the innocent firefighter, the innocent corrections officer, the innocent E.M.S. person whose [sic] had their life needlessly taken in a homicide" (Baker 2004).

The first substantive changes to New York's capital punishment laws were initiated by the legislature prior to the U.S. Supreme Court's decision to suspend the practice nationwide in 1972. Nevertheless, the judiciary, led by the Court of Appeals, consistently altered those policy choices, though refused to go so far as to find the death penalty unconstitutional in all cases. In terms of the rhetorical frames that were most common among the elected and judicial branches, the former focused heavily on the use of capital punishment as a deterrent to murder, while the latter spoke in more legal terms, albeit also consistently highlighting that the ultimate decision regarding the existence of the death penalty in the state rested with the legislature. Notably, most of the major Court of Appeals decisions relied heavily on the application of decisions from the U.S. Supreme Court rather than interpretations of the state Constitution. This may have been the result of a Court that was suspicious of the use of capital punishment—a conclusion suggested by its willingness to overturn death sentences—but was nonetheless reluctant to overturn completely a policy that the legislature had been so active in developing. It is also worth noting that, somewhat in contrast to *Roe*, the U.S. Supreme Court's death penalty rulings in *Furman* and *Gregg* offered a wide array of both political and legal frames for capital punishment, perhaps encouraging both courts and lawmakers to choose those that were most expedient for their purposes. While abortion was "constitutionalized" in *Roe*, particularly for those on the pro-choice side of the debate, the multitude of opinions offered in *Furman* and Justice Stewart's opinion in *Gregg* provided no such unifying theme. Indeed, this plethora of legal and political arguments on both sides of the capital punishment debate is even more evident in New Jersey, a state that saw its first policy change located in the courts.

CAPITAL PUNISHMENT IN NEW JERSEY

Just as New York would a year later, New Jersey Governor Richard Hughes established the Commission to Study Capital Punishment in 1964 whose charge was "to study capital punishment and to weigh the question of its place in present-day society, and to inquire into possible substitutions therefor." Chaired by former Assembly Member William F. Tompkins, the Commission, in contrast to its New York counterpart, recommended that the death penalty remain a sentencing option for those convicted of murder or treason. Prior to this report, the only meaningful legislative action that had taken place in the state dealing with the issue of capital punishment were calls to establish the Commission itself. The first substantive change to New Jersey's death penalty laws, then, did not occur until the *Furman* decision in 1972.

The New Jersey Supreme Court, however, would weigh in on the matter in 1968 following the U.S. Supreme Court's ruling in *United States v. Jackson*, which had struck down portions of a federal kidnapping act providing that a defendant who insisted on a jury trial could face the death penalty. In *State v. Forcella*, the Court ultimately found that New Jersey's capital punishment statute differed sufficiently from the law at issue in *Jackson* and therefore remained a valid sentencing option. What is perhaps most interesting about this case, though, is the heavy emphasis Chief Justice Weintraub placed on deferring to the legislature when it came to the issue of the death penalty. Leaving little doubt about this view, Weintraub wrote that:

> The history of capital punishment in this State is well documented. In that light, we could hardly accept the extraordinary proposition that the 1893 act or the 1917 act, or any general revision of the laws, spelled out an intent that the death penalty should fall if the introduction of the non vult plea created a constitutional impasse. Capital punishment lies within the authority and the responsibility of the Legislature, and the Legislature has expressly and continuously dealt with the subject. There have been numerous efforts to abolish it. As recently as 1964 a study commission created by joint resolution of the Legislature recommended that the death penalty be retained. It is not our responsibility, or authority, whatever our individual views on capital punishment, to impute to the Legislature a repeal it has consistently refused to enact during more than a century of agitation upon this subject (282, 283).

The Court also rejected several other claims raised by the defendant, including a Due Process violation related to the non-bifurcated nature of the trial and sentencing phases as well as an Eighth Amendment violation also related to the non-bifurcation issue as well as a claim that the death penalty "serves no justifiable end" (293). As it had in the quote above, the Court also highlighted that it saw the determination of what might constitute "cruel and unusual punishment" as a question entirely within the purview of the legislature.

The *Forcella* decision was appealed to the U.S. Supreme Court, which overturned the death sentence in a memorandum disposition citing *Jackson*, as well as *Witherspoon v. Illinois*, (1968), *Boulden v. Holman* (1969), and *Maxwell v. Bishop* (1970). With the case remanded, the New Jersey Supreme Court wrote in *State v. Funicello* that "[w]e therefore accept the conclusion that the United States Supreme Court has declared the death penalty to be unconstitutional under our statute" (67). The issue of course would become moot several months later when the High Court's *Furman* decision stayed all executions throughout the country, though it is interesting to note that it was in fact *Jackson* that ultimately eliminated capital punishment as a sentencing option in New Jersey. The remainder of the Court's Per Curium opinion in *Funicello* made no reference to the death penalty, but instead focused on the maintenance of the first degree murder statute and its provision for life without parole.

The response from lawmakers to the elimination of New Jersey's capital punishment statute was relative swift, with a bill to reinstate the sentence passing the state Senate in 1972, though the measure was never brought to the Assembly. Following the U.S. Supreme Court's decision reinstating the death penalty in *Gregg* in 1976, however, a bill did pass both houses of the legislature, though it was ultimately pocket-vetoed by Governor Byrne. The public statements made by lawmakers during the debate surrounding the reinstatement bill are notable for the drastically different tone they took when compared to those in New York. Rather than framing the issue as one focused on the deterrent potential of capital punishment, legislators in New Jersey explicitly rejected this view, instead emphasizing the notion of death as an appropriate punishment for the most heinous crimes. Illustrating this well, Senator John Russo (D) wrote in a *New York Times* op-ed that "I support the reinstatement of capital punishment in New Jersey not so much as a deterrent to murder but primarily as a fulfilment of a need and demand of society. Certainly I cannot subscribe to the deterrent value of capital punishment in murder perpetrated by those who act in passion" (Russo 1976). Senator Matthew Feldman (D), the president of the state senate, made a democratic argument for the death penalty bill, saying of the governor that "I think he's reading the polls. It's what the people want, even if maybe only out of frustration and a sense of helplessness" (Sullivan 1976).

Also in contrast to the New York debate, opponents of the death penalty in New Jersey highlighted questions surrounding the disproportionate application of capital punishment against minorities and the poor. Senator James Dugan (D) argued during a floor debate that the death penalty statute was likely to be applied to those who "don't have the money to buy a life sentence." In response, Senator Anthony Imperiale (I) claimed that "[a] murderer is a murderer, no matter what his race, creed or color" (Waldron 1976). Assembly Members Aldridge Hawkins (D) and Robert Owens (D), echoing this sentiment, urged their fellow lawmakers during debate to watch the then-airing mini-series "Roots" for insight into "why black folks get a little upset when some laws are passed." Hawkins continued, saying "[w]e know some laws are going to hit us harder. We know. We know" (Waldron 1977). Finally, in speaking about his decision not to sign the reinstatement bill into law, Governor Byrne argued that "[c]apital punishment is chiefly an emotional response to crime, especially when offered in the absence of any meaningful attempt at penal reform" (Waldron 1978).

With the election of Thomas Kean as governor in 1981, successful passage of a reinstatement law became considerably more likely as the Republican was a much stronger supporter of capital punishment than Byrne had been. Indeed, the following year the Senate and Assembly passed a capital punishment bill that was quickly signed by the new governor. Lawmakers' rhetoric in the early 1980s was almost identical to what it had been following *Gregg* and the opportunity to reinstate the death penalty in 1976. In terms of deterrence, Assembly Member Martin Herman (D) said during a floor debate that "[a]nyone who votes for the bill because he feels it is a deterrent is 180 degrees off base. The evidence clearly doesn't support this. I support the death penalty because I feel it is the proper penalty for the crime" (Barry 1981). Assembly Member Wayne Bryant (D), for his part, echoed Owens' and Hawkins' earlier concern regarding proportionality, stating during the floor debate that "opposition to the death penalty stems primarily from the inability of these statutes to impose penalties in an even-handed, nondiscriminatory manner." Fellow Assembly Member Martin Herman (D), perhaps coming closest to a deterrence frame, argued that "[v]iolent crime is occurring at an accelerated rate. Society has a responsibility to cure itself of the cancer that is causing it" (Narvaez 1982).

Other supporters increasingly used what might be termed an antagonistic frame, with Senator Wayne Dumont (R) during a committee hearing claiming that "[f]or the last 20 years, I found too many people have been too concerned about the rights of the accused and not enough concerned about the rights of the victims. It's time to go back to what we used to have" (Norman 1982). Perhaps reflecting the emerging narrative of the Reagan era regarding crime, Assembly Member Thomas Paterniti (D) said that "[f]or too long, criminals have been looked upon as supercitizens with superrights, and this bill sends the message that the public will no longer stand for it" (Sullivan 1982). In a somewhat more measured tone, Governor Kean said in signing the bill that "[t]his is a terrible, serious step, but it is necessary and emphasizes the seriousness of the crime problem that faces our country and our state. People must know if they take a life, they may have to forfeit theirs in return" (Sullivan 1982a). Finally, Senator Russo (D), who had previously authored a New York Times article in support of capital punishment, said after passage in the Senate that "[t]here will be few executions under this bill—I hope there are none—but I am convinced that our system of criminal justice must include this ultimate punishment" (Sullivan 1982b).

Up to this point, the courts had played little, if any, role in determining New Jersey's death penalty policy, with the application of the *Jackson* ruling to the state's law being the only meaningful intervention. When the state's Supreme Court had spoken on the subject, it had made it clear that it understood capital punishment as falling squarely within the policy making authority of the elected branches. Members of the legislature seem to have taken this message to heart and spent the ten years after New Jersey's statute was originally struck down debating the merits of reinstatement with little reference to the courts. Indeed, the rhetorical frames employed by lawmakers consisted almost entirely of appeals to ultimate justice and the proper punishment of offenders as well as concerns about the disproportionate impact the death penalty might have on the poor and racial minorities. This would begin to change following passage of the reinstatement law, however, as the courts became somewhat bolder in their willingness to at least alter the contours of how the death penalty was to be carried out in the state, if never actually challenging its constitutionality directly.

The first case involving the 1982 capital punishment statute was decided by the New Jersey Supreme Court in the 1987 case of *State v. Ramseur*.

Substantively, Chief Justice Wilentz's opinion for the Court can be broken up into two major portions, with the first overturning two death sentences for murder on the grounds that the jurors were said to have been coerced into a unanimous sentence of death when a non-unanimous decision would have resulted in a prison term. The second, and perhaps more important portion, articulated the Chief Justice's view on a number of constitutional issues related to capital punishment in general that had been raised by the defendant. Here again the Court refused to find the death penalty unconstitutional and remained committed to the position that such a determination was entirely the province of the legislature. Leaving little doubt about this view, Wilentz wrote that "[i]t is not for this Court to pass on the wisdom or the ultimate morality of the death penalty. That issue is for the Legislature and the Governor, and for them alone" (331). Similarly, when discussing the deterrent potential of capital punishment, the Chief Justice argued that "the Legislature could reasonably find that the death penalty deters murder, just as it could find that it does not . . . The wisdom of the death penalty is not for this Court to decide" (180). Notably, though, the Court did invoke what can fairly be described as a legal frame at one point, arguing that the idea of "contemporary standards of decency" might be useful in determining whether or not the death penalty violated the Eighth Amendment's Cruel and Unusual Clause, though still offering considerable deference to elected officials. Here Wilentz writes that "[o]ne of the strongest indicators of this contemporary standard is the fact that the Legislature passed the Act in 1982. Obviously, passage of that law cannot be dispositive. Such an interpretation would render the constitutional ban on cruel and unusual punishments a mere tautology, eliminating its function as a limitation on legislative power. Nevertheless, since contemporary community standards are the test, such recent legislation, enacted by those who represent the community, must be given great deference" (172).

The following year, the Court further limited the application of the death penalty in New Jersey, finding in *State v. Gerald* (1988) that imposition of the death penalty for non-premeditated murder violated the cruel and unusual provision of the New Jersey State Constitution. Here Justice Clifford wrote that:

> The legislature has made an aggravated assault, such as we have in this case, a second-degree crime, see N.J.S.A. 2C:12-1(b), and a defendant convicted of that crime faces a term of imprisonment ranging from five to ten years, with a presumptive term of seven years. See, respectively, N.J.S.A. 2C:43-6(a)(2) and N.J.S.A. 2C:44-1(f)(1)(c). Where an actor commits an offense that is identical in all material respects except for the victim's unintended death, it is grossly disproportionate to subject that actor to the death penalty. Because the actor's conduct, mental state, and intended result in both instances are virtually identical, the victim's fortuitous survival in one case and unfortunate demise in

> the other cannot provide an adequate basis for subjecting one actor to a term of imprisonment and executing the other (86, 87).

By 1990, eight years after passage of the reinstatement law, the State Supreme Court had overturned each of the twenty-five death sentences that had been handed down in that time on a variety of grounds, though often related to problems it saw with jury instructions. The Court did finally sustain a death sentence in *State v. Marshall* (1991), a high-profile case involving a husband's contract killing of his wife. The only mention of the constitutionality of capital punishment in the 267-page opinion, though, consisted of a brief reference to the Court's previous finding in *Ramseur* that the death penalty did not violate the cruel and unusual provision of the New Jersey Constitution.

Frustrated with what it saw as the Court's interference in the application of the death penalty, in 1992 the Assembly passed a bill aimed at limiting the appeals process in capital cases. Specifically, the measure would have forestalled challenges to the constitutionality of the method of execution, required that a proportionality review of death sentences only include cases where the death penalty was imposed rather than all murder cases, allowed for capital punishment in cases involving murders connected to drug trafficking, and a proposed constitutional amendment stating that the death penalty was not cruel and unusual punishment (King 1992). Ultimately, only the proportionality review provision was signed into law by Governor Florio, though a somewhat revised version of the constitutional amendment allowing for the death penalty to be imposed in cases of non-premeditated murder was approved by voters in the 1992 election (Gray 1992). The purpose behind these measures was made clear by Assembly Speaker Garabed (Chuck) Haytaian (R) who argued that that the state's High Court "has taken the death penalty statute and turned it into a meaningless piece of paper. Unless we amend the Constitution, the scale of justice will be tipped in favor of murderers" (King 1992). Florio had expressed a similar sentiment in a speech to a group of police chiefs and prosecutors, saying that "[m]aybe the criminals are happy, but the rest of us want to know what the hell is going on," adding that the role of courts was "not [to] frustrate [the law]" (King 1992).[3]

In 1999, the constitutionality of New Jersey's revised proportionality review statute was challenged in *State v. Loftin*, with the State Supreme Court upholding it as applied in that case as well as sustaining the death sentence of the defendant. In a lengthy analysis that included consideration of a number of statistical models, various U.S. Supreme Court standards that had been articulated, and the practices of other states, the Court found insufficient evidence to demonstrate a racial bias in the defendant's sentence. Five years later, though, the Court did place additional limits on the applicability of New Jersey's capital punishment statute, finding in *State v. Fortin* (2004) that aggravating factors that could lead to a death sentence must be presented to a grand jury seeking indictment. As in *Loftin*, the vast majority of the Court's opinion was focused on the specifics of the case at issue, with little mention of what might be considered political or legal rhetorical frames. Near the end of the decision, Justice Albin wrote that "[w]e, therefore, hold that our State Constitution requires that aggravating factors be submitted to the grand jury and returned in an indictment. In a criminal justice system in which all of the elements of a crime must be submitted to the grand jury it would be odd to make capital murder the one exception. Our analysis of the development of federal law does not compel this result; logic and fairness and the historical importance we attach to our grand jury system do" (1035). The *Loftin* and *Fortin* decisions, then, in many ways represent something of a continuation of previous capital punishment rulings from the State Supreme Court in that it continued to defer to the legislature's authority regarding the constitutionality of the death penalty itself, though promulgating strict criteria for its implementation.

Fortin would prove to be the final word from the courts on the death penalty as the following year legislation was passed to establish a commission to study the continued use of capital punishment in New Jersey. Asked "to study all aspects of the death penalty as currently administered in New Jersey and to report its findings and recommendations, including any recommended legislation, to the Legislature and the Governor" (New Jersey 2007), the commission ultimately advised in January 2007 that the state abolish its capital punishment statute. The Assembly and Senate passed a repeal bill during a lame-duck session following the 2007 election and Governor Corzine signed the law on December 17, 2007, making New Jersey the first state to repeal its death penalty statute legislatively since 1976 (Peters 2007a).

Senator Richard Codey (D), who had sponsored the reinstatement bill in 1982 but had supported the repeal effort in 2007, argued that "[p]eople's opinions since 1981 have changed. And I can't intelligently make the argument that it's going to deter anybody because they know they're never going to be executed" (Peters 2007b). Speaking in opposition to the repeal bill, Senator Gerald Cardinale (I) claimed the measure was supported by lawmakers representing "an uninformed electorate in certain parts of this state. It forms the base of support for the majority party in both houses. That uninformed electorate is moved in certain emotional directions by the fact that they think the death penalty disproportionately affects their inner-city residents" (Peters 2007c). Finally, after signing the repeal bill, Governor Corzine said "[f]or me the question is more fundamental. I believe society must first determine if its endorsement of violence begets violence, and if violence undermines our commitment to the sanctity of life. To these questions, I answer 'Yes.' . . . Other good people will describe today's actions in quite different terms—in terms of injustice—particularly those who carry heavy hearts. Broken hearts from their tragic losses. This bill does not forgive or in any way condone the unfathomable acts carried out by the eight men now on New Jersey's death row. They will spend the rest of their lives in jail" (Peters 2007a). In passing the repeal law, then, it seems that lawmakers continued to conceptualize the death penalty in many of the same ways they had in the 1970s and 1980s. Specifically, Senator Cardinale's statement addresses the ongoing critique of capital punishment as disproportionately affecting minorities—albeit in a particularly tactless way—while the Governor makes a moral argument regarding the value of life. Even Senator Codey's remarks, while alluding to deterrence, actually seem to reflect a sense of resignation regarding the likelihood that a death sentence would ever be carried out.

In many ways, the progression of capital punishment policy making in New Jersey and New York followed a similar pattern. Both saw their old statutes fall with the U.S. Supreme Court's ruling in *Furman*, followed by ultimately successful efforts to reinstate the practice, and ultimately reversing course again such that neither state currently maintains a death penalty law. The reinstatement process did happen more quickly in New Jersey, though this is almost entirely attributable to a long series of gubernatorial vetoes in New York until Governor Pataki finally signed a renewed measure into law in 1995. It is, of course, notable that abolition was accomplished legislatively in New Jersey and, though somewhat indirectly, by the Court of Appeals in New York. A closer examination of the decisions of both courts does nevertheless reveal that in neither case were judges willing to find their states' capital punishment statues unconstitutional in all cases. Indeed, this is true of the *Furman* decision itself, a fact that is made clear subsequently in *Gregg*, upholding a number of revised death penalty provisions. Returning to the theoretical framework proposed in earlier chapters, the New York and New Jersey capital punishment cases would seem to reinforce the idea that rhetorical frames matter inasmuch as the courts' use of political language may be taken by lawmakers as a message that they hold the primary authority to make policy decisions in a particular issue area. Recall that Justice Stewart's majority opinion in *Gregg* was framed to a large extent around concerns of democratic legitimacy, a position that was also adopted by the courts in New York and New Jersey. So while the first substantive change to capital punishment policy was located in the judiciary in both states—albeit at the federal level—this change was framed in political terms, in stark contrast to *Roe*. This difference in the institutional location of change has important implications for the theory on offer here and will be addressed later in this chapter; however, we turn now to the case of abortion policy making in two Midwestern states that, like New York and New Jersey, share a number of commonalities in terms of demographics, history, and political structures.

ABORTION POLICY IN MINNESOTA

As was the case in New York and New Jersey, there were a number of legislative efforts to repeal Minnesota's abortion law in the late 1960s and early 1970s, though none were successful, due in large part to the efforts of a local pro-life group called Minnesota Citizens Concerned for Life (MCCL). Indeed, the group was founded in 1968 as a direct result of increasing pressure to liberalize the state's abortion laws and continued to play an influential role in politics surrounding reproductive rights throughout the next forty years (Segers and Byrnes 1995). Minnesota's abortion law did not change, then, until the U.S. Supreme Court's *Roe* decision and several state Supreme Court rulings interpreting its applicability. The first of these, *State v. Hodgson* (1973) offered only a brief Per Curiam opinion overturning the conviction of a doctor convicted under the state's abortion statute and providing an overview of the federal decision, while the second, *State v. Hultgren* (1973), upheld the four-year sentence of a man charged with performing an illegal abortion in 1969.

The same year that *Roe* was handed down, a bill calling for a constitutional convention to overturn the decision passed the state House of Representatives, though it ultimately failed in the Senate. The following year, a series of abortion restrictions, including mandatory counseling, the identification of a fetus as viable at four-and-a-half months, at which point physicians must attempt a live birth during an abortion, and a requirement that abortions occurring after three months be performed in a hospital, passed both houses and were signed into law by Governor Wendell Anderson. Lawmakers debating these measures spoke both in medical and more legal terms, with Rep. Robert Bell (R) saying during a floor session dealing with the constitutional amendment that "[n]ot once was a woman ever prosecuted under this statute . . . [abortion bans deprive] some people of proper medical care" (Shellum 1973). Rep. Thaddeus Jude (DFL), for his part, argued for the resolution, saying "for those who did not accept the Supreme Court decision, this is a legitimate exercise in their right to petition Congress" (Bemidji Pioneer 1973a). Senator David Schaff (DFL), speaking of the viability bill, similarly asked his colleagues to "[t]hink about that, a bill to regulate medical practice, and no medical testimony was allowed" (Shellum 1974). Minnesota House Judiciary Chairman Richard Parish, again echoing a more legal view, said shortly after *Roe* that "[o]ur first step, I would think, is to find out what the state Supreme Court is going say before we rush too hurriedly into any amendment of our law . . . The legislature will be guided by the Supreme Court's decision in defining what [the federal ruling] means" (*Bemidji Pioneer* 1973b). While some of the more medical concerns expressed by lawmakers may have been a reflection, particularly in the case of the viability bill, of the law's subject matter itself, which concerned questions of viability and hospital requirements, these quotes suggest that at least during the early stages of discussion of abortion by Minnesota lawmakers, members of the House and Senate were thinking both in legal and political terms.

All of these measures were quickly challenged in federal court, with the District Court finding all three main provisions of the Minnesota law incompatible with the framework articulated in *Roe*. Following the U.S. Supreme Court's decision in *Planned Parenthood of Central Missouri v. Danforth* (1976), which had upheld a similar counseling requirement in that state, an Eighth Circuit Court of Appeals panel partially overturned the District Court's holding, though it maintained that the viability provision was unconstitutional. The Court took particular issue with the wording of the Minnesota law, writing that "[h]ad 'viable' been defined simply as 'ability to live outside the womb even though artificial aid may be required' and had the word 'viable' instead of the term 'potentially viable' been used in the operative sections of the Minnesota abortion law, then the offending sections of the statute . . . could have been sustained" (*Hodgson v. Lawson* [1976] at 1354). In terms of the counseling requirement, the majority argued that "[w]e believe that the particularly stressful nature of the decision to abort distinguishes it sufficiently from other medical decisions to justify additional state regulation insuring that the woman's consent has been freely and intelligently given" (1356). Finally, Judge Heaney authored a highly political dissent, writing that:

> The Supreme Court's decisions in *Roe v. Wade* and *Doe v. Bolton* were premised on the concept that a decision to abort would be made in the traditional doctor-patient setting. There was not to be abortion on demand; rather, the abortion decision was to be made only after the doctor and the patient had carefully reviewed the physical, emotional, psychological and familial factors relevant to this extremely important and stressful decision. The realities are altogether different. It is estimated that more than half of the nearly one million abortions performed in 1975 took place in non-hospital clinics, under circumstances where the doctor performing the operation often sees the patient once and then only for a brief period. The result is that we do have abortion on demand, and the decisions of the doctor and patient to abort are not being made with the same degree of care and thoughtfulness that accompanies other surgical procedures (1359).

While much of this decision was clearly based on, and therefore to some extent limited by, the Court's understanding of *Danforth*, the language employed by both the majority and Judge Heaney in dissent seemed focused on relatively "political" concerns related to what it saw as the best medical and emotional interests of women seeking abortion, rather than a concern about strictly constitutional issues.

The next major issue confronted by lawmakers in Minnesota concerned the question of Medicaid financing for abortions, with a law banning all public funds for the procedure eventually passing both houses of the legislature and being signed into law by Governor Perpich. Interestingly, the state already maintained a ban on such funding as a result of the Minnesota Supreme Court's ruling in *McKee v. Likins* (1977) in which a taxpayer had successfully sued to stop the state Medicaid for abortions program.[4] As with the call for a constitutional convention and viability measures that had been debated several years earlier, statements from elected officials surrounding the Medicaid ban reflected both legal and political concerns. Senator George Perpich (DFL), brother of then-Governor Rudy Perpich, said of the ban while it was first being considered that "[y]ou're cutting out the poor and that's the easy thing to do. They haven't got the world's best lobby" (Charnley 1977). Rep. Ray Kempe (DFL), for his part, countered a legal argument against the ban by claiming that "[i]t is not class discrimination against the poor, nor is it violating any equal protection clause of the U.S. Constitution. This bill will simply take Minnesota out of the abortion business and say to those who want to have an abortion that it is their moral responsibility and their fiscal responsibility" (*Evening Tribune* 1978). Finally, Governor Perpich appealed to democratic values in signing the bill, asserting that "[t]he Legislature has debated this issue in detail in extensive public hearings. It is clear the Legislature does not support the use of public funds to finance elective abortions. The bill passed both houses of the legislature by substantial margins. With these facts in mind I have decided to sign it" (Brandt 1978).

The following year Minnesota passed another abortion restriction, this time banning public funding for any individual or organization that provided elective abortions. The law was challenged shortly after passage with the Eighth Circuit Court of Appeals striking it down in *Planned Parenthood of Minnesota v. Minnesota* (1980). The case turned almost entirely on the question of whether the law ought to be subjected to a strict scrutiny or simply rational basis standard of review, ultimately finding that it failed even the latter's less demanding benchmark. Illustrating this position, Judge Lay wrote for the Court that "[t]he record demonstrates that Planned Parenthood of Minnesota in its abortion stance has made itself unpopular among some segments of the population. The legislative history of [the statute] indicates that Planned Parenthood's unpopularity played a large role in its passage. Planned Parenthood's unpopularity in and of itself and without reference to some independent considerations in the public interest cannot justify subdivision 2" (361). The Eighth Circuit, however, sustained the Medicaid ban that had been passed in 1978 that same year in *Hodgson v. Board of County Commissioners* (1980). While conceding that the ban violated the Medicaid Act and Title XIX of the Social Security Act, the Court ultimately ruled that the Hyde Amendment substantively altered these provisions in a manner that no longer required states to fund abortion.

It is notable that Judge Stephenson's opinion argued rather forcefully that Title XIX did in fact require Minnesota to fund abortion services, with only a brief discussion near the end of the opinion concerning the Hyde Amendment. Indeed, the majority wrote that "[t]his holding does not save the Minnesota statute. Minnesota's refusal to subsidize medically necessary abortions may or may not be 'reasonable' under *Beal*. It is clear, however, that Minnesota's abortion subsidy restriction is inconsistent with Title XIX's objectives in that it denies medical assistance on the basis of the type of medical disorder and not on the degree of medical need. Our conclusion is in harmony with *Beal*. We therefore hold that Minnesota's welfare scheme, which subsidizes medical assistance services generally but which subjects abortions to a 'life-threatening' standard, is inconsistent with and superseded by Title XIX. Abortions, like other medical services, must be subsidized on the basis of the recipient's financial and medical need" (610,611). The portion of Stephenson's opinion that did assess the relevance of the Hyde Amendment focused for the most part on previous courts' consideration of the legislative history of the statute, concluding that it was in fact Congress' intent to disallow abortion funds under Medicaid. Likely as a result of the pending decision in *Harris v. McRae*, the Court did not consider the constitutionality of Minnesota's Medicaid ban, writing that "we acknowledge, as plaintiffs assert, that our statutory interpretation raises the serious constitutional question whether a state subsidizing only Hyde Amendment abortions under its medicaid program is acting in violation of the Equal Protection Clause, and that in the case, we should avoid constitutional questions where statutory construction makes this 'fairly possible.' . . . Like the First and Seventh Circuits in *Preterm* and *Zbaraz*, however, we do not think that this doctrine compels us to accept a narrow interpretation of the Hyde Amendment that contradicts clear evidence of congressional intent" (615). Given its focus on levels of scrutiny in the 1980 *Planned Parenthood* case and legislative intent in *Hodgson*, it seems reasonable to attribute a largely legal rhetorical frame to the Eighth Circuit's decisions at this point, somewhat in contrast to the earlier rulings discussed above.

In 1981, the legislature passed, and the governor signed, a parental notification law that required both parents be informed of a minor's abortion forty-eight hours prior to the procedure, as well as a provision providing for a judicial bypass in the event that the parental notification statute was found unconstitutional. In considering the statements from lawmakers during the lead-up to passage of the parental notification law, it is again evident that elected officials were speaking both in legal as well as political terms. In terms of the latter, Senator Gene Waldorf (DFL) argued that "[w]e're simply trying to bring back some loving parental support" (Sturdevant 1981a) while

Rep. John Brandl (DFL), after co-sponsoring a protest amendment that would require parental notification of the would-be father's parents as well, argued that "what we're doing in this bill is attributing to young women the inability to make decisions, something we're not attributing to young males" (Sturdevant 1981b). Senator Eugene Waldorf (DFL), echoing an abortion frame prominent in legal discourse, asked during a Senate hearing on the parental notification bill "[w]hat support does this bring to the minor who is pregnant? This would just invade the young woman's privacy. By taking it outside of the family unit" (Sturdevant 1981b), with Senator Linda Berglin (DFL) commenting that the state could not "enforce [a] contract between parents and teenagers" (*Star Tribune* 1981).

The rest of the 1980s saw somewhat of a lull in legislation or litigation dealing with abortion in Minnesota with the exception of the passage of a fetal disposal law in 1987 after pro-life protesters had displayed fetal parts found in a dumpster outside of a Minneapolis abortion clinic (Segers and Byrnes 1995). During this time, though, a challenge to the state's parental notification law had been making its way through the courts, finally culminating in the U.S. Supreme Court's ruling in *Hodgson v. Minnesota* (1990). The Court ruled that the two-parent provision of the statute was unconstitutional, but, in a separate majority, sustained the law on the basis that the judicial bypass procedure provided sufficient protection for a minor's access to abortion. Justice Stevens' partial majority focused largely on the question of whether the state had a compelling interest in requiring both parents be notified of a minor's abortion, an issue that also formed the basis of Justices Marshall's and Kennedy's analyses. Specifically, Stevens wrote that

> It is equally clear that the requirement that both parents be notified, whether or not both wish to be notified or have assumed responsibility for the upbringing of the child, does not reasonably further any legitimate state interest. The usual justification for a parental consent or notification provision is that it supports the authority of a parent who is presumed to act in the minor's best interest, and thereby assures that the minor's decision to terminate her pregnancy is knowing, intelligent, and deliberate. To the extent that such an interest is legitimate, it would be fully served by a requirement that the minor notify one parent, who can then seek the counsel of his or her mate or any other party when such advice and support is deemed necessary to help the child make a difficult decision. In the ideal family setting, of course, notice to either parent would normally constitute notice to both. A statute requiring two-parent notification would not further any state interest in those instances. In many families, however, the parent notified by the child would not notify the other parent. In those cases, the State has no legitimate interest in questioning one parent's judgment that notice to the other parent would not assist the minor or in presuming that the parent who has assumed parental duties is incompetent to make decisions regarding the health and welfare of the child (450).

In addition to this largely legal rhetorical framework, Stevens also cites a number of social scientific studies regarding the impact of parental notification laws on familial communications, abortion rates, and other measures. Kennedy's partial concurrence also offers some political arguments in support of the two-parent requirement, writing that "the Court errs in serious degree when it commands its own solution to the cruel consequences of individual misconduct, parental failure, and social ills. The legislative authority is entitled to attempt to meet these wrongs by taking reasonable measures to recognize and promote the primacy of the family tie, a concept which this Court now seems intent on declaring a constitutional irrelevance" (501). Nevertheless, the thrust of the opinions is clearly centered on a legal framing of a minor's right to abortion and, perhaps unsurprisingly, resembles in this regard the Court's understanding in *Roe*.

The same year the U.S. Supreme Court issued its decision in *Hodgson*, an Eighth Circuit Court of Appeals panel upheld the fetal remains statute that Minnesota had passed in 1987. In *Planned Parenthood of Minnesota v. Minnesota* (1990), the Court rejected the plaintiff's arguments regarding the law's vagueness and its violation of the Due Process Clause, partly based on the recent High Court ruling in *Webster v. Reproductive Health Services* (1989). Interestingly, Chief Judge Lay wrote that "[w]e acknowledge that this statute is not a model of clarity, and for some facilities, may pose compliance difficulties. However, we cannot say that the statute is impermissibly vague in all its applications such that it does not fairly warn of the conduct prohibited. We therefore find that the statute is not unconstitutionally vague" (486). In terms of the Due Process challenge, Lay went on to write that "[r]ather than regulating abortion, this statute acknowledges the existence of abortion and regulates an issue related to abortion. While the statute admittedly touches on abortion, we cannot say it interferes with or burdens a woman's right to choose to have an abortion" (487). While the case likely had little impact on the actual availability of abortion in Minnesota, it is clear from the Court's opinion that legal, rather than political or policy, concerns dominated its reasoning and conceptualization of the issue in this decision.

Throughout most of the 1990s, Minnesota lawmakers had been focused on a proposed bill requiring a twenty-four-hour waiting period as well as state-mandated counseling before a woman could obtain an abortion. Statements from members of the State House and Senate during this period reflect a combination of legal and political concerns, both from opponents as well as supporters of the measure. In response to a questionnaire from the St. Paul *Pioneer Press* in 1992 that included the question "Do you favor any additional restrictions on women's access to abortion? If so, what?", for instance, Rep. Edward Schones (DFL) stated "I oppose using abortion as a method of birth control but believe that abortion should be legal in case of rape, incest or to save the life of the mother. The answer to unwanted pregnancies is prevention through education and accessible birth control. Women considering abortion should have the right to sufficient information about options." Rep. Al Bachel (DFL) expressed a more democratic view, answering that "I feel maybe it's time for the people of the state to vote on the abortion issue. My feelings are that it's a moral issue and the final decision should be up to the woman, her family and her religious beliefs" (*Pioneer Press* 1992a, 1992b). Before passage of the twenty-four-hour waiting period and mandatory counseling bill, Governor Arne Carlson spoke in much more legal terms, stating that "[t]wenty-four hours we would have no problem with. A 24-hour waiting period is not an undue burden. That doesn't mean I'm going to approve of it, but it's not an unreasonable restriction" (Whereatt and Halvorsen 1992). While still debating the measure in 2000, Sen. Jane Ranum (DFL) argued that "I believe the real purpose behind this bill is to shut down clinics and providers" while Sen. Linda Scheid, (DFL) decried that "[t]his bill is a hurdle, an obstacle disguised as a right" (O'Connor and Devine 2000).

It was not until April of 2000 that the bill finally passed the House and Senate, though it was vetoed by Governor Jesse Ventura who, perhaps unsurprisingly, took a notably libertarian position on the issue, stating that "I have decided it is wrong for the government to assume a role in something I have always believed was between a woman, her family, her doctor, and if she chooses, her clergy" (Whereatt and McAuliffe 2000). With the election of Tim Pawlenty in 2002, though, the legislature again passed the measure and it was signed onto law by the new Republican governor. Specifically, the law requires a twenty-four-hour waiting period before an abortion, as well as mandatory counseling informing women of the risks of abortion and childbirth and alternatives to abortion available in the state. This proved to be the last major piece of legislation related to abortion passed in Minnesota during the period under consideration and the state today is often seen as among those with the fewest restrictions in the Midwest (NARAL 2017).

The last major action taken by the courts in Minnesota saw the rare involvement of the State Supreme Court, which had not been the site of litigation related to abortion for the majority of the previous twenty-five years. In *Women of the State of Minnesota v. Gomez* (1995), the Court struck down the state's Medicaid ban, a full fifteen years after the Eighth Circuit Court of Appeals had sustained the statute. Reflecting perhaps the rhetorical frames of lawmakers in Minnesota more than those adopted by previous—and almost exclusively federal—courts, the State Supreme Court conceptualized the issue both in highly political as well as legal terms. Focusing on policy concerns in the first part of the majority opinion, Chief Justice Keith wrote that

> The State concedes that one study has found that Medicaid-eligible women who are denied funding delay abortion while they seek alternative funds.

> Plaintiffs' affidavits suggest that such women may delay for several weeks to obtain funding from other sources. Women commonly cancel and reschedule appointments for the procedure a number of times while they seek funding. Plaintiffs' affidavits further demonstrate that delay in the performance of an abortion increases the health risks women face in connection with the procedure . . . The mortality risk of abortion increases with gestational age, and one study suggests that the mortality risk of abortion increases 50 percent with each week after the eighth week of pregnancy (26).

In addressing the Due Process argument put forward by the plaintiffs, Keith rejects the U.S. Supreme Court's opinion in *Harris v. McRae,* writing that "[t]he fundamental flaw in the Court's due process analysis, then, is its failure to acknowledge that the discriminatory distribution of the benefits of governmental largesse can discourage the exercise of fundamental liberties just as effectively as can an outright denial of those rights through criminal and regulatory sanctions" (29). Indeed, much of the majority's critique on *McRae* is drawn directly from Justice Brennan's dissenting opinion in that case, adding that the Minnesota Constitution affords greater protection to the indigent than does its federal counterpart. In any event, the only major decision from the State Supreme Court dealing with abortion is notable for its use of both political as well as legal understandings of the issue, somewhat at odds with the same institutions in New York and New Jersey.

Indeed, the development of abortion policy in Minnesota in some ways represents a sort of middle ground between the experiences of New York and New Jersey. The courts were certainly not unwilling to make policy dealing with the issue, as can be seen in *Hodgson v. Anderson*, striking down a viability law; *Planned Parenthood of Minnesota v. Minnesota*, overturning a ban on abortion funding for nonprofits; and *Gomez*, finding the state's Medicaid ban unconstitutional. At the same time, the courts sustained the parental notification requirement and left undisturbed the twenty-four-hour waiting period and mandatory counseling requirement. This middle ground can also be seen in the rhetorical frames adopted by lawmakers and, to a lesser extent, judges in Minnesota, which made use of both political and legal language in discussing abortion. Finally, unlike the New York and New Jersey cases presented in the previous chapters, the state courts played a very limited role in litigation treating abortion restrictions, with the single exception of *Gomez*. Instead, almost all of the court battles were fought at the federal level, a fact that may help account for the more common use of legal frames in the judicial context as compared to the legislature, as well as Minnesota's relatively moderate abortion policies. With that in mind, the final case study in this chapter considers a state where the courts played a very limited role in policy development surrounding reproductive rights.

ABORTION POLICY IN WISCONSIN

Initial efforts to repeal Wisconsin's nineteenth-century abortion statute might best be described as confused. In 1970, a federal District Court found the state's abortion ban unconstitutional in *Babbitz v. McCann*, and reversed the conviction of a doctor charged with performing the procedure. Specifically, the Court rejected the argument that the law was void for vagueness, but instead found an Equal Protection violation based on the disproportionate impact of abortion bans on poor women. Indeed, the Per Curium opinion argued that it found:

> more cogency in the argument that a wealthy woman, but not a poor one, is able, upon demand, to secure a safe and legal abortion in Japan or some other locale in which abortion is permitted. We take judicial notice of the fact that there are a number of places throughout the world where legal abortions are available. We have also considered the argument that an affluent woman, unlike the poor one, may enjoy a long-standing, personal relationship with a well-paid physician, who might more likely be willing or able to persuade his fellow doctors to authorize a therapeutic abortion (298).

Following this judgment, however, E. Michael McCann, the district attorney for Milwaukee County and the state's Attorney General issued statements that they would not adhere to the District Court's decision until the U.S. Supreme Court issued a decision regarding the constitutionality of abortion restrictions and planned to continue their prosecution of Dr. Babbitz (see *Babbitz v. McCann*, 320 F. Supp. 219—1970). Another hearing before the District Court saw the same three-judge panel reiterate their finding of the law's unconstitutionality and enjoining the prosecution of Dr. Babbitz. The state then appealed the decision to the U.S. Supreme Court, which in *McCann v. Babbitz* (1971) vacated the District Court's ruling. In the end, Wisconsin's abortion law remained in force until *Roe*, despite an unruly start to efforts at repeal.

Following the *Roe* decision, the state legislature moved quickly to pass several laws and resolutions aimed at challenging the ruling. In October 1973, the Senate and Assembly passed a bill that would allow doctors and hospitals to refuse to perform abortions and sterilization and in February 1974, approved a resolution calling for a constitutional amendment to overturn *Roe*. Assembly member Carl Otte (D), speaking of the hospital refusal bill argued that "[a]s much as many of us oppose abortion, we are still required to follow the ruling laid down by the U.S. Supreme Court. If refusal to perform an abortion is based on moral or religious grounds, it is extremely necessary that the physician, hospital employee, or hospital not be required to act counter to this moral reasoning" (*Sheboygan Press* 1973). GOP State Senator Gordon Roseleip, defending the constitutional amendment proposal was blunter, claiming that "[n]o church and no party is influencing me on this resolution. God is telling me to support it" (*Sheboygan Press* 1974). Clearly, the initial tone of lawmakers when discussing abortion was somewhat more confrontational and uncompromising—at least in the case of Senator Roseleip—though Otte's comments do reveal some degree of deference to the courts. This latter type of rhetoric would become increasingly uncommon, though, as legislators continued to press their attack on abortion access.

Banning the use of state Medicaid funds for abortion quickly became the focus of lawmakers following passage of the hospital conscience and constitutional amendment measures, though this effort faced some opposition from the governor. Several bills ending funding for the procedure passed the Senate between 1975 and 1977, only to stall in the Assembly. Both houses finally agreed to a bill that would have banned Medicaid funding for abortions except in the case of rape or incest or to save the life of the mother in 1978, though it was initially vetoed by Governor Schreiber. A revised measure was signed into law later that year, though, with the addition of "grave, long lasting physical health damage" to the definition of Medicaid-eligible abortions. The debate surrounding the funding ban was noteworthy largely for the difference in the ways in which supporters and opponents of the bill framed their arguments. Sen. James Devitt (R), for instance, stated that "[t]hose of us who believe abortion is murder don't want state funds used for it" while Assembly member Lloyd Barbee (D), an opponent of the bill, argued that "[i]t certainly would discriminate against the poor people who disproportionately receive medical healthcare. This is clearly class and economic discrimination" (*Sheboygan Press* 1975). Senator Timothy Cullen (D) said after the Medicaid funding ban had passed the Senate that "I hate abortion. But after an enormous amount of soul-searching, I'm convinced we're setting up a second-class society" (Srb 1978), while Assembly member Joanne Duren (D) claimed that "[the Department of Health and Social Services] are calling killing 'appropriate healthcare.' I think this might be a little disturbing to the people of the state" (*Sheboygan Press* 1977). Carl Otte, who had shepherded the bill though the Assembly, made a practical case for the compromise bill, saying "[p]olitics is the art of the possible and I am convinced that we have passed the best possible abortion law in light of the makeup of this Legislature whose members are quite evenly split on this issue" (*Sheboygan Press* 1978a). Finally, Governor Shreiber, in his veto message of the first bill, claimed to "continue to personally oppose abortion, but society cannot tolerate a situation in which a woman's ability to protect her health is determined by her ability to pay. Our constitution was not designed to accommodate such a double standard" (*Sheboygan Press* 1978b).

The Medicaid funding ban was challenged in court the following year, with a District Court finding in *Doe v. Percy* (1979) that the law was unconstitutional on a number of grounds. Touching on a wide array of legal issues, Chief Judge Doyle wrote that:

> [w]ithout more, it appears that the statutory classification challenged in the present case impairs the fundamental interest of plaintiff Doe in her freedom to choose whether to terminate her pregnancy, that strict scrutiny is required, that defendant must show a compelling governmental interest in making the classification, and that defendant must show that the particular classification has been narrowly drawn to express only the legitimate state interests at stake (330).

The decision relied very heavily on *Roe* with much of the opinion dedicated to distinguishing the present case from *Maher v. Roe* (1977), which had upheld a similar Connecticut ban on Medicaid funding for abortion. The case was remanded by the 7th Circuit Court of Appeals without opinion in 1980, however, the same year the U.S. Supreme Court upheld the Hyde Amendment in *Harris v. McRae*. Indeed, *Harris* was handed down in March 1980, a mere four months before the 7th Circuit decision overturning the District Court's ruling in July 1980. Wisconsin's ban on Medicaid funding for abortion therefore remained intact and would not face any serious challenges again in state or federal courts.

The remainder of the 1980s saw little activity in terms of lawmaking or litigation related to abortion in Wisconsin, with the exception of passage of a viability statute and FACE statute, both in 1985.[5] The former defined this as "that stage of fetal development when, in the medical judgment of the attending physician based on the particular facts of the case before him or her, there is a reasonable likelihood of sustained survival of the fetus outside the womb, with or without artificial support" (Section 940.15, Wisconsin Statutes). Assembly member John Medinger (D) said of the viability clause that "[m]edical technology will advance to the state when you can save these children at 12 weeks instead of 24" (*Sheboygan Press* 1985), framing the measure in clearly political terms. The viability statute was never challenged in court, though in 1989 the Wisconsin Supreme Court upheld the FACE law in the case of *State v. Migliorino*. Justice Day's majority opinion in this decision was somewhat unremarkable in that it dealt with many of the same issues as other courts had when considering similar laws, coming to the conclusion that the law was constitutional. Day wrote that:

> Section 943.145, Stats., is content neutral. We also conclude that it is a reasonable regulation when assessed in the light of the purpose of medical facilities and the circumstances surrounding them . . . It is a reasonable regulation in furtherance of significant state interests such as privacy, health, property, and security. The legislature may constitutionally protect these interests and this statute does so (528).

Indeed, a focus on content neutrality, the state's interest in privacy and health, and the reasonableness of the regulation may be considered hallmarks of most FACE law litigation, and First Amendment challenges in general.

After several years of debate in both houses of the legislature, Wisconsin did pass a parental consent law with a judicial bypass that, like the viability statute, was never challenged in court. In an op-ed piece published in the *Sheboygan Press*, Assembly member Susan Vergeront (R) argued in support of the parental consent law, claiming it was "incredible that in a society where it is illegal for a trained medical doctor to pierce a child's ears or dispense an aspirin without the knowledge and written consent of the parents or guardian, that a minor of any age can demand and receive an abortion without even notification of parent of guardian . . . A number of other states have constitutionally sound laws on the books that protect the rights of both parents and children. Through a series of court cases, the Supreme Court has defined what is needed to have an enforceable parental consent law while also protecting the rights of minors" (Vergeront 1989). Assembly member Calvin Potter (D) said after the Assembly passed the parental consent bill that "[t]hose among us who are getting out among the people are sensing a great deal of support. The general public feels that their parents ought to be involved with their kids" (*Sheboygan Press* 1990). At least surrounding the issue of parental involvement, then, we see lawmakers using both legal, in Vergeront's case, and political rhetorical frames.

A series of abortion restrictions were passed in the mid- to late-1990s, the first of which being a twenty-four-hour waiting period and informed consent measure that also included an ultrasound requirement if the fetus had reached viability. Senator Timothy Weeden (R) said of the waiting period bill that "[a] person ought to think three, four, five, six times [before an abortion]. I think the bill serves a useful public purpose." In opposition to the same bill, Senator Gary George (D) made an almost libertarian argument, calling the measure "government interference in what is purely a private affair . . . a right-wing reactionary agenda that we should not be a part of" (*Sheboygan Press* 1996a). Senator Alice Clausing (D) said after passage of the bill, and considerable debate regarding rape and incest exceptions, that "[w]hat has not even been mentioned today is that rape and incest is all about power and control. It is power and control over women by men. And now my colleagues are going to go on and exercise that same power and control over women that have been violated" (*Sheboygan Press* 1996b). Finally, then–Assembly Member Tammy Baldwin made a similarly political argument, noting that "[m]ost other states have conceded that doctors know more than the Legislature about medical issues and are willing to trust them" (Beulow 1995).

In 1998 the state also passed a late-term abortion ban that included an exception only for the life of the mother and mandated a punishment of life imprisonment for those convicted of performing the procedure (Sections

895.038 and 940.16, Wisconsin Statutes). Proponents of the measure framed the issue in highly political, and even emotional, terms, with Assembly member Robert Goetsch (R) saying "[i]t's time now to do the right thing, to get rid of what we consider an abomination, the practice of partial-birth abortion" (*Sheboygan Press* 1997). Striking a similar tone, Assembly member Scott Fitzgerald (R) argued that lawmakers were "talking about a fully formed human baby that is sometimes less than three months away from a normal delivery." Senator Gwendolynne Moore (D) also used almost graphic language in opposition to the bill, claiming that it endangered women's lives "because it's less liability for a physician to just let her lay there and bleed to death than to save her life by making an abortion" (Theimer 1998). Finally, upon signing the late-term abortion bill, Governor Tommy Thompson called the practice a "morally repugnant and ethically corrupt procedure that will not be tolerated in Wisconsin" (*Sheboygan Press* 1998). Both the twenty-four-hour waiting period and informed consent laws, as well as the late-term abortion ban, represent examples of lawmakers framing the abortion issue using politically charged language, somewhat in contrast to the parental consent bill. While these particular issues may lend themselves well to this brand of fiery speech, recall that in New Jersey, even the late-term abortion ban saw lawmakers using considerably more legal language. The reasons for this difference are not entirely clear, but some possibilities will be discussed in the following section.

A preliminary injunction against the late-term abortion ban was issued by the 7th Circuit Court of Appeals shortly after the law's passage, with Judge Posner articulating several constitutional deficiencies in the measure. In *Planned Parenthood v. Doyle* (1998), the Court argued that the statute's lack of an exception for cases of fetal unviability and the health of the mother, as well as its vagueness, together amounted to an "undue burden" on women's access to abortion. Posner also seemed to take issue with the severity of the punishment imposed by the law, writing that:

> [e]ven if the mother would become sterile if an alternative procedure were used (or if she carried the fetus to term)—even if she would become paralyzed, or, as the state's lawyer affirmed at argument, put at a risk though not a certainty of death—the physician who performed the abortion would still be guilty of a crime that is punished as severely as Wisconsin, which does not have capital punishment, punishes murder (467).

The Circuit Court did not offer a final judgment on the constitutionality of the statute, however, and on remand of the case, the District Court found that physicians could reasonably be expected to understand that the law prohibited only the D&X procedure. Indeed, Chief Judge Shabaz wrote for the Court that:

> [i]n light of this substantial evidence, the Court concludes that partial birth abortion is never medically necessary to preserve the health or life of a woman and abolition of the procedure does not subject women to materially greater health risks. D&E is nearly always an option and there has been no credible showing that D&E is riskier that D&X. Moreover, induction is safer than even D&E and can be used in those rare pregnancies, if any, where D&E would be problematic (*Planned Parenthood of Wisconsin v. Doyle*, 44 F. Supp. 2d 975 at 982).

Shabaz also wrote in notably political terms as well, though, arguing that:

> [p]erhaps, as plaintiffs argue, the child will endure a gruesome death through some other method of abortion. This does not detract from the legitimacy of Wisconsin's partial birth abortion law, however, because it is apparently beyond Wisconsin's power to eliminate those other methods of abortion. Wisconsin can eliminate this one method. Given the national groundswell of opposition to partial birth abortion and the ethical concerns raised within the medical community concerning the procedure, the State cannot be faulted for acting where it can to outlaw an unnecessary procedure that in most cases in which it is used is literally inches away from being infanticide (983, 984).

The 7th Circuit Court of Appeals heard the case again, this time in consolidation with a similar Illinois law, in *Hope Clinic v. Ryan* (1999). This time the Court found that "both laws can be applied in a constitutional manner. Whether that will occur depends on state courts, which alone can settle questions about the construction of the statutes" (861). Most of Judge Posner's opinion in this case was dedicated to explaining why the Court felt the law may not be unconstitutionally vague—as it was susceptible to judicial construction and narrowing; does not seem to have deterred physicians from using other late-term abortion methods; and was an undue burden. In terms of the last point, Posner wrote that "[i]t is always difficult for a court of appeals to predict how Justices of the Supreme Court will apply a phrase with as much plasticity as 'undue burden.' But our best estimate is that 'undue' rather than 'burden' is the key word, and that 'undue' means not only 'substantial' (a small cost or inconvenience is not 'undue') but also that the burden must be undue in relation to the woman's interests, rather than undue in relation to the court's assessment of society's interests" (874). Ultimately, this decision was appealed to the U.S. Supreme Court, which denied review, remanding in light of its striking down of a similar Nebraska law in *Stenberg v. Carhart* (2000).

The last substantive case from Wisconsin treating abortion policy came with the 1999 case of *Karlin v. Foust*, upholding the twenty-four-hour waiting period and informed consent laws which had been passed several years earlier. The vast majority of the Court's opinion in this case focused on the question of the law's vagueness with Judge Kanne writing that:

> [i]n sum, we hold that AB 441's 'reasonable medical judgment' standard is not void for vagueness for three reasons: (1) the standard clearly conveys to physicians that their emergency medical determinations will be judged on an objective basis; (2) physicians are accustomed to having their medical decisions adjudged under an objective standard; and (3) this same objectivity, we believe, provides an adequate safeguard against any risk of arbitrary and unfair enforcement (468).

The remainder of the Court's opinion applied *Casey*'s "undue burden" test to various aspects of the law including the waiting period and the lack of a mental health exception to the informed consent requirement, finding that the law was not likely to result in preventing substantial numbers of women from obtaining abortions and therefore meeting the undue burden standard.

What is perhaps most notable about the Wisconsin case is that the courts sustained almost all of the statutes passed by lawmakers related to abortion, with the sole exception of the late-term abortion ban, which itself was only found unconstitutional indirectly via the U.S. Supreme Court. In terms of rhetorical frames, legislators seemed to use both political and legal language in discussing the issue, though the choice of which often depended on the particular aspect of abortion being debated. The courts, for their part, spoke mostly in legal terms such as undue burdens, vagueness, overbreadth, and least restrictive means, though the District Courts' opinions in *Doyle* and *Babbitz* were notable exceptions. Having discussed these four cases, the final section of this chapter will offer some preliminary analysis of how these fit with the abortion cases in New York and New Jersey and the broader theoretical framework on offer here.

CONCLUSION

The theoretical framework on offer here can be understood as having two major components, the first emphasizing the institutional location of decisions—and in particular which institution initiates policy change—while the second focuses on the rhetorical frames that members those institutions employ in discussing policy as a means of maintaining an institutional path. What, then, to make of the case studies described in this chapter? The story of the development of capital punishment policy in New York and New Jersey followed a somewhat different path than did the abortion issue. New York saw some changes surrounding the death penalty in the late 1960s, before the U.S. Supreme Court's decision in *Furman* temporarily ended executions nationwide, while in New Jersey, the first major change came via *Furman* itself. Ultimately, though, it was the legislature that abolished capital punishment in the Garden State while a Court of Appeals decision technically halted executions in New York. At this point, however, it is important to distinguish what the courts did in the cases of abortion and the death penalty. *Roe*, of course, overturned the abortion laws of forty-six states by extending the right to privacy to cover a woman's right to terminate her pregnancy before viability. *Furman*, however, explicitly ruled that capital punishment, as it was being practiced, was unconstitutional due to its bias and capricious implementation. In short, abortion bans before viability were, by their nature, unconstitutional, whereas the death penalty, as the Court later affirmed in *Gregg*, could be constitutional given adequate safeguards. This difference is crucial as it did not, strictly speaking, represent a fundamental change in policy—in New York and New Jersey or, for that matter, in any other state—leaving lawmakers free after 1976 to alter policy largely as they saw fit. And this is precisely what happened with the reinstatement measures in 1982 and 1995, followed ultimately by the New York Court of Appeals decision in *LaValle* and the repeal law in 2007 in New Jersey. In the latter, then, the process of capital punishment policy making can reasonably be said to have begun and ended with the elected branches, despite significant involvement by the courts throughout this period. For New York's part, while the Court of Appeals did place a *de facto* ban on the death penalty in 2004, it has never ruled that the practice is unconstitutional under any circumstances and very clearly left the door open to reinstatement. The status of capital punishment in New York as of this writing, then, is the result of the legislature's choice not to pass a law remedying the deficiencies identified by the Court.

Comparing the rhetorical frames used by the courts and lawmakers surrounding the death penalty in the two states to abortion is also instructive. As has been argued throughout this work, the decision in *Roe* was framed largely in legal terms centered on the right to privacy and Due Process concerns. The *Furman* and *Gregg* decisions, however, consisted of lengthy discussions of both legal issues such as the equal protection of the law and the concept of cruel and unusual punishment, as well as political considerations including analyses of statistical and social scientific data and more ephemeral questions of human dignity and the morality of state-sanctioned killing. What the Court's analysis of capital punishment did not provide, in contrast to the abortion issue, was a clearly legal way of conceptualizing the central questions of the debate. This, I argue, left the framing door open to a much broader set of rhetorical choices, resulting in lawmakers speaking in their "native tongue" of political and policy concerns. Indeed, the courts too followed the *Furman* and *Gregg* lead, often finding relatively obscure legal fault with the practice of capital punishment, but insisting that the ultimate decision as to its use fell to the elected branches. Simply put, the development of capital punishment policy in New York and New Jersey may have been influenced by the landmark U.S. Supreme Court decisions on the issue, but concrete policy change remained located where it had begun, the state legislature.

Abortion policy change in Minnesota and Wisconsin, however, was clearly situated initially in the courts with the decision in *Roe* overturning both states' ban on the procedure. Subsequent policy making, however, was much more likely to be located in the courts in Minnesota, with the Wisconsin legislature being significantly more successful in enacting its policy choices. In the case of the former, judicial actors were crucial in setting the state's policy treating Medicaid funding, the four-and-a-half-month abortion ban, and funding restrictions on nonprofits offering abortion services, while sustaining only the parental notification and informed consent statutes. Courts in Wisconsin, by contrast, struck down only the state's late-term abortion ban and were never even presented with a challenge to the parental involvement law. In this sense, Minnesota largely followed the same policy making path as New Jersey, at least in terms of the institutional location of policy development. Despite the courts being the first to alter policy in Wisconsin, however, judges seemed much more inclined to sustain abortion provisions passed by lawmakers in that state.

The ways in which lawmakers and courts framed their understanding of abortion in the two states, for their part, were much more complicated than was the case in New York or New Jersey. Both judges and lawmakers tended to make their arguments in political as well as legal terms in Minnesota, while in Wisconsin, courts seemed more inclined to frame their decisions in a legal context with legislators often choosing their rhetoric based on the specific issue at hand and their position on abortion generally. When discussing the late-term abortion ban or the twenty-four-hour waiting and counseling requirement, for instance, both opponents and supporters of these measures relied on highly emotional, political language. This was also true for the most part of supporters of the parental consent and Medicaid funding bans, though opponents of these measures relied on noticeably more legal frames. In short, lawmakers and courts in Minnesota largely conceptualized abortion in the same terms, though these were neither fully political nor fully legal. Legislators and judges in Wisconsin, by contrast, differed significantly in their framing choices, with the latter employing more legal understandings and the former a combination of both political and jurisprudential frameworks.

Why, then, did Minnesota largely follow New Jersey in terms of the location of institutional decision making, though not framing, while Wisconsin did not, despite initial policy change being situated in the courts in both cases? Two specific factors seem likely as starting points in explaining this difference: the political situation in the two Midwestern states and the role of federal versus state courts. New York and New Jersey, as discussed in the introduction to this study, are among the most liberal states in the country, making both simply more likely to develop less restrictive abortion policies, whether through the courts or the legislature. According to Gallup data from 2016, Minnesota ranked as the sixteenth most liberal state in the union, ahead of Wisconsin at twenty-second, though putting both largely in the middle of the national political spectrum.[6] While this clearly does not reflect where these states stood during the most active periods of abortion policy making between 1970 and 2010, recall that Erickson et al. (2007) have demonstrated that a state's respective ideological position is largely constant over time. At the same time, there is some evidence to suggest that the Seventh Circuit Court of Appeals, of which Wisconsin is a part, is among the more conservative federal appeals courts in the country (Broscheid 2011). This is not to suggest that ideology alone is determinative of a state's abortion policy—indeed, Montana, arguably one of the most conservative states in the country, has comparatively few abortion restrictions—or the institutional location of policy making. Nevertheless, the partisan and ideological makeup of a state will undoubtedly have a meaningful impact on its policy outputs. A complete account of the role of the courts and legislatures in abortion policy making in Minnesota and Wisconsin would therefore need to take account of this variable in a way that is not possible here.

It is also worth noting that unlike New York and New Jersey, litigation related to abortion took place overwhelmingly in federal courts in Minnesota and Wisconsin. In fact, state courts weighed in on the matter only once in each case, upholding a Wisconsin FACE statute in *State v. Migliorino* and overturning Minnesota's Medicaid funding ban in *Women of the State of Minnesota v. Gomez*. Every other challenge to an abortion statute in both states was made exclusively in federal court. This fact may help account for the lack of rhetorical uniformity between the legislatures and courts in Minnesota and Wisconsin that was much more common in New York and New Jersey. Lawmakers may very well be attuned to the narratives and frames emanating from the federal bench, as was the case with *Roe*, though this influence could be stronger when it comes from an institution more closely affiliated with state government. This of course leaves the question of why litigation was so actively pursued in federal courts in Minnesota and Wisconsin compared to their Northeastern counterparts; however, I leave that inquiry to future scholarship.

It ought to come as no surprise that different jurisdictions would follow different developmental paths in the construction of their policies related to abortion, capital punishment, or any other issue given the vast array of variables that can potentially play into the institutional location of decision making. Nonetheless, the cases presented in this chapter are instructive for the theoretical framework presented in this study. Comparing the development of death penalty policy in New York and New Jersey with the abortion issue suggests that the rhetorical frames and policy pronouncements of the courts matter for how issues will be discussed subsequently and the institutions that will lead further development. In *Roe*, we saw a clear statement from the U.S. Supreme Court that abortion was a right that could not be restricted, at least up to a certain point. Going forward, lawmakers and judges, to a greater extent in New Jersey but also in Minnesota and Wisconsin, took this narrative seriously and incorporated it into their own debates, while New York, which had altered its policy prior to the 1973 ruling, retained its politically focused rhetoric. In *Furman* and *Gregg*, the Court made no similar pronouncement, and spoke broadly in both legal and political terms, an approach that was mirrored by state courts in New York and New Jersey and could be found in the issue frames adopted by lawmakers. The cases discussed in this chapter share some things in common with the story of abortion policy development in New York and New Jersey, though they also reveal that further refinement of the theoretical framework on offer here is certainly warranted.

NOTES

1. The case was decided along with *Jackson v. Georgia* and *Branch v. Texas*.
2. As of this writing in July 2017.
3. In 1993 Governor Florio also signed a bill extending the death penalty to terrorists, largely in response to the World Trade Center attacks that year. The rhetoric surrounding this bill centered on deterring and punishing terrorism, making it somewhat of an outlier in terms of issue frames (Sullivan 1993).
4. The Court did not, in fact, directly address the question of the state's abortion funding requirement but rather found that the rules promulgated by the Director of Public Welfare authorizing the use of state funds for abortion did not follow the Minnesota Administrative Procedure Act.
5. Unfortunately, no record of floor debates in either chamber of the Wisconsin Legislature exists either of these measures, or indeed any other abortion legislation, with Assembly member John Medinger's comments being the only publicly available record from lawmakers.
6. New York, for its part, ranked fourth while New Jersey placed twelfth.

Chapter Five

Talking Rights or Talking Politics?

Courts in New York and New Jersey played vastly different roles in the development of abortion policy over the course of the forty years between 1970 and 2010. In the case of the former, despite the initiation of a challenge to the state's 140-year-old ban on the procedure in federal district court in 1969 (*Abramowicz v. Lefkowitz*), the legislature passed the landmark liberalization law the following year, making New York one of only a handful of states to allow abortion before the *Roe* decision. Lawmakers could have avoided the politically toxic issue quite easily had they simply chosen not to act and allowed the case to continue making its way through the courts. Instead, the Senate and Assembly passed, and Governor Rockefeller signed, the most liberal abortion statute yet in the country. This action, coupled with the *Byrn* decision two years later, helped set a norm in the state where the question of reproductive rights came to be seen by the courts as one best settled by elected officials; even one to be discussed and decided in terms much more in line with the other branches than the language of rights, Equal Protection, and fundamental liberty that are the *modus operandi* of common law jurisprudence. As Brandwein (2011) has pointed out, ideas and institutions are indeed inseparable and the rhetorical frameworks courts adopt will have a profound impact not only on the decisions they make but the role they play in the wider political system.

Despite formulating what are in practical terms identical abortion policies to those in New York, New Jersey's laws today are the result almost exclusively of rulings by the state Supreme Court and federal Courts of Appeal. Nevertheless, the same mechanism that led New York's judicial branch to take such a passive role in abortion policy making seems to have been at work in the Garden State. Instead of legislating on the issue before the courts had a chance to weigh in, as their northern counterparts had, lawmakers in

New Jersey consistently failed to address the question. The first changes to that state's abortion policy, therefore, were made by judges and it was consequently the language and frameworks inherent to the mandate of courts that came to dominate the discourse surrounding that issue not only for the judicial, but for the elected branches as well. In addition, while there is good reason to suspect that legislators were engaging in what Lovell (2003) calls legislative deferral in some instances—most notably in the case of the late-term abortion ban passed over Governor Whitman's veto in 1997—other examples seem to represent genuine efforts to create policy. By the time these laws were passed, however, the norm of abortion as a fundamental right in general, and one enjoying heightened protection through the state Constitution in particular, had been so firmly established in the state that it is doubtful that any substantive limit on the procedure would have survived judicial scrutiny.

The case studies presented in the preceding chapters offer a unique opportunity to consider the question at the heart of this study, specifically, when, and under what circumstances, courts are likely to play a meaningful role in the development of policy, particularly treating a highly contentious and divisive social issue. New York and New Jersey share a host of characteristics that social scientists have traditionally identified as relevant in explaining the behavior of courts and legislatures. Both are liberal Northeastern states with comparable racial, religious, and other demographic populations. The two states are also often seen as culturally progressive strongholds of the Democratic Party at the national level, though also being home to an influential, albeit moderate, state level Republican Party. And yet the role of the courts in creating abortion policy in New York could not have been more divergent from the same institution in New Jersey. Given these similarities, these social, demographic, and political characteristics are insufficient in explaining this striking difference. What is different in the story of abortion policy making in the two states is the initial location of policy decisions and the ways in which courts came to think about and understand this issue in their respective jurisdictions.

The following section will summarize the findings presented in chapters 2, 3, and 4 with a particular focus on the critical decision points and how the various institutional actors influenced the role that the court was to play in developing abortion policy. Following this, the implications of the New York and New Jersey case studies for some of the most closely related work on interbranch relations will also be discussed. Related to this, there are some notable implications of this study for several broader questions of interest to law and courts scholars, which will also be touched upon. Finally, some promising areas of future research will be suggested.

Having eliminated the most likely explanatory phenomena for the question at issue in this study, chapters 2 and 3 demonstrate that what was different in the case of abortion policy making between the two states was both the timing of the involvement of the judiciary, as well as the framing of the issue adopted by both the courts and the elected branches. Indeed, the difference could not be starker. New Jersey, of course, saw a very different ordering of events. Chapter 2 demonstrates that there is considerable evidence that the elected branches in that state were making every effort to avoid creating policy dealing with abortion in the 1970s, despite a report they had commissioned suggesting that the nineteenth-century law be amended, the need for policy articulation following the *Roe* decision, and pleas from the Attorney General, as well as the state's medical community, to clarify what the law was in the state. At the same time, the *Kugler* decision in 1972 struck down the state's ban on abortion, a ruling that was indirectly upheld the following year in *Roe*. With the legislature still having yet to pass any meaningful statute on the matter, the state Supreme Court in 1976 issued its first decision dealing directly with abortion in *Doe v. Bridgeton Hospital Association*. Nevertheless, that same year the Assembly and Senate finally did pass legislation that included several restrictions on the procedure, including a ban on Medicaid funding, which was quickly enjoined by a federal District Court. The ban was ultimately struck down by the state's High Court in 1982, relying heavily on the argument articulated five years earlier by Justice Pashman in *Planned Parenthood of New York City v. State*. The late 1990s saw further restrictions passed by the legislature, including a late-term abortion ban and a parental notification law, both of which were struck down in 2000.

New York, however, saw a very different chain of events. Following the recommendations of the Froessel committee, the legislature passed the 1970 liberalization law before the resolution of the *Abramowicz* case or the *Roe* decision. The legislature voted to repeal the statute two years later and was prevented from accomplishing this only through Governor Rockefeller's veto. It was not until after these two critically important developments that the Court of Appeals finally issued its first decision on the matter when it upheld the liberalization law in the landmark *Byrn* decision. Notably, all of these developments had taken place before *Roe*, unlike in New Jersey where only the *Kugler* case had addressed the abortion question before 1973. In the years that followed, the Court reiterated its deference to the legislature in *Robin* and *Hope*, the latter upholding the state's prohibition on the use of PCAP funds for abortions. The last fifteen years of the period considered in this study saw several other laws related to reproductive rights passed by the Assembly and Senate, most importantly the state's FACE statute and a bill allowing over-the-counter sale of RU-486, though the latter was vetoed by Governor Pataki.

Comparing these two cases, then, it is apparent that institutional first movement was critically important in determining what role the courts were to play in resolving the abortion question in New York and New Jersey.

Indeed, perhaps the single most important event in the present study was the passage of the liberalization law in New York in 1970. The occupation of this issue area by the elected branches before either federal or state courts had handed down rulings treating abortion appears to have been crucial in framing this question and consequently the position taken by the courts.[1] As the discussion of the opinion delivered in *Byrn* reveals, the judges on that state's High Court made numerous references to the prerogative of the legislature to determine the legal status of abortion and, by extension, the nonjusticiable nature of the question. Recall, by way of example, Judge Breitel's statement at the end of his opinion in that case that the questions presented "are issues outside the law unless the Legislature should provide otherwise" (203). Indeed, New York is very much an outlier in the national context inasmuch as its abortion policy saw so little judicial involvement in abortion policy making. The Empire State is also one of only four to have legalized abortion in a manner consistent with *Roe* prior to that decision. In this sense, the idea described in the first chapter of this work that the courts will tend to adopt the issue frame inherent in the mandate of the institution that first developed policy in that area seems to have been borne out in the New York case. Again, Judge Jasen's concurring opinion reveals a distinctly political bent when he writes that the regulation of abortion "is a value judgment not committed to the discretion of judges, but reposing instead in the representative branch of government" (205). Conversely, the fact that New Jersey's policy on abortion was first altered by the courts, and that the judiciary continued to play an active role in the development of this policy, also supports the path dependent component of the theoretical framework on offer here. While there were legislative efforts to regulate the procedure in that state in the mid-1970s, these were consistently struck down by the courts. Just as the opinions issued by the New York Court of Appeals reveal a consistent trend of viewing abortion in political terms, those in New Jersey were equally inclined to think and write in ways that reflected a "legal" understanding of the issue. Again recalling some of the main features of Justice Pollock's ruling in *Byrne*, the majority argued that the "statute denies equal protection to those women entitled to necessary medical services under Medicaid" (306) and "discriminates between those for whom medical care is necessary for childbirth and those for whom an abortion is medically necessary" (305).

The second component of the importance of timing, that of self-reinforcing sequences, can also clearly be seen in both cases. The jurisprudential development of abortion policy in New York demonstrates this well as the cases that followed *Byrn* all relied on the understanding of the issue reflected in that decision, in most cases explicitly, and consequently maintained the attitude of deference to the legislature that formed the basis of the 1972 ruling. As the analysis of the majority opinions in *Robin* and *Hope* described above reveal, the norm that, when it came to the abortion question, the "issues in this litigation . . . are not legal or justiciable. They are issues outside the law unless the Legislature should provide otherwise" (*Byrn v. New York City Health & Hospitals Corporation* at 203). When Judge Fuld wrote in *Robin* that "[t]here can be no doubt that the State has reserved to itself regulation of the practice of medicine in general and of the performance of abortions in particular" (351), the process of reinforcing the *Byrn* understanding had already clearly begun. Two decades later, Judge Kaye's opinion upholding the exclusion of abortion from PCAP funding took a remarkably similar tone, arguing that "It is not the role of the courts to pass upon the wisdom of the Legislature's policy choice, even though there may be differences of views about the decision to exclude a medically necessary service from an otherwise comprehensive prenatal care program" (*Hope v. Perales* at 575). As policy was developed, each consecutive decision by the New York Court of Appeals further reinforced the frame adopted in 1972, an understanding of its role in relation to the legislature that can ultimately be traced back to the ideas inherent in the elected branches.

A critical component of the path dependent portion of the theory on offer here is that subsequent decisions will tend to adopt the issue frames articulated at the early stages of policy change, and are just as apparent in the self-reinforcing sequence seen in the New Jersey case. The same year the New York Court of Appeals had issued its *Byrn* decision, New Jersey's nineteenth-century abortion statute was struck down in *YWCA of Princeton v. Kugler*, with the District Court writing that "the New Jersey abortion statute, 2A:87-1, is unconstitutionally vague on its face and as applied; that it chills and deters the plaintiff-physicians in the exercise of protected First Amendment activities; and that it violates plaintiff-physicians' rights under the Fourteenth Amendment to freely practice the profession of their choice" (1066). Four years later, when the New Jersey Supreme Court first weighed in on the abortion issue in *Doe v. Bridgeton Hospital Association*, it both reinforced the line of reasoning articulated in *Kugler* and *Roe* and began to establish its own conceptualization of itself as a proper institutional venue for the development of policy in this area. In terms of the former, the Court wrote that "[t]he federal constitutional right to an abortion during the first trimester is now well-settled . . . For the state to frustrate that right by its action would be violative of the constitutional guarantee" (647). Reinforcing this understanding in *Right to Choose v. Byrne* (1982), Justice Pollock wrote that "[b]y granting funds when life is at risk, but withholding them when health is endangered, the statute denies equal protection to those women entitled to necessary medical services under Medicaid" (306). During the mid-1990s, the courts continued to assert their role as a principal location for abortion policy making in a series of clinic obstruction cases, the most notable being *Horizon Health Center v. Felicissimo* (1994). This was particularly noteworthy considering the active role the legislature had taken on this issue in New York, with the courts in that state largely upholding FACE laws passed by Congress and the state legislature. The courts in New Jersey instead acted independently of the elected branches and issued a series of injunctions barring aggressive clinic protests. Finally, in 2000, both the federal and state *Farmer* cases continued to sustain the institutional role of the courts, with the former finding that "the Act's chilling effect on a woman's ability to obtain a conventional and constitutionally permissible method of abortion, coupled with the attendant health risks, creates an undue burden under Casey" (145,146) and the latter ruling that "Article I, paragraph 1, of the New Jersey Constitution does not permit the State to impose disparate and unjustifiable burdens on different classes of young women when fundamental constitutional rights hang in the balance" (638).

The governors in both New York and New Jersey also played an important role in influencing the possibility of the courts involving themselves in the abortion question as well, primarily by vetoing several key bills that would have increased restrictions on the procedure. That being said, gubernatorial involvement was likely a more important factor in the former as it kept two very significant issues off the court's agenda, whereas in the latter, one provision that was vetoed was eventually passed by a subsequent legislature and signed into law while the other saw a successful override vote. Specifically, Governor Rockefeller vetoed the repeal of the liberalization law in New York in 1972 while Governor Carey similarly refused to sign the parental consent bill passed in 1976. It is, of course, impossible to know what would have been the result of passage of either law, though some distinct possibilities are worth considering. In terms of the first veto, its absence would likely have meant simply that New York's abortion law would have been struck down the following year, just as New Jersey's had been. The outcome of the inevitable litigation that would have followed passage of the parental consent bill is slightly less certain; however, it seems relatively unlikely that the law would have survived judicial scrutiny. Indeed, several months after the passage of the New York law, a very similar statute was struck down by the U.S. Supreme Court in *Planned Parenthood of Central Missouri v. Danforth* (1976). The practical effect of the vetoes therefore may have been rather minimal as neither law was likely to survive in the courts.[2]

What impact the absence of these vetoes would have had on the larger role of the courts in New York, however, is less clear. As it happened, no law passed by the legislature in the state was ever struck down or otherwise altered by the actions of the judicial branch, though this would almost certainly have not been the case had either the 1972 or 1976 laws been enacted. In addition, the presence of a major court decision early in the process of abortion policy making in New York may have had a highly significant impact on the role that institution would play going forward. A key prediction of the path dependence perspective that forms much of the basis of the theoretical framework proposed here is that developments that occur early in a process have a disproportionate impact on subsequent actions (see Skocpol 1999; Pierson 2004; North 1990). Just as important, though, is the adoption of a particular discursive frame by the courts, which, it is argued, will depend to a large extent on the understandings inherent in a given institution's mandate. Taken together, it seems at least plausible that the absence of the two key vetoes described above may have fundamentally changed the way abortion was viewed by the courts in New York and potentially led to a more robust role for that institution in the process of policy making treating that issue.

Conversely, the gubernatorial vetoes observed in New Jersey may have been considerably less important in determining the role of the courts in that state. The first of these occurred in 1980 when Governor Byrne refused to sign a package of restrictions, the most significant of which required parental notification before a minor could obtain an abortion and an informed consent provision emphasizing the "negative aspects" of the procedure. To again consider the counterfactual, some portions of this law were considerably more likely to have been sustained than the vetoed 1976 New York statute, at least at the federal level, as the U.S. Supreme Court would rule in *H.L. v. Matheson* (1981) that parental notification was a permissible restriction on abortion. The informed consent portion of the law may have fared more poorly, though, as a similar statute passed in Pennsylvania was struck down by the High Court in *Thornburgh v. American College of Obstetricians and Gynecologists* (1986). The potential fate of the 1980 bill in state court is more difficult to assess, though there is considerable reason to suspect that it would have been invalidated. In the 1982 *Byrne* decision, the New Jersey Supreme Court had explicitly indicated that the state constitution afforded greater protection for abortion rights than its federal counterpart. Indeed, the Court would eventually rule on both issues, striking down the parental notification law passed in 1999 and refusing to require doctors to inform women of the "negative aspects" of abortion in its 2007 *Acuna* decision. Finally, Governor Whitman's veto of the 1997 late-term abortion ban was overridden and consequently had little meaningful impact on the court's agenda, though her refusal to defend the law was noted in the federal *Farmer* case in 2000. In any event, unlike in New York, gubernatorial vetoes in New Jersey did not prevent critical issues from going before the courts, though as discussed below, they may have had some influence on the issue frames adopted by the judicial branch.

The final component of the theoretical framework proposed in this work that can be seen in the cases presented here is the remarkable consistency of the framing choices employed by the courts in New York and New Jersey, as well as the extent to which these differed between the two states. While the preceding summaries highlighted the importance of the timing of institutional involvement in the abortion debate for the role the courts were to play, it bears emphasizing here that of equal importance is the mechanism by which this timing shaped the courts' behavior. Fundamental to the argument proposed in this study is that the lens through which the courts viewed the abortion question was largely determinative of the role they were to play. Once again, the opinions excerpted above and discussed at length in chapters 2 and 3 are instructive. The overriding theme of the *Byrn*, *Robin*, *Hope*, and other abortion decisions handed down by the courts in New York was that the issue was a political question or, at the very least, not a legal one. Beyond this, the focus of the arguments put forward in these opinions largely relied on what might be termed a policy frame and tended to emphasize considerations such as the potential impact on women's health that might result from restrictions on abortion, the proper function of hospitals and other healthcare facilities, and the propriety of judicial preemption of the choices of the elected branches. The courts in New Jersey, however, spoke much more often in terms of the right to abortion, the protections afforded by the concepts of Equal Protection and Due Process, both in the state and federal constitutions, and the defects of overbroad language—in short, the frames and concepts indigenous to legal institutions. Further demonstrating the way in which these frames came to be reinforced over time, subsequent decisions in both states treating abortion often made reference to these earlier arguments in reduced form, suggesting a "winning" rhetorical scheme.

Indeed, it was not only the courts in the two states that seemed to consistently view abortion through very different lenses. As demonstrated in the veto messages of the various governors of New York and New Jersey, as well as the memoranda and statements to the media delivered by members of the state Assemblies and Senates, officials in the elected branches also framed their understandings of the issue in very disparate terms. Governor Rockefeller, for example, spoke of seeing "no justification now for repealing this reform and thus condemning hundreds of thousands of women to the dark age once again" and that "the extremes of personal vilification and political coercion brought to bear on members of the Legislature raise serious doubts that the vote to repeal the reform represented the will of a majority of the people of New York State" (Greenhouse and Siegel 2012, 159, 160). Governor Carey similarly wrote that "a higher proportion of early teenage pregnancies are among those who lack a secure home. It is with respect to these children that the bill's defects are most glaring, since it would impose upon them a cruel and intolerable burden" (1976, 456) when vetoing the parental consent bill passed by the legislature. Four years later, Governor Byrne of New Jersey would write that parental notification, a twenty-four hour waiting period, and a hospital requirement would be "in direct conflict with pertinent regulations of the State Department of Health and the State

Board of Medical Examiners" (1980, 2) and that "the cumulative effect of the provisions of Assembly Bill No. 1285 would not be to regulate reasonably but rather to erode substantially the right of a woman to choose to have an abortion in this State" (1980, 1). Explaining her reasoning for vetoing the late-term abortion ban passed in 1997, Governor Whitman claimed that "because the ban applies throughout pregnancy, and severely restricts medical options by applying to several distinct procedures, it is unconstitutional under United States Supreme Court precedent" and wrote that "the ban violates settled precedent holding that even when a fetus is viable, the state must permit abortions that are 'necessary, in appropriate medical judgment, for the preservation of the life or health of the mother'" (2). The point, in any event, is that courts were not operating in a vacuum but rather in the context of the wider political environment in both states. In Kahn's (2006) terms, the "social construction" of the abortion question adopted by judges in New York and New Jersey was informed as much by the conceptualizations of the other branches as by the understandings articulated by previous decisions.

Considering the early developments related to abortion policy in the national context is also revealing, both to illustrate the competing issue frames that were being put forward in the time leading up to the *Roe* decision, as well as how the timing of that decision may have affected the behavior of the courts in New York and New Jersey. While a vast array of arguments in support or opposition to legalized abortion have been offered since the issue first came to the fore of political debate in the 1960s, the period before 1973 saw several dominant narratives offered by proponents and opponents of liberalization. Among the most common were debates about fetal personhood, the harms associated with illegal "back-alley" abortions, feminist claims drawing on the autonomy of women over their reproductive choices, the ability of doctors to make appropriate medical decisions for their patients, and the right to privacy (see Greenhouse and Siegel 2012). All of these informed the *Roe* decision itself and were presented in amicus briefs, with Blackmun's opinion also referencing many of these competing claims. Ultimately, though, the U.S. Supreme Court's decision rested for the most part on the implied right to privacy first articulated in *Griswold v. Connecticut* (1965). Subsequent rulings by the High Court have alternately upheld or struck down restrictions placed on abortion by a host of states since the landmark decision, with the most substantive change to *Roe* coming in 1992 when the trimester framework developed in that decision was replaced by the undue burden test in *Casey v. Planned Parenthood of Southeastern Pennsylvania*.

In this sense, beyond striking down the abortion statutes then in force in most states, the most important impact that *Roe* had on abortion jurisprudence was to articulate a national standard and conceptualization of the question as one best understood in terms of substantive due process. What makes the experience in New York so different from that in New Jersey, then, may very well be that the laws in the former were altered before *Roe* while those in the latter were only changed after 1973. When New York began considering changes to its abortion law, the rhetorical field was wide open, and the basis on which it ultimately chose to act, via the legislature, was precisely what would be expected from the elected branches—a policy-oriented frame that emphasized the harms associated with the law as it stood at the time. While there is no record of the floor debate that preceded the vote on the liberalization bill in 1970, the memorandum distributed by Assemblywoman Constance E. Cook discussed in chapter 3 may be illustrative of the rationale that informed the legislature's decision making. In particular, the document makes mention of three main arguments in favor of legalized abortion: that the procedure was already common and available to women who could afford them; that the law interfered with the ability of doctors to make necessary medical decisions; and that "the state [ought to be kept] out of the business of decreeing who is to be born" (Nossiff 2001, 66). Besides the passage of the liberalization law, the Court of Appeals too would have a chance to rule on the abortion question prior to *Roe*, and it chose to defer to the choices made by the legislature. By acting before 1973, then, a norm was established in New York's political and legal interpretive community that abortion was to be understood as best left to the elected branches.

In New Jersey, however, the only policy movement that preceded *Roe* was the District Court decision in *Kugler* in 1972. While that court did indeed find the state's abortion statute unconstitutional, it refused to issue an injunction and the law was not officially struck down until 1974 when the Third Circuit Court of Appeals upheld the District Court's ruling, almost entirely on the basis of *Roe*. Virtually all of the policy changes that took place in New Jersey therefore occurred after 1973. In other words, the terms of the debate over abortion in that state were heavily influenced by the recognition that there existed in the U.S. Constitution a right to reproductive freedom. This understanding, coupled with the reasoning in *Kugler*, meant that, just as abortion had been framed by the social construction process—to borrow again from Kahn (2006)—in New York as a "political" question, the issue in New Jersey was inextricably linked to the narrative of abortion as a right. Going forward, the courts, as well as the elected branches, would increasingly view abortion in these terms. The consequence of this was not only that the decisions of the court were framed by this lens, but that the role of the judiciary would be one of robust involvement in policy making in this area.

To reiterate, the level of analysis that forms the basis of both case studies presented in this work is indeed the policy making community at the state level, defined as all three branches of government. At the same time, the theoretical framework on offer in this study highlights the importance of initial policy change following a lengthy period of inaction in a given issue area. Because of the nature of the federal system, then, it is possible that such change might be the result of institutions outside of the state in question, as was the case in New Jersey. Nevertheless, the influence of the rhetorical frame articulated by the Court in *Roe* unquestionably informed the understanding of the judicial and elected branches in the Garden State, as can be seen in the language employed in major state cases such as *Bridgeton*, *Byrne*, and *Farmer*, as well as the veto messages issued by Governors Byrne and Whitman and comments by members of the legislature. This fact becomes even starker when taking into account the rare examples of federal intervention in New York. For example, several district and appellate court rulings in the late 1980s and early 1990s issued injunctions against abortion clinic protesters, some of which were later overturned by the U.S. Supreme Court. These decisions, however, did not appear to change the assertive role the elected branches in that state had come to adopt as the legislature passed a FACE law in 1998. The difference in the latter case of course was that the "winning" rhetorical frame in New York had by that time largely become one of legislative predominance, as reflected in the twenty-five years of jurisprudence on the Court of Appeals since the 1972 *Byrn* decision. So while federal intervention did take place in both states, the influence of that involvement was considerably less important in New York than in New Jersey due, according to the argument presented here, to the temporal ordering of the relevant events.

In terms of the implications of the preceding analysis for the relevant law and courts literature, this study speaks most directly to the debate regarding the importance of the separation of powers model, albeit in a way somewhat similar to the claims that Lovell (2003), Graber (1993), and Whittington (1997) make regarding this approach. Clearly, the interactions between the Court and the elected branches in the cases presented in this work do not fit the pattern that would be predicted by proponents of this model such as Eskridge (1991), Clark (2009), and Clinton (1994). While on the surface it may appear that the New York Court of Appeals might have been constrained by the preferences of the legislature inasmuch as it never substantively altered the choices of this branch, it seems unlikely that this was a strategic choice on the part of the judges. In the *Byrn* case, for instance, the Court upheld a law that the legislature had a mere two months earlier voted to repeal, suggesting that the judiciary was not taking its cues from the Senate and Assembly. Similarly, by sustaining the exclusion of abortion financing from the PCAP program, the Court was actually voting against the policy preferences of both the Assembly and Governor. The New Jersey case provides even less support for the separation of powers approach. In striking down the parental notification law in the state *Farmer* decision, the Court was overruling a statute that had been passed with a large majority of support in both houses, the blessing of Governor Whitman, and the majority of New Jersey residents. Setting aside for the moment the obvious and almost certainly intentional flaws in the statute struck down in the federal *Farmer* case, this law too was, at least on paper, also supported by an overwhelming majority in the Assembly and Senate, as evidenced by the super-majority that overrode the Governor's veto. Nevertheless, the Third Circuit Court of Appeals ruled the ban on late-term abortions unconstitutional. If, as the separation of powers model claims, courts are unlikely to stray too far from the policy preferences of the median member of a given legislature, the judges and justices of the High Courts in New York and New Jersey were particularly poor at assessing the views of lawmakers.

One approach commonly employed in this tradition, perhaps most famously Robert Lowry Clinton's (1994) discussion of *Marbury v. Madison*, is to view the relationship between courts and elected officials in game-theoretic terms where the expected reaction to a particular ruling by the president or Congress is gauged and the justices vote as closely to their policy preferences as possible. Looking again at both *Farmer* cases, it seems unlikely that this type of reasoning was being practiced by the members of either the New Jersey Supreme Court or the federal Appeals Court. While it is impossible to know with certainty what these jurists expected the response from the legislature to be, there was some evidence that their decisions may have been overturned. Certainly in the case of the late-term abortion ban, there were apparently enough votes in the Senate and Assembly to pass an amended statute that might have been sustained with more precise wording. Following the state Court's decision striking down the parental notification requirement, there was in fact a push by some lawmakers to amend the state constitution in order to circumvent the ruling, though this was never brought to the floor and became much less likely following the landslide Democratic wins in both chambers in 2001. The New York case does not provide an equivalent opportunity to assess this aspect of the separation of powers model, however, making it difficult to draw any conclusions regarding this behavior one way or the other.

That being said, the relationship between the elected branches and the judiciary highlighted by proponents of the separation of powers approach was nonetheless very important, though not in the strategic sense generally articulated by these scholars. Instead of the competitive view that the game theory and other versions of this model take, it seems that cooperation was a much more accurate description of the interactions between the courts and the legislature. Indeed, the legislative deferral hypotheses posit that elected officials actively seek to have their policies altered by the much less accountable judiciary, and this does seem to have been the case in several of the New Jersey decisions. Interestingly, Whittington's (2007) take on the cooperative nature of the Court–President–Congress relationship as one where the dominant national coalition uses the Supreme Court to legitimize its policy choices at the state level may have been operative in New York, though on a smaller scale. In *Byrn*, the Court rejected the argument that the unborn were entitled to the Due Process protection of life, something that had been, and still remains, a cornerstone of the pro-life argument. Similarly, in *Robin*, the Court ruled that a municipality could not overturn the policy articulated by the legislature, thereby helping to further establish the choices made by the Senate and Assembly. Finally, the Attorney General used the courts on several occasions during the 1980s and early 1990s to prosecute so-called "pregnancy crisis centers" for falsely advertising themselves as abortion providers. In this sense, something akin to Whittington's view of the court as a legitimizing force working hand in hand with the executive and legislative branches seems to have been at work in the New York case.

Most of the critiques of the separation of powers approach have come from the attitudinal model most closely associated with Segal and Spaeth (2002). The findings reported here, though, offer a theoretically distinct reason to question the utility of this view that is completely separate from the attitudinalist take on the issue. To reiterate, the claim from proponents of this approach is that the separation of powers approach downplays the institutional position of the Court in the American political system that allows the justices to decide cases entirely on the basis of their policy preferences. Simply put, the president and Congress do not have sufficient means at their disposal to override or otherwise disincentivize members of the High Court from pursuing their policy goals unencumbered. The theoretical framework on offer here, however, argues that the court is not necessarily constrained by the other branches by virtue of its ability to essentially ignore the legislature and executive in handing down its rulings, but that it often works in cooperation with the elected institutions of government. Furthermore, even when this is not necessarily the case, as it may not have been in several of the major decisions in New Jersey, the judiciary can maintain its primary role in the policy making process because of the way a given controversy is framed, which in turn leads that issue to be understood as falling within the institutional orbit of the courts. So while the theory presented in this work in some ways shares the argument of proponents of the attitudinal model that the separation of powers approach is often insufficient in explaining the role of the courts in relation to the other branches, it is based on a very different understanding of interbranch relations.

The separation of powers view has been challenged, albeit somewhat less directly, by the legislative deferral approach associated with Lovell (2003), Graber (1993), and Whittington (2007). The study presented in this work, however, also seems to call much of this approach into question. In particular, the New York case appears very difficult to square with many of the predictions that follow from this theory, despite the presence of most of the characteristics that Lovell and Graber identify as likely to result in deferral behavior. Perhaps most obviously, a clear opportunity to defer to the courts via the *Abramowicz* case and avoid what was clearly a politically damaging vote, which cost several of the members of the legislature their careers, the liberalization bill was passed in 1970. Indeed, Graber explicitly uses the example of abortion policy making in his piece, arguing that this issue will be likely to engender deferral behavior not only at the national level but also among state lawmakers (1993, 58). This expectation is articulated well when Graber writes that:

> mainstream politicians in virtually every Western democracy responded to the emergence of the abortion issues by adopting strategies which emphasize 'abstinence, postponement, and depoliticization.' Judicial review . . . is merely the particular device that American public officials have used to remove this politically unpalatable issue from electoral debate (1993, 53, 54).

Clearly, however, this was not the case in New York, either at the stage of initial policy development, or at later points in this process. In terms of the latter, Graber (1993) argues that pro-choice members of Congress had voted for the Hyde Amendment with the, albeit mistaken, belief that it would be struck down by the courts. The equivalent to this restriction in New York, though, was instead separated from the budget bill and defeated in the Assembly.

While there is some evidence for legislative deferral behavior in New Jersey, most notably in the case of the late-term abortion ban where legislators were clearly aware that they were passing a law that would almost certainly be struck down by the courts, other instances do not seem to fit this pattern either. In particular, lawmakers appeared to take great care in crafting the parental notification statute signed by Governor Whitman in 1999. The original version of the bill had contained no provision for a judicial bypass or exceptions in cases where there was evidence of physical or sexual abuse, though these were added at the request of the Governor. The intentions of legislators in passing the Medicaid funding ban in 1976 are more difficult to assess, though it seems plausible here too that lawmakers may have been attempting to craft legislation that they believed would be sustained by the courts. On the one hand, the New Jersey law was very similar to the original Hyde Amendment passed by Congress and upheld by the U.S. Supreme Court in *Harris v. McRae* (1980). On the other hand, however, the statute allowed funding only in cases where the life of the mother was endangered, excluding these funds for instances of "severe and physical health damage" and cases of rape and incest, as Congress had done in the 1977 version of the Hyde Amendment. The law was in fact upheld in federal court, again on the basis that it comported with the *Harris* ruling, though it was eventually struck down by the state Supreme Court in *Byrne* in 1982. In the New Jersey case, then, we find mixed support for the deferral model, with one example appearing to be an obvious instance of lawmakers deferring to the courts, another seeming to represent a genuine attempt to enact a limit on abortion supported by a majority of New Jerseyans, and a third where the intentions of legislators appear somewhat unclear.

Despite little evidence of legislative deferral to the courts in New York, there is some reason to suspect that lawmakers may have engaged in a similar type of behavior aimed at the executive. As described in chapter 3, it seems highly plausible that members of the Senate and Assembly voted for bills that they were keenly aware would be vetoed by the chief executive. This is particularly evident in the case of the liberalization repeal legislation passed in 1972 as Governor Rockefeller had repeatedly made it clear that he would not sign any such bill that reached his desk. Ultimately, Rockefeller made good on his promise, writing a forceful veto message that reiterated his support for reproductive rights, and it was known in the upper and lower houses that there was no chance of an override. Indeed, Alfonso Narvaez of the *New York Times* wrote at the time that it was common knowledge within the legislature that a number of lawmakers had voted in favor of the repeal only with the understanding that it would not become law on account of Rockefeller's expected veto (1972a). Linda Greenhouse (1976) had made a similar suggestion regarding Governor Carey's veto of the 1976 parental consent bill, though this is somewhat less clear as Carey had not been as vocal about his opposition to the legislation and had waited until the last minute to reject the measure. Nevertheless, there is substantial evidence that something similar to legislative deferral had taken place in regards to the 1972 and 1976 votes, with the executive playing a role akin to that of the courts in Lovell's (2003) and Graber's (1993) frameworks. The difference, of course, being that the governor, unlike the judiciary, is not unaccountable to the electorate and therefore the dynamics of such a "deferral" would be somewhat different. Indeed, it seems just as likely that the lawmakers who voted in favor of the repeal and parental consent bills were simply engaging in a form of political posturing aimed at placating the vocal anti-abortion lobby at the time led by the Catholic Church.

One possible example of this difference is related to what is, after all, the overriding goal of deferral as understood by Lovell (2003), Graber (1993), and Whittington (2007): the avoidance of roll call votes that have the potential to alienate important constituents. What may be a politically costly policy choice for a legislator in a particular district may not be as dangerous for another elected official, particularly one elected on a statewide basis. In the case of abortion in New York, for example, a member of the Assembly or Senate may represent a group of voters who are closely split on the issue and therefore wish to vote in support of a measure restricting access to the procedure while at the same time remaining confident that the bill will not be signed into law. The governor, for his part, may not face the same pressure to "play both sides" in a state that has consistently seen a sizeable pro-choice majority. While both Governors Rockefeller and Carey faced vocal opposition from pro-life groups throughout their tenures, neither ever suffered electorally for their support of abortion rights, suggesting that they were better positioned to absorb any political fallout from their vetoes than many state legislators. There does exist some evidence that lawmakers will defer some policy making authority to the executive under certain circumstances (see Epstein and O'Halloran 1996; Volden 2002; Huber, Shipan, and Pfahler 2001), however, this research has tended to focus on the role of executive agencies at the policy formation stage rather than in a manner approximating legislative deferral to the courts. Borrowing from some of the separation of powers literature (Clinton 1994, Eskridge 1991), it may also be the case that the governor and the legislature—as measured by the policy preferences of the median member—had differing ideal points, in a game-theoretical sense, resulting in passage of the 1972 and 1976 abortion restrictions in the Assembly and Senate followed by a gubernatorial veto by a chief executive who was considerably more pro-choice. In any event, there is evidence for the presence of this type of behavior in both the New York and New Jersey cases presented in this study. A more complete consideration of the precise mechanisms and nature of legislative deferral, or some other related phenomenon, to the chief executive, if in fact it did occur, would require a considerably more detailed analysis of the interplay between these two branches than is possible here, though future research may prove fruitful in determining when and how this phenomenon takes place.

The theories put forward by Lovell (2003), Graber (1993), and Whittington (2007) rest to a greater or lesser extent on the assumption that lawmakers are concerned with ensuring that they do not alienate constituencies that have strong feelings on controversial issues. In several instances in the case studies presented here, however, we see examples of legislators knowingly taking these political risks and some indeed losing their reelection bids on the basis of a vote they could have avoided. The liberalization bill in New York is no doubt the best example of this, with several members of the Assembly and Senate failing to retain their seats based almost entirely on their affirmative votes in 1970 and others facing much closer races, both in the primary and general elections, than they would have had they similarly attempted to defer the issue to the courts (Knowles 1970; Kovach 1970a; Farrell 1972b). This is not to suggest that lawmakers were not sincere in their vote choices on the liberalization bill—indeed, George Michaels seems to have been quite so—or did not wish to enact policies that they genuinely supported. The difficulty faced by many legislators following their support of the 1970 bill simply serves to illustrate that the political costs Lovell and Graber claim that elected officials seek to avoid through legislative deferral were quite real, at least for several members of the Assembly and Senate in New York, yet they still chose to act.

The case studies presented in this work also have some implications for other areas of research, both in law and courts, as well as other substantive topics in American government. In terms of what is perhaps the most common source of inquiry among the former group of scholars, accounting for the decision making of judges, this work provides further support for the view of many in the Law and APD tradition (Gillman 2002, 2006; Tushnet 2006; Smith 1988; Frymer 2008; *inter alia*), as well as some taking a more positivist approach (Maltzman et al. 2000; Epstein and Knight 1998), that these choices are the product of much more than simply the policy preferences of individual members of the Court. Taken in the aggregate, the story of the judiciary's role in the development of abortion policy in New York and New Jersey was the product of a complex series of interaction between elected officials in the executive and legislative branches and the courts. In some cases, such as the federal *Farmer* case and the *Byrne* decision, there is relatively conclusive evidence that lawmakers sought to invite judges to make policy and, at least in the former case, it seems unlikely that any court would have upheld the extremely overbroad restrictions contained in the late-term abortion ban. Similarly, a careful reading of the *Hope* decision suggests that Chief Judge Kaye herself did not support the exclusion of abortion from PCAP funding but felt bound by prior commitments on the part of the Court to providing broad latitude to the legislature on the abortion question. This is not to suggest that the policy preferences of the members of both states' High Courts played no role in influencing their decision making. It is likely no accident that the New York Court of Appeals and the New Jersey Supreme Court, both considered among the more progressive in the country, relatively consistently handed down pro-choice rulings. Nevertheless, there was undoubtedly more behind these decisions than mere policy preferences, particularly when they are considered in the context of the wider abortion debate in the two states.

While the focus of this work has been the role of the courts, the events surrounding the passage of the liberalization law in New York are also interesting in light of one of the most dominant views from the legislative decision making literature. Specifically, a number of prominent scholars (Miller and Stokes 1963; Mayhew 1974; Kingdon 1973; McCrone and Kuklinski 1979; Fenno 1978; *inter alia*) have argued that reelection is the overriding goal of lawmakers, a proposition that seems intuitive given that virtually all other goals these officials have depend on retaining their positions. While some (Parker 1989; Abramowitz 2001) have questioned this conventional wisdom, it remains one of the most important assumptions of much work in this area. Nevertheless, a number of lawmakers in both the Assembly and

Senate voted in favor of the reform legislation despite the danger it posed to their reelection chances. The most obvious example of this was of course George Michaels, the moderate Democrat from central New York, who famously acknowledged that changing his vote would end his career. A full account of why some legislators in this case chose to take the risk of a vote they knew would harm them politically is well beyond the scope of this investigation, though it does present an interesting counterpoint to one of the most ubiquitous claims in the legislative decision making field.

Finally, this study has aimed to further refine some of the major works in the Law and APD field, particularly in relation to the work of Kahn (2006) and Brandwein (2011), while also drawing on path dependence conceptualizations from the work of Pierson (2000, 2004) and Orren (1991). In terms of the former, the theoretical framework that forms the basis of the present work is partially built on, and adds to, the argument that "cognitive structures cannot be pried apart from forms of institutional authority" (Brandwein 2011, 194). As discussed in the introduction to this investigation, Brandwein rejects Orren and Skowronek's (2004) assertion that institutions must be understood independently from ideas—also referred to in this context as ideologies and discursive formations. To illustrate this point, Brandwein discusses previous work dealing with race and the law during the Jim Crow era, demonstrating that "state action (what the state does) is inseparable from . . . (what the state is)" (200). The cases of abortion policy making in New York and New Jersey represent the application of this understanding to a very different set of historical, institutional, and policy settings. Despite a change in temporal location (from the late nineteenth and early twentieth centuries to the late twentieth and early twenty-first centuries), levels of government (national to state), and issue areas (race to abortion), much of what Brandwein claims regarding how the mandates or "stable sets of ideas" (188, 189) that constitute institutions guide their behavior seems to be borne out. Thinking again of the vastly different rhetorical schemes employed by the courts, as well as other actors, throughout the development of abortion policy in New York and New Jersey, it seems likely that this divergence had a significant impact on what the courts did. While further research would clearly add to the robustness of Brandwein's argument regarding the close linkages between ideas and institutions, this study at the very least suggests that this conceptual framework can be instructive across a wide range of times and issues.

Somewhat related to Brandwein's (2011) focus on the interconnectedness of ideas and institutions is Kahn's notion of the social construction process (SCP). To briefly reiterate this view, Kahn (2006) suggests that judges engage in both an internal and external dialogue that takes account of factors such as the prior understandings of issues that previous courts have taken as well as the importance of their jurisprudence for the lived lives of the average citizen. Something akin to the SCP seemed to be at work in the New York and New Jersey cases as well, though the dialogue that Kahn describes was not one between the elected branches and the courts. The workability of the right articulated by the courts for the citizens of New York and New Jersey may not have been as important in these cases as in those considered in Kahn's analysis, but his focus on the importance of external as well as internal dialogue certainly was. In decisions such as *Byrn*, *Robin*, and *Hope* in New York and *Byrne*, *Farmer*, and *Acuna* in New Jersey, we see a type of SCP where both past decisions as well as issue frames adopted by the other branches were largely determinative of how the court saw the abortion question and consequently what role it played. In other words, the courts were "simultaneously inward (legal) and outward (society) [as reflected by elected officials] looking" (Kahn 2006, 67). Recall, however, that the argument on offer here is not one of increasing returns path dependence, but rather that the frames adopted by the policy making community as a whole were largely self-reinforcing across institutions, as can be seen in the statements of both elected officials and the major court opinions treating abortion. What the present study adds to this understanding, then, is that the SCP seems to be operative both at the level of courts and society, as well as courts and the elected branches. The point is that social construction, and its impact on judicial behavior, can come from multiple outside sources, depending on the configuration of the social and political worlds.

In addition to describing the SCP, Kahn (2006) also provides a critique of path dependent approaches to understanding the behavior of courts in general and their likelihood of overturning precedent in particular. The theoretical framework proposed here offers somewhat of a response to this as well. Specifically, Kahn argues that because courts are able to engage in "path switching" more easily than the elected branches simply by overturning previous decisions and that there are fewer start-up costs for novel approaches to policy questions, the forces driving path dependent processes in other arenas are not present in the judiciary. What the cases described in chapters 2 and 3 demonstrate, however, is that path dependence in the courts setting is not necessarily a function of doctrinal development and direction, as Kahn supposes, but rather one of issue framing defined by both internal and external factors. While courts may very well alter their previous rulings or develop novel conceptualizations of specific issues, their understandings of policy questions and hence the frameworks they adopted when confronted by similar issues are nonetheless framed by antecedent actions. Consider again the *Byrn* and *Hope* decisions in New York. The former reflected a norm of deference to the choices made by the legislature and the propriety of allowing that body wide latitude in choosing to expand access to abortion reflected in the 1970 liberalization law. The latter, for its part, similarly spoke in terms of the legislature's prerogative in terms of appropriate limits on abortion funding, despite Chief Judge Kaye's apparent disagreement with the policy in question.

Hope, then, is not clearly explicable in terms of either policy preferences or adherence to precedent. The Court could have struck down the PCAP restriction and switched paths, as Kahn argues the unconstrained judiciary may, but it chose instead to continue the norm of deference to the choices of the legislature. *Hope* seems best explained as the result not of reliance on stare decisis, but a more informal process by which abortion was viewed in political terms and hence properly located within the purview of the elected branches. Furthermore, these understandings are formed, along lines similar to those described by Brandwein (2011) by the ideas inherent in the institutions that first treated a given policy question. In this sense, what Kahn fails to consider in his critique of path dependent approaches to judicial decision making is the larger issue framing and dialectic environment within which courts operate. Put simply, decisions are not made in a vacuum but are situated in a policy making environment populated by other actors, such as elected officials, who can influence how judges understand particular issues. The decisions judges make occur within the context of the ideas and mandates of the other branches and the temporal ordering of these actions matter for how and what courts do.

Related to this, of course, is the contribution to the path dependence approach that this study aims to make. While traditional versions of the theory, reflecting their intellectual heritage within the APD school, have focused on how institutions and institutional behavior, particularly at early stages of policy development, shape subsequent actions, the present work shifts the focus to the level of discourse and issue framing. To be sure, the idea that norms can be responsive to path dependent forces is not entirely new (see Pierson 2000; Acharya 2004; Paul 2008). Nevertheless, this specific way of seeing this phenomenon has not been extensively investigated by scholars and it seems to have been highly relevant for the development of abortion policy in New York and New Jersey. Additionally, the idea that institutional first movement can influence the behavior of other branches of government in a path dependent sense has not been explored in great detail as this approach has tended to focus on particular policies as the level of analysis rather than institutions.[3] Finally, while some scholars have attempted to apply the assumptions of path dependence to the courts and jurisprudential development (Orren 1991; Hathaway 2001), these efforts have tended to consider the courts in isolation from the other branches of government. By expanding the scope of analysis to include not simply the courts and their successive decisions, but also the ongoing dialogue between that institution and the elected branches, this study has attempted to demonstrate how a path dependent approach, when considered in a broader context that includes the totality of the political environment can be a useful tool for explaining the role of the judiciary in policy development.

The cases of capital punishment in New York and New Jersey as well as the abortion issue in Minnesota and Wisconsin add further layers to our understanding of the importance of institutional first movement and the role of rhetorical frames in structuring the actions of lawmakers and judges. Perhaps most notably, the story of death penalty policy development suggests that *how* a court acts as first mover may be as important as *when* it acts. Despite issuing a moratorium on executions in *Furman* in 1972, the U.S. Supreme Court did not find capital punishment unconstitutional in all cases, making the identification of this particular juncture as critical in the policy making process somewhat more difficult. Indeed, the development of death penalty policy may better be characterized as one of largely legislative decision making, punctuated by occasional limitations placed on this process by the courts. Nevertheless, judges at both the federal and state level were consistently careful to insist that decision making in this issue area was the responsibility of elected officials. Unlike abortion, there was no sudden and fundamentally policy altering shock coming from the judiciary following a long period of inaction, leaving the choices of rhetorical frames, and institutional involvement, much more open than was the case following *Roe*.

Abortion policy development in Minnesota and Wisconsin also helps refine the theoretical framework proposed here, though in a more complex way. Policy change in the former followed much the same path as was the case in New Jersey, with the courts initiating a change and continuing to play a dominant role throughout the following decades. Wisconsin, however, witnessed the same policy shock as Minnesota with the decision in *Roe*, though the courts in the state seemed considerably less inclined to play an active role in the subsequent development of abortion policy. As discussed in the previous chapter, both states differed from New York and New Jersey in the level of state court involvement, with neither seeing any significant intervention from their own judiciaries. The reasons for this are not entirely clear, though the impact, at least in the case of Wisconsin, may very well have been a greater level of deference by the court to the choices legislators made. It may also be the case that, for political or electoral reasons, lawmakers in Minnesota were engaging in a sort of legislative deferral of the type described by Lovell (2003), Graber (1993), and Whittington (2007), while those in Wisconsin were more genuinely interested in enacting legislation that would pass judicial scrutiny. Perhaps the most important lesson, though, is that the interaction between state legislatures and the courts is likely to be a fruitful location for further study and testing of a number of theories related to policy formulation.

A final possibility regarding the behavior of the courts in New York and New Jersey bears addressing here and represents an alternative interpretation of the preceding study. Rather than the story of abortion policy development in the two states being one of choices between possible rhetorical frames, and the location of decision that these imply, New York's decision to legalize abortion pre-*Roe* might be seen as a broader attempt to establish a pro-choice regime, while New Jersey's legislative failure to act, and the restrictions it placed on abortion after the Supreme Court's 1973 ruling, an attempt to establish a more pro-life regime. In this telling, the courts in the latter felt obligated to protect the right to abortion in a jurisdiction where the elected branches were not committed to this right, while New York's judiciary felt no similar pressure. This view, however, does not account for the persistence of the legal frame that runs throughout the major abortion decisions in New Jersey. As the discussion of the Minnesota and Wisconsin cases demonstrate, courts interested simply in countering what they saw as legislative efforts to undermine abortion rights could, and did, rely as often as not on policy rather than legally centered narratives. What is interesting about the New Jersey case is that the latter frame was used almost exclusively by the courts, as well as by elected lawmakers, an observation that seems unlikely to be a coincidence. Perhaps more importantly, however, is that early in the process of abortion policy development, there seems to be little evidence that New York was particularly committed to a pro-choice regime. Indeed, the legislature repealed the liberalization law in 1972 and passed a highly restrictive parental involvement law in 1976, both of which were blocked only by gubernatorial vetoes. At the same time, the New York Court of Appeals did sustain an abortion restriction in *Hope*, albeit a relatively minor one, a development that seems more in line with a judiciary concerned with leaving abortion regulation in the hands of the legislature, as it had for the preceding twenty-five years.

The preceding study of abortion policy development in New York and New Jersey, as well as the theoretical framework proposed here, offers considerable opportunities for future research. Most immediately, a consideration of the formulation of policy in this issue area in several other states would have the potential to greatly improve the robustness of the findings presented in this work. As mentioned above, both Washington and Hawaii seem to have followed much the same developmental path as New York in that they too saw little meaningful involvement by the courts. By the same token, California and Montana appear to have much in common with New Jersey in that their respective judicial branches were quite active in this area and saw many state laws struck down by their High Courts. The latter is particularly interesting given the traditional view of Montana as a socially conservative, rural state with a small and homogenous population. If the same processes that appear to have driven the development of abortion policy in New York and New Jersey are found to be operative in these states as well, it would add considerably to the reliability of the theory articulated here.

Beyond this, the study of the court's role in abortion policy making in general, at both the state and federal levels, may benefit from the application of some of the theoretical propositions put forward in this investigation. With litigation being extremely common following the passage of any laws involving the procedure, a fuller understanding of the relationship between the elected branches and the judiciary ought to provide much in the way of a better accounting of when these laws might be struck down or sustained. Given the precipitous rise in the number of abortion restrictions that have been passed at the state level in recent years following the rise of Tea Party conservatism, scholars have ample opportunity to consider the political and legal, or even normative, aspects of policy making in this issue area. Indeed, a number of states, including Oklahoma (SB 1433), Virginia (HB 1), and North Dakota (ND 4009), have passed or are considering so-called "personhood" bills that would directly challenge *Roe*, the latter example being a proposed amendment to the state's constitution that would establish an "inalienable right to life of every human being at every stage of development" (ND 2009). The renewed push to test the limits of the landmark 1973 ruling, whether they ultimately come before the U.S. Supreme Court or not, underscores the importance for legal scholars and other researchers concerned with reproductive rights of formulating a clear set of theoretical tools for understanding these developments. Expansion of the theoretical framework proposed here would undoubtedly require some modifications to account for the vastly different political and legal environments of these other states, as well as the large amount of case law from both federal and state courts, though such an undertaking has the potential to yield important insights into this ongoing policy development.

Similarly, expanding the number of issues considered through the lens proposed in this study would also lend greater credibility to its findings. Abortion is a relatively unique political and legal question in the American context as it has remained, at least at the level of public opinion, rather stagnant over the course of the last forty years. Courts, too, have issued a wide range of rulings on the issue, variously upholding, striking down, or narrowing a broad selection of laws on the question; in some cases reversing previous holdings that had rejected limits on the procedure shortly after the original decision.[4] Unlike some of the other issues mentioned earlier such as same-sex marriage, gun control, and healthcare policy, public views on reproductive rights have not changed markedly as various laws have been passed and court decisions rendered. This fact may mean that the processes that drive the behavior of courts when dealing with this issue do not hold in other areas as the dynamics described in this work are influenced by the interfering variable of shifting societal views. It would, however, be possible to take these differences into account, which would provide a richer understanding of the interplay between the elected branches—which would presumably be more responsive to such changes—and the courts. Indeed, this expansion of issue areas need not be confined to social issues, which themselves often involve considerations not present in other areas with which the government deals, but could also examine how frame adoption, institutional first movement, and jurisprudential development operate in the economic, social welfare, or even foreign policy realms.

Finally, the theoretical framework developed through the combination of the Law and APD approach described by Kahn (2006) and Brandwein (2011) and some of the assumptions of path dependence proposed here may be of use to law and courts scholars concerned with comparative legal studies. While the dynamics of this theory would of course be different within systems operating under disparate governmental structures, most democratic countries maintain an independent judiciary that nonetheless influences, and is in turn influenced by, its relationship with the elected branches. For example, the Supreme Court of Canada decision in *R. v. Morgentaler*, often referred to as the "Canadian *Roe v. Wade*," that struck down that country's abortion law in 1988 was quickly followed by the passage of a bill to recriminalize the procedure in the House of Commons, only to fail in a tie vote in the Senate (Richer 2008). Indeed, the abortion debate in Canada has had much in common with the American experience, including subsequent Supreme Court and provincial High Court rulings clarifying the legal status of reproductive rights (see *Tremblay v. Daigle* [1989], *Winnipeg Child and Family Services v. [G.] D.F.* [1997], and *Morgentaler v. New Brunswick* [2008]; *inter alia*) and the passage of clinic obstruction laws (see Access to Abortion Services Act R.S.B.C. 1996 c. 1). Beyond the potential such future research would have for better understanding the policy making role of courts in foreign contexts, a clearer picture of how methodological tools such as frame analysis, historical-institutionalism, and Law and APD may also emerge.

Returning the question posed at the outset of this investigation, it is clear that the role of the courts in resolving important policy questions will differ depending on both the configuration of certain key political and legal factors, as well as the timing of institutional involvement. By the same token, whether a controversy plays out within the judicial rather than legislative or executive branches will have major implications for specific issue areas going forward. A significant policy change resulting from a court decision will influence how further alterations to that policy take place, as well as the strategies employed by interest groups and activists on both sides. To use the abortion question again as an example of this, efforts to expand or curtail reproductive rights following the *Roe* decision have often revolved around the understandings articulated in that ruling and have almost always found their way to state or federal court. In the case of abortion policy making in New York and New Jersey specifically, the foregoing case studies demonstrate that policy change occurs in a markedly different manner when it is undertaken by judges rather than legislators. In the federal *Farmer* case, for instance, the Third Circuit Court of Appeals struck down the state's late-term abortion ban as unconstitutionally overbroad. As the legislature was considering the bill, however, it could have narrowed the language of the statute, as suggested by Governor Whitman, to include only the D&X procedure. The point, in any case, is that policy change occurring in a court setting is often zero sum—either a statute is constitutionally valid or it is not—while lawmakers have much more latitude in including or excluding specific provisions or otherwise tailoring laws in ways that may not be available to courts.[5] In this sense, decisions taken by judges are often qualitatively different than those made by legislators, and understanding when and under what circumstances courts create policy is of significant empirical, as well as normative, importance.

What, then, leads courts to play a more or less active role in policy development? According to the theoretical framework proposed here, a combination of institutional first movement, the internal and external dialogue within courts and between judges and elected officials, and the ideas and norms, or, to use Brandwein's (2006) term, discursive formations, which are inherent to institutional mandates will meaningfully influence that role. When policy change, whether in a novel issue area or following a long period of inactivity, is first initiated by the courts, that issue going forward will tend to be understood in legal terms, as it is this rhetorical framework that is indigenous to the judiciary. As a consequence, further changes will tend to be located in the courts as these are viewed as the proper institutional venue for debate. Conversely, the "cognitive frameworks" inherent to the elected branches will tend to become dominant if these institutions initiate policy change and the courts will be inclined to adopt these norms as well, reducing the likelihood that they will alter the choices made by the legislature. This combination of path dependent processes and some of the more recent scholarship from the Law and APD field seems to be borne out in the case studies of abortion policy making presented in this work. What emerges from this analysis is a starkly different role for the New York Court of Appeals and the New Jersey Supreme Court, with the latter frequently weighing in on the question while the former consistently deferred to its elected counterparts. Having eliminated other potentially explanatory mechanisms that may have accounted for this difference, thoroughly analyzed the order of institutional involvement, and considered the relevant historical and legal documents, the theoretical approach proposed here would seem to offer the best account for the behavior observed in these cases.

Further testing and refinement of the model presented in this work would of course add considerably to the robustness of its conclusions. This, however, as they say, is a feature, not a bug. The questions and implications that follow from this study provide the potential for a rich research agenda going forward. Much work remains to be done in the relatively nascent field, at least in its current incarnation, of Law and APD, and this investigation seeks to add theoretical and methodological tools to the endeavor. It had also been the aim here to help bridge some of the divides that remain between the historical-institutionalist, APD, and positivists schools. Such a pluralist approach is too often neglected by scholars who, as Brandwein (2011) writes, often "talk past each other." The story of abortion policy development in New York and New Jersey can tell us much both about how this question can, and has been, treated by courts at the state level while also informing larger concerns regarding how judges deal with important policy questions and what approaches may yield the most complete answers to these inquiries.

NOTES

1. It is worth noting that both Hawaii and Washington had also liberalized their abortion statutes before 1973 and the courts in those states seem to have played a similarly passive role.
2. The precise form that such a challenge might have taken, however, is not clear. While Planned Parenthood had stated publicly that they would seek an injunction against the consent law if it had been enacted, whether this suit would have been brought in federal or state court was not mentioned. If the former route had been chosen, it may have represented an even more significant event in the development of abortion policy in New York as virtually all of the litigation in that case took place in state courts.
3. One notable exception to this is Skocpol's (1999) study of membership groups during the twentieth century.
4. Litigation involving state laws that mandated parental involvement being one particularly salient example of this.
5. This is not to suggest that judges have no leeway to narrow or selectively limit the impact of their holdings, particularly in the case of statutory interpretation, simply that this latitude is greater for legislators.

Bibliography

Abortion. 2012. "Abortion In American Law: The Nineteenth Century." Law Library—American Law and Legal Information. Accessed March 23, 2012. http://law.jrank.org/pages/446/Abortion-Abortion-in-American-law-nineteenth-century.html.

Abramowitz, Alan A. 2001. "'Mr. Mayhew, Meet Mr. Delay,' or the Electoral Connection in the Post-Reform Congress." *PS: Political Science and Politics*. 34(2): 257-258.

Abramowitz, Alan I., and Kyle L. Saunders. 1998. "Ideological Realignment in the U.S. Electorate." *Journal of Politics* 60 (3): 634–52.

Acharya, Amitav. 2004. "How Ideas Spread: Whose Norms Matter? Norm Localization and Institutional Change in Asian Regionalism." *International Organization* 58 (2): 239–275.

American Judicature Society. 2013. "Methods of Judicial Selection." Accessed Nov. 4, 2013. http://judicialselection.us/judicial_selection/methods/selection_of_judges.cfm?state=.

Andelman, David. 1974. "State Senate Votes Death Penalty Bill, More Limited One Than Assembly's." *New York Times*. May 1, 1974.

Apple, R.W., Jr. 1965a. "Surprise Action." *New York Times*. June 2, 1965.

———. 1965b. "Zaretzki Pledges Vote." *New York Times*. February 25, 1965.

Baker, Al. 2004. "Effort to Reinstate Death Penalty Law Is Stalled in Albany." *New York Times*. November 18, 2004.

Baker, Al; Raymond Hernandez. 2005. "Both Parties Attack Pataki's Stand on Morning-After Pill." *New York Times*. August 2, 2005.

Balkin, Jack M. 2005. "Plessy, Brown, and Grutter: A Play in Three Acts." Faculty Scholarship Series. Paper 237.

Barnum, David G. 1985. "The Supreme Court and Public Opinion: Judicial Decision Making in the Post-New Deal Period," *Journal of Politics* 47 (2): 652–66.

Barry, Michael. 1981. "Death Penalty: Its Prospects Have Improved." *New York Times*. April 5, 1981.

Bebout, John E.; Joseph Harrison. 1968. "The Working of the New Jersey Constitution of 1947." 10 *Wm. & Mary L. Rev*. 337.

Bell, Stephen. 2012. "Where are the Institutions? The Limits of Vivien Schmidt's Constructivism." *British Journal of Political Science*. 42 (3): 714–719.

Bemidji Pioneer. 1973b. "Legislators Will Wait to Act on Abortion Ruling." *The Pioneer*. January 26, 1973.

Bemidji Pioneer. 1973a. "State House Urges Abortion Ban." *The Pioneer*. April 13, 1973.

Bennett, James. 1993. "Council Considers Penalties for Abortion Clinic Violence." *New York Times*. April 22, 1993.

Bernstein, Andrea. 2012. "NJ Has Fastest Growing Commuter Counties." *WNYC*. March 22, 2012.

Buelow, Michael C. 1995. "State's Abortion Bill Too Limiting: Critics." *Sheboygan Press*. October 2, 1995.
Bird, David. 1977b. "Death Penalty Bill Is Vetoed by Carey." *New York Times*. July 3, 1977.
Bird, David. 1977a. "State Senate in Albany Approves Measure Broadening Coverage of the Death Penalty." *New York Times*. June 15, 1977.
Blomberg, Thomas G.; Karol Lucken. 2000. *American Penology: A History of Control*. Aldine Transaction.
Bobbitt, Phillip. 1982. *Constitutional Fate: Theory of the Constitution*. New York: Oxford University Press.
Bonventre, Vincent M. 1992. "State Constitutional Adjudication at the Court of Appeals, 1990 and 1991: Retrenchment Is the Rule." 56 *Ala. L. Rev*. 119, 121–23.
Bonventre, Vincent M.; John D. Powell. 1994. "Changing Course at the High Court." *Empire St. Rep*. 55 55–57.
Bower, Anne. 1996. "Bill Baird: The 30 Year Crusade: Conversations, Clippings and Remembrances." *The Body Politic* 6 (3): 10
Boylan, Michael J. 1973. "Suit Demands State Permit Abortions Under Medicaid: No Claims Refused Two Named in Suit." *New York Times*. June 27, 1973.
Brace, Paul R.; Melinda Gann Hall. 1997. "The Interplay of Preferences, Case Facts, Context, and Rules in the Politics of Judicial Choice." *The Journal of Politics* 59 (4): 1206–1231.
Brace, Paul; Kellie Sims-Butler; Kevin Arceneaux; Martin Johnson. 2002. "Public Opinion in the American States: New Perspectives Using National Survey Data." *American Journal of Political Science* 46 (1): 173–189.
Brace, Paul; Kevin Arceneaux; Martin Johnson; Stacy G. Ulbig. 2004. "Does State Political Ideology Change over Time?" *Political Research Quarterly* 57 (4): 529–540.
Brace, Paul; Laura Langer; Melinda Gann Hall. 2000. "Measuring the Preferences of State Supreme Court Judges." *The Journal of Politics* 62 (2): 387–413.
Brace, Paul; Melinda Gann Hall. 1995. "Studying Courts Comparatively: The View from the American States." *Political Research Quarterly* 48 (1): 5–29.
Brandt, Steve. 1978. "Perpich Signs Abortion Fund Cut." *Star Tribune*. March 22, 1978.
Brandwein, Pamela. 2006. "Studying the Careers of Knowledge Claims: Bringing Science Studies to Legal Studies." In *Interpretation & Method: Empirical Research Methods and the Interpretive Turn*, edited by Dvora Yanow and Peregrine Schwartz-Shea, 228–243. New York: M. E. Sharpe.
———. 2011. "Law and American Political Development." *Annual Review of Law Social Science* 7: 187–216.
Broscheid, Andreas. 2011. "Comparing Circuits: Are Some U.S. Courts of Appeals More Liberal or Conservative Than Others?" *Law and Society Review* 45 (1): 171–194.
Brozan, Nadine. 1991. "Court Allows Clinic Advice on Abortion: Court Delays Federal Ban on Abortion Counseling." *New York Times*. July 26, 1991.
Buckley, Tom. 1973. "Both Sides Gird for Battle on Abortion." *New York Times*. January 3, 1973.
Buelow, Michael C. 1995. "State's Abortion Bill too Limiting: Critics." *Sheboygan Press*. October 2, 1995.
Burns, Gene. 2005. *The Moral Veto: Framing Contraception, Abortion, and Cultural Pluralism in the United States*. London: Cambridge University Press.
Campbell, John L. 2002. "Ideas, Politics, and Public Policy." *Annual Review of Sociology* 28: 21–38.
Capoccia, Giovanni; R. Daniel Kelemen. 2007. "The Study of Critical Junctures: Theory, Narrative, and Counterfactuals in Historical Institutionalism." *World Politics* 59 (3): 341–369.
Carey, Hugh. 1976. "Governor's Memoranda on Bills Vetoed." *New York State Legislative Annuals—1976*.
Carmines, Edward G., and James Woods. 2002. "The Role of Party Activists in the Evolution of the Abortion Issue." *Political Behavior*, 24(4): Special Issue: Parties and Partisanship, Part Three. 361–377.

Carroll, Maurice. 1985. "Abortion-Clinic Case Is Lost by Albany Catholic Diocese." *New York Times*. December 18, 1985.
Cerra, Frances. 1978. "Suffolk Legislature Votes to End Medicaid Abortions." *New York Times*. March 1, 1978.
Charnley, Blair. 1977. "Abortion Foes Plan Drive for Anti-Funding Law." *Minneapolis Star*. July 16, 1977.
Clarity, James F. 1968. "Governor Backs Report Urging Major Abortion Law Reforms." *New York Times*. March 31, 1968.
Clark, Tom S. 2009. "The Separation of Powers, Court Curbing, and Judicial Legitimacy." *American Journal of Political Science* 53 (4): 971–989.
Clines, Francis X. 1974. "Wilson Criticized on Abortion Issue." *New York Times*. September 20, 1974.
Clinton, Robert Lowry. 1994. "Game Theory, Legal History, and the Origins of Judicial Review: A Revisionist Analysis of Marbury v. Madison." *American Journal of Political Science* 38 (2): 285–302.
Collier, David. 2011. "Understanding Process Tracing." *PS: Political Science and Politics* 44 (4): 823–830.
Cunningham, Bradley E. 2001. "Implications of FDA Approval of RU-486: Regulating Mifepristone Within the Bounds of the Constitution." *Kentucky Law Journal* 90: 229.
Dahl, Robert A. 1957. "Decision-Making in a Democracy: The Supreme Court as a National Policy-Maker." *J. of Pub L.* 6: 279.
Dao, James. 1995a. "A Vow Fulfilled: Law Takes Effect Sept. 1—Its Foes Promise a Court Challenge Pataki Signs Bill Restoring Death Penalty After 18 Years." *New York Times*. March 8, 1995.
———. 1995b. "New York Senate Approves Revival of Death Penalty." *New York Times*. March 7, 1995.
———. 1994. "Pataki's Abortion Stance Draws Fire From Both Sides." *New York Times*. June 4, 1994.
Davis, Alvin; Don Wycliff. 1979a. "The Region: In Summary Gibson and Council In a Showdown Over Extra Police N.J. Would Tighten." *New York Times*. November 18, 1979.
Davis, Alvin; Don Wycliff. 1979b. "The Region: In Summary Koch Identifies His Targets for Hospital Closings N.J. Tightens Abortion." *New York Times*. June 17, 1979.
Dellapenna, Joseph W. 2006. *Dispelling the Myths of Abortion History*. Durham, NC: Carolina Academic Press.
Dionne, E. J., Jr. 1979a. "Albany Deadlocked on Abortion Funds." *New York Times*. April 3, 1979.
———. 1979b. "State Budget Voted as Albany Approves Aid for Abortions: Action on $12.6 Billion Spending Follows Meeting by Anderson With Fellow Republicans Local Assistance Budget Albany Reaches Abortion Pact; Budget Is Passed Brooklyn Hospital Bill Pay Checks Delayed." *New York Times*. April 6, 1979.
Doyle, Sir Arthur Conan. 1890. *The Sign of the Four*. Spencer Blackett.
Druckman, James N. 2001. "The Implications of Framing Effects for Citizen Competence." *Political Behavior* 23 (3): 225–56.
Dudziak, Mary L. 2004. "Brown as a Cold War Case." *The Journal of American History* 91 (1): 32–42.
Dullea, Georgia. 1976. "Teen-age Abortions Without Family Consent Hang in the Balance." *New York Times*. June 22, 1976.
Dworkin, Ronald. 1982. "The Politics of Interpretation." *Critical Inquiry* 9 (1): 179–200.
Emmert, Craig F.; Traut, Carol Ann. 1992. "State Supreme Courts, State Constitutions, and Judicial Policymaking." *Justice System Journal*. 16 (1): 16–37.
Empire Center. 2012. "Legislative Salaries per State." *Empire Center for New York State Policy*. Accessed 1 July, 2013. https://www.empirecenter.org/publications/legislative-salaries-per-state/.
Epstein, David; Sharyn O'Halloran. 1996. "Divided Government and the Design of Administrative Procedures: A Formal Model and Empirical Test." *The Journal of Politics* 58 (2): 373–397.

Epstein, Lee; Jack Knight. 1998. *The Choices Justices Make*. Washington, DC: CQ Press.

Epstein, Lee, Jack Knight; Andrew D. Martin. 2001. "The Supreme Court as a Strategic National Policy Maker." *Emory Law Review*. 50 (2): 583–612.

Erikson, Robert S.; Gerald C. Wright; John P. McIver. 2007. "Measuring the Public's Ideological Preferences in the 50 States: Survey Responses versus Roll Call Data." *State Politics & Policy Quarterly* 7 (2): 141–151.

Ertelt, Steven. 2007. "New Jersey Assembly Forces Pharmacists to Fill Morning After Pill Orders." *LifeNews.org*. June 13, 2007.

Eskridge, William N., Jr. 1991. "Reneging on History? Playing the Court/Congress/President Civil Rights Game." *California Law Rev* 79: 613.

Evening Tribune. 1978. "Abortion Bill up to Perpich." *Sunday Tribune*. March 19, 1978.

Farrell, William E. 1972a. "Assembly Votes to Repeal Liberalized Abortion Law." *New York Times*. May 10, 1972.

Farrell, William E. 1972b. "High-Ranking State Legislators Facing Challenges in Primaries." *New York Times*. June 14, 1972.

Felzenberg, Alvin S. 2006. *Governor Tom Kean: From the New Jersey Statehouse to the 9-11 Commission*. New Brunswick, NJ: Rutgers University Press.

Fenno, Richard F., Jr. 1978. *Home Style: House Members in Their Districts*. Boston: Little, Brown.

Flemming, Gregory N.; David B. Holian; Susan G. Mezey. 1998. "An Integrated Model of Privacy Decision Making in State Supreme Courts." *American Politics Quarterly* 26 (1) 35–58.

Flemming, Roy B.; B. Dan Wood. 1997. "The Public and the Supreme Court: Individual Justice Responsiveness to American Policy Moods," *American Journal of Political Science* 41 (2): 468–98.

Frymer, Paul. 2008. "Law and American Political Development." *Law & Social Inquiry* 33 (3): 779–803.

Funston, Richard. 1975. "The Supreme Court and Critical Elections." *The American Political Science Review* 69 (3): 795–811.

Gallup. 2016. "State of the States." Gallup, Inc. Accessed July 25, 2017. http://www.gallup.com/poll/125066/State-States.aspx.

Gallup. 2010. "State of the States." Accessed July 1, 2013. http://www.gallup.com/poll/125066/State-States.aspx.

Gallup. 2013a. "Guns." Accessed September 3, 2013. http://news.gallup.com/poll/1645/guns.aspx.

Gallup. 2013b. "Death Penalty." Accessed September 3, 2013. http://news.gallup.com/poll/1606/death-penalty.aspx.

Gamson, William A. 2001. "Foreword." In *Framing Public Life: Perspectives on Media and Our Understanding of the Social World*, edited by Stephen D. Reese, Oscar H. Gandy, Jr., and August E. Grant, ix-xi. London: Lawrence Erlbaum.

Gargan, Edward A. 1983. "Assembly Passes Death Penalty Bill." *New York Times*. March 1, 1983.

Gaylord, Thomas Wayne. 1994. "The Scope of Abortion Rights Since Roe v. Wade and the Next Tier: The Right to Access." *Honors Projects*. Paper 24.

Gerring, John. 2007. *Case Study Research: Principles and Practices*. Cambridge, MA: Cambridge University Press.

Gillman, Howard. 1993. *The Constitution Besieged: The Rise & Demise of Lochner Era Police Powers Jurisprudence*. Durham, NC: Duke University Press.

———. 1999. "The Court as an Idea, Not a Building (or a Game): Interpretive Institutionalism and the Analysis of Supreme Court Decision-Making." In *Supreme Court Decision-Making: New Institutionalist Approaches*, edited by Cornell W. Clayton and Howard Gillman. Chicago & London: University of Chicago Press, 65–87.

———. 2002. "How Political Parties Can Use the Courts to Advance Their Agendas: Federal Courts in the United States, 1875–1891." *American Political Science Review* 96 (3): 511–24.

———. 2006. "Political Parties and Constitutional Change: The Political Origins of Liberal Judicial Activism." In *The Supreme Court & American Political Development*, edited by Ronald Kahn and Ken I. Kersch. Lawrence, KS: University of Kansas Press, 138–168.

Ginsberg, Thomas. 1997. "Assembly Overrides Abortion Ban Veto After An Earlier Setback, A N.J. Bill Banning 'partial-birth' Abortions Moved Closer To Passage." *Philadelphia Enquirer*. December 5, 1997.

Glaeser, Edward L.; Matt Resseger; Kristina Tobio. 2008. "Urban Inequality." Working Paper. *Harvard Kennedy School, Taubman Center for State and Local Government*.

Glendon, Mary Ann. 1991. *Rights Talk: The Impoverishment of Political Discourse*. New York: The Free Press.

Gober, Patricia. 1994. "Why Abortion Rates Vary: A Geographical Examination of the Supply of and Demand for Abortion Services in the United States in 1988." *Annals of the Association of American Geographers* 84 (2): 230–250.

Gold, R. B., and E. Nash. 2007. "State Abortion Counseling Policies and the Fundamental Principles of Informed Consent." *Guttmacher Policy Review*, 10(4), 6-13.

Goldman, Sheldon. 1975. "Voting Behavior on the United States Courts of Appeals Revisited." *The American Political Science Review* 69 (2): 491–506.

Goodnough, Abby. 1998. "Abortion Bill Is Dropped in About-Face by Silver." *New York Times*. May 21, 1998.

Goodnough, Abby. 1997. "Somerset Lawyer Is Chosen to Defend New Jersey's Late-Term Abortion Law." *New York Times*. December 24, 1997.

Gorski, Ashley. 2009. "The Author of Her Trouble: Abortion Nineteenth- and Early-Twentieth Century Judicial Discourses." *Harv. J.L. & Gender* 32: 431.

Graber, Mark A. 1993. "The Non-Majoritarian Problem: Legislative Deference to the Judiciary." *Studies in American Political Development* 7: 35.

———. 2006. "Legal, Strategic or Legal Strategy: Deciding to Decide during the Civil War and Reconstruction." In *The Supreme Court & American Political Development*, edited by Ronald Kahn and Ken I. Kersch. Lawrence: University of Kansas Press, 33–66.

———. 1999. *Rethinking Abortion: Equal Choice, the Constitution, and Reproductive Politics*. Princeton, NJ: Princeton University Press.

Grafstein, Robert. 1997. "Thick Rationality and the Missing 'Brute Fact': The Limits of Rationalist Incorporations of Norms and Ideas." *The Journal of Politics* 59 (4): 1040–1047.

Gray, Jerry. 1991. "Bill Shields Abortion Clinics From Protests." *New York Times*. December 23, 1991.

Gray, Jerry. 1992. "Florio Defends Gun Control." *New York Times*. August 20, 1992.

Gray, Jerry. 1992. "Voters Approve Broader Use of the Death Penalty." *New York Times*. November 4, 1992.

Greenhouse, Linda. 1976. "No Chance Is Seen of Overriding Carey's Veto of Abortion Bill." *New York Times*. June 24, 1976.

Greenhouse, Linda; Reva B. Siegel. 2012. *Before Roe v. Wade: Voices that Shaped the Abortion Debate Before the Supreme Court's Ruling*. New Haven, CT: Yale Law School.

Greif, Avner. 1994. "Cultural Beliefs and the Organization of Society: A Historical and Theoretical Reflection on Collectivist and Individual Societies." *Journal of Political Economy* 102 (5): 912–950.

Gross, Jane. 1987. "Pregnancy Centers: Anti-Abortion Role Challenged: Pregnancy Centers: Anti-Abortion Efforts at Center of Controversy." *New York Times*. January 23, 1987.

Guiraudon, Virginie. 2000. "European Courts and Foreigners' Rights: A Comparative Study of Norms Diffusion." *International Migration Review* 34 (4): 1088–1125.

Gutis, Philip S. 1989. "Albany Pact on Prenatal Care Excludes Abortion." *New York Times*. June 30, 1989.

Guttmacher Institute. 2012. "State Policies in Brief: State Funding of Abortion Under Medicaid." September 1, 2012. Accessed September 29, 2012. https://www.guttmacher.org/state-policy/explore/state-funding-abortion-under-medicaid.

Guttmacher Institute. 2013. "State Policies in Brief: An Overview of Abortion Laws." 6 June 2013. Accessed 25 June 2013. https://www.guttmacher.org/state-policy/explore/overview-abortion-laws.

Habel, Philip D. 2008. "The Consequences of Electoral Institutions for Careerism." *Legislative Studies Quarterly* 33 (3): 471–494.

Habermas, Jürgen. 1988. "Law as Medium and Law as Institution." In *Dilemmas of Law in the Welfare State*, edited by Gunther Teubner, 203–220. Berlin: Walter De Gruyter & Co.

Hacker, Jacob S. 2002. *The Divided Welfare State: The Battle Over Public and Private Social Benefits in the United States*. New York: Cambridge University Press.

Haider-Markel, Donald P.; Kenneth J. Meier. 2003. "Legislative Victory, Electoral Uncertainty: Explaining Outcomes in the Battles over Lesbian and Gay Civil Rights." *Review of Policy Research* 20 (4): 671–90.

Hall, Melinda Gann. 1987. "Constituent Influence in State Supreme Courts: Conceptual Notes and a Case Study." *The Journal of Politics*. 49 (4): 1117–1124.

Hall, Melinda Gann. 2007. "Voting in State Supreme Court Elections: Competition and Context as Democratic Incentives." *The Journal of Politics* 69 (4): 1147–1159.

Hall, Melinda Gann; Paul Brace. 1992. "Toward an Integrated Model of Judicial Voting Behavior." *American Politics Quarterly* 20 (2): 147–68.

Hanley, Robert. 2000. "Assembly Moves to Restore Parental Notification of Abortion." *New York Times*. November 21, 2000.

Harris, Gardiner. 2009. "FDA Easing Access to 'Morning After' Pill." *New York Times*. April 22, 2009.

Hathaway, Oona A. 2001. "Path Dependence in the Law: The Course and Pattern of Change in a Common Law Legal System." *Iowa Law Review* 86: 1.

Hawking, Stephen. 1988. *A Brief History of Time*. New York: Bantam Dell Publishing Group.

Hays, Constance L. 1990. "Suit Seeks New Abortion Protection." *New York Times*. April 24, 1990.

Henshaw, S.K.; T.J. Joyce; A. Dennis; L.B. Finer; K. Blanchard. 2009. *Restrictions on Medicaid Funding for Abortions: A Literature Review*. New York: Guttmacher Institute.

Herman, Robin. 1981a. "Budget Is Passed in Albany, 42 Days Late: Tax Rebates to Resume." *New York Times*. May 13, 1981.

Herman, Robin. 1981b. "Assembly Backs Funds for Abortions." *New York Times*. April 3, 1981.

Hernandez, Raymond; Al Baker. 2005. "Pataki Will Veto New Rule on Pill." *New York Times*. August 1, 2005.

Hernandez, Raymond. 1996. "Assembly May Debate a Measure on Abortion." *New York Times*. December 13, 1996.

Howell, William G. 2003. *Power Without Persuasion: The Politics of Direct Presidential Action*. Princeton, NJ: Princeton University Press.

Hu, Winnie. 1999. "New Jersey's New Abortion Law Regarding Minors Is Blocked." *New York Times*. September 26, 1999.

Huber, John D.; Charles R. Shipan; Madelaine Pfahler. 2001. "Legislatures and Statutory Control of Bureaucracy." *American Journal of Political Science* 45 (2): 330–345.

Jacoby, William G. 2000. "Issue Framing and Public Opinion on Government Spending." *American Journal of Political Science* 44 (4): 750–767.

Jalsevac, John. 2007. "No Freedom of Conscience for Pharmacists Says Bill Passed by New Jersey Legislature." *LifeSiteNews*. June 12, 2007.

Jones, Jeffrey M. 2013. "Same-Sex Marriage Support Solidifies Above 50% in U.S." Gallup Politics. Accessed May 13, 2013. http://news.gallup.com/poll/162398/sex-marriage-support-solidifies-above.aspx

Jones-Correa, Michael. 2000–2001. "The Origins and Diffusion of Racial Restrictive Covenants." *Political Science Quarterly* 115 (4): 541–568.

Kaheny, Erin B.; Susan Brodie Haire; Sara C. Benesh. 2008. "Change Over Tenure: Voting, Variance, and Decision Making on the US Courts of Appeals." *American Journal of Political Science* 52 (3): 490–503.

Kahn, Ronald. 2006. "Social Construction, Supreme Court Reversals, and American Political Development: *Lochner*, *Plessy*, *Bowers*, but Not *Roe*." In *The Supreme Court & American Political Development*, edited by Ronald Kahn and Ken I. Kersch. Lawrence: University of Kansas Press, 67–113.

Kahn, Ronald; Ken I. Kersch. 2006. "Introduction." In *The Supreme Court & American Political Development*, Edited by Ronald Kahn and Ken I. Kersch. Lawrence: University of Kansas Press, 1–30.

Karl, Terry. 1997. *The Paradox of Plenty: Oil Booms and Petro-States*. Berkeley: University of California Press.

Kasindorf, Jeanie. 1989. "Abortion in New York." *New York Magazine*. September 18, 1989.

Katzenstein, Peter. 1996. "Introduction: Alternative Perspective on International Security." In *The Culture of National Security: Norms and Identity in World Politics*, edited by Peter Katzenstein, 1–32. New York: Columbia University Press.

Keck, Thomas M. 2004. *The Most Activist Supreme Court in History: The Road to Modern Judicial Conservatism*. Chicago and London: University of Chicago Press.

Keck, Thomas M. 2006. "From *Bakke* to *Grutter*: The Rise of Rights-Based Conservatism." In *The Supreme Court & American Political Development*, edited by Ronald Kahn and Ken I. Kersch. Lawrence: University of Kansas Press, 414–442.

Kerr, Peter. 1989. "Kean Urges Ending 'No Fault' Car Insurance." *New York Times*. January 11, 1989.

King, Wayne. 1992. "Assembly Passes Bills Supporting Executions." *New York Times*. May 1, 1992.

Kingdon, John. 1973. *Congressmen's Voting Decisions*. New York: Harper & Row.

Knowles, Clayton. 1970. "Each Party Registers Gain of Seat in a House." *New York Times*. November 4, 1970.

Kocieniewski, David. 1999a. "Abortion-Rights Groups Surprised by Whitman." *New York Times*. June 15, 1999.

———. 1999b. "Whitman Quietly Signs Bill Limiting Teen-Age Abortions." *New York Times*. June 29, 1999.

Kolbert, Elizabeth. 1989. "In Albany, the Line Against The Death Penalty Falls Back." *New York Times*. March 5, 1989.

Kovach, Bill. 1970a. "Primaries May Decide Control of Legislature." *New York Times*. June 19, 1970.

———.1970b "Abortion Reform Approved, 31–26, by State Senate." *New York Times*. March 19, 1970.

———. 1970c. "Abortion Reform is Voted by the Assembly, 76 to 73; Final Approval Expected." *New York Times*. April 10, 1970.

Lawless, R. M.; D. L. Murray. 1997. "An Empirical Analysis of Bankruptcy Certiorari." *Missouri Law Review* 62: 101–134.

Lawrence, C. R., III. 1995. "The Epidemiology of Color-Blindness: Learning to Think and Talk About Race, Again." *Boston College Third World Law Journal*, 15(1): 1-18

Legge, Jerome S., Jr. 1983. "The Determinants of Attitudes toward Abortion in the American Electorate." *Western Political Quarterly* 36:479-90.

Lehne, Richard; John Reynolds. 1978. "The Impact of Judicial Activism on Public Opinion." *American Journal of Political Science* 22 (4): 896–904.

Lentol, Robert; Helene Weinstein; Jeffrion Aubry. 2005. "The Death Penalty in New York." Report, New York State Assembly, April 3, 2005.

Levi, Margaret. 1997. "A Model, a Method, and a Map: Rational Choice in Comparative and Historical Analysis." In *Comparative Politics: Rationality, Culture, and Structure*, edited by Mark I. Lichbach and Alan S. Zuckerman. Cambridge: Cambridge University Press, 19–41.

Levy, Clifford J. 1996. "Albany Senate Backs Ban On Late-Term Abortions: But Bill Has Little Chance to Become Law." *New York Times*. May 1, 1996.

Levy, Clifford J. 1999 "With Senate Gone, Albany Has a Deal." *New York Times*. August 6, 1999.

Lewin, Tamar. 1988 "U.S. Abortion Rule is Upheld by Judge: Decision on Federal Funds for Health Clinics Conflicts With 2 Other Rulings." *New York Times*. July 2, 1988.

Lieberman, Robert C. 2002. "Ideas, Institutions, and Political Order: Explaining Political Change." *American Political Science Review* 96 (4): 697–712.

Llewellyn, Karl N. 1934. "The Constitution as an Institution." *Columbia Law Review* 34 (1): 1–40.

Lovell, George I. 2003. *Legislative Deferrals: Statutory Ambiguity, Judicial Power, and American Democracy*. Cambridge, MA: Cambridge University Press.

Madison, James. 1788. "The Federalist 51: The Structure of the Government Must Furnish the Proper Checks and Balances Between the Different Departments." Library of Congress. February 8, 1788. Accessed Nov. 1, 2013. https://www.congress.gov/resources/display/content/The+Federalist+Papers.

Maeder, Jay. 2001. "Repealing the Abortion Law." *Daily News* (New York). July 10, 2001.

Maestas, Cherie. 2000. "Professional Legislatures and Ambitious Politicians: Policy Responsiveness of State Institutions." *Legislative Studies Quarterly* 25 (4): 663–690.

Mahoney, James. 2000. "Path Dependence in Historical Sociology." *Theory and Society* 29 (4): 507–548.

Maioni, Antonia. 1998. *Parting at the Crossroads: The Emergence of Health Insurance in the United States and Canada*. Princeton: Princeton University Press.

Maltzman, Forrest; James F. Spriggs II; Paul J. Wahlbeck. 2000. *Crafting Law on the Supreme Court: The Collegial Game*. Cambridge, MA: Cambridge University Press.

Mansnerus, Laura. 2001. "Push Resumes for Notifying Parents of Abortions." *New York Times*. December 18, 2001.

Matern, Camille. 1996. "Abortion and Politics in WA State." Feminist Women's Health Center. Accessed April 3, 2012. http://www.fwhc.org/abortion/camille.htm.

Mauro, Frank J. "Understanding and Evaluating the New York State Legislature's Proposed Budget Process Constitutional Amendments." Accessed July 27, 2012. http://www.fiscalpolicy.org/FrankMauro~BudgetProcessConstitutionalAmendments.pdf.

Mayhew, David R. 1974. *Congress: The Electoral Connection*. Yale University Press: Princeton, NJ.

McCann, Michael W. 1994. *Rights at Work: Pay Equity Reform and the Politics of Legal Mobilization*. Chicago: University of Chicago Press.

McCloskey, Robert G. 2010. *The American Supreme Court*. Chicago: The University of Chicago Press.

McCrone, Donald J.; James H. Kuklinski. 1979. "The Delegate Theory of Representation." *American Journal of Political Science* 23 (May): 278–300.

McKinley, James C., Jr. 2001. "Family Fined in First Ruling Based on State Abortion Clinic Access Law." *New York Times*. August 28, 2001.

Means, Cyril C. 1968. "The Law of New York Concerning Abortion and the Status of the Foetus, 1664–1968: A Case of Cessation Constitutionality" 14 *N.Y.L.F.* 411.

Mears, Bill. 2013. "Feds Drop 'Morning-After Pill' Appeal." *CNN Health*. June 11, 2013. Accessed July 29, 2013. http://www.cnn.com/2013/06/10/health/court-birth-control/index.html.

Meislin, Richard J. 1978. "Approval of Budget Is Voted in Albany: Medicaid Abortion Ban Is Defeated After Separation From Bill Final Part of Budget Is Approved After Bill on Abortion Is Defeated." *New York Times*. April 6, 1978.

Melvin, Tessa. 1985. "Decision Awaited on Abortion Clinic." *New York Times*. July 14, 1985.

Miller, Warren E.; Donald E. Stokes. 1963. "Constituency Influence in Congress." *American Political Science Review* 57 (1) 45–56.

Mishler, William; Reginald S. Sheehan. 1993. "The Supreme Court as a Countermajoritarian Institution? The Impact of Public Opinion on Supreme Court Decisions." *American Political Science Review* 87: 87–101.

Moakley, Maureen W. 1986. "Political Parties." In *The Political State of New Jersey*, edited by Gerald M. Pomper. New Brunswick, NJ: Rutgers University Press, 45–66.

Mohr, James C. 1979. *Abortion in America: The Origins and Evolution of National Policy, 1800–1900*. Oxford: Oxford University Press.

Mooney, Christopher Z., and Mei-Hsien Lee. 2000. "The Influence of Values on Consensus and Contentious Morality Policy: U.S. Death Penalty Reform, 1956–82." *The Journal of Politics* 62 (1): 223–39.

Mosher, Dan. 2013. "Abortion Stalemate in Senate." *The Legislative Gazette*. June 17, 2013.

Murphy, Walter. 1964. *Elements of Judicial Strategy*. Chicago: University of Chicago Press.

Myers, Steven Lee. 1993. "Assembly Passes Bill to Outlaw Blockades of Abortion Clinics. *New York Times*. March 23, 1993.
Nackenoff, Carol. 2006. "Constitutionalizing Terms of Inclusion: Friends of the Indian and Citizenship for Native Americans, 1880s–1930s." In *The Supreme Court & American Political Development*, edited by Ronald Kahn and Ken I. Kersch. Lawrence: University of Kansas Press, 366–413.
Nagourney, Adam. 1998. "Pataki Plans Bill to Protect Abortion Clinics From Harassment." *New York Times*. November 20, 1998.
NARAL. 2017. "State Government: Minnesota." Accessed July 17, 2017. https://www.prochoiceamerica.org/state/minnesota/.
Narvaez, Alfonso. 1972a. "Abortion Repeal Passed by Senate, Sent to Governor." *New York Times*. May 11, 1972.
———. 1972b. "Abortion Repeal Urged in Albany." *New York Times*. April 18, 1972.
———. 1974a. "Abortion Curbs Signed by Wilson" *New York Times*. June 16, 1974.
———. 1974b. "Assembly Votes for a Death Penalty Bill." *New York Times*, April 24, 1974.
———. 1982. "Jersey Assembly Votes Death-Penalty Bill, 54–19." *New York Times*. June 22, 1982.
National Center for State Courts. 2013. "State Court Organization." Accessed Nov. 11, 2013. http://www.ncsc.org/sco.
Nelson, Thomas E.; Zoe M. Oxley. 1999. "Issue Framing Effects on Belief Importance and Opinion." *Journal of Politics* 61 (4): 1040–1067.
Neustadt, Richard E. 1991. *Presidential Power and the Modern Presidents*. New York: Free Press.
New Jersey State Democrats. 2006. "Madden/Vitale Bill to Protect Patients' Rights Clears Senate." Press Release. June 26, 2006.
New Jersey. 2007. Office of Legislative Services. *New Jersey Death Penalty Commission Report*. By M. William Howard et al. Trenton: State House Annex, 2007.
New York State Medicaid Program. 2011. "Inpatient Manual Policy Guidelines." December 5, 2011. Accessed September 29, 2012. https://www.emedny.org/ProviderManuals/Inpatient/Pdfs/Inpatient_Policy_Guidelines.pdf.
New York State Unified Court System. 2013. "Lower Appellate Courts." *NYCourts.gov*. March 15, 2013. Accessed Nov. 11, 2013. https://www.nycourts.gov/courts/lowerappeals.shtml.
New York Times. 1972. "Doctor Who Defied Antiabortion Laws Indicted in Bergen." *New York Times*. August 25, 1972.
———.1973a. "Hospitals Ease Abortion Policy: Pickets Fail to Deter Move in Atlantic City." *New York Times*. May 25, 1973.
———.1973b. "Abortions for 2 Blocked by Judge: Court's Order Sanctioning Operations Is Stayed." *New York Times*. June 30, 1973.
———.1974. "A Death Penalty Gaining in Albany." *New York Times*. April 3, 1974.
———.1974a. "Anti-Abortionists Step Up Drive Against Court Ruling: Right to Life Group Seeks Restrictive State Laws and National Amendment - Opposition Also Voices Militancy Unity Is Sought." *New York Times*. August 19, 1974.
———.1974b. "Disputed Measure on Abortion Advances: Forcing the Hands Measure Called Bias." *New York Times*. May 12, 1974.
———. 1975. "Abortion Witness Cites Procedure." *New York Times*. January 18, 1975.
———. 1975a. "Curb on Abortion Voted in Jersey: Legislature Would Restrict Payments by Medicaid." *New York Times*. April 15, 1975.
———.1975b. "Byrne Signs a Medicaid Abortion Curb: Byrne Signs a Bill Curbing Use Of Medicaid Funds in Abortions." *New York Times*. December 19, 1975.
———.1975c. "The ACLU Challenged the Conscience Bill in Court, Though the Trial Court, At Least Upheld It. Bill Proposes Local Votes to Allow Abortion Clinics." *New York Times*. February 11, 1975.
———.1976. "Assembly Revives an Abortion Bill." *New York Times*. June 3, 1976.
———.1979. "The Region: Pinelands Housing Brewery Employees Reach Pact Upstate County Legislators Set Salary." *New York Times*. December 13, 1979.

———. 1985. "Two Films Enter the Debate on Abortion Issue in Albany." *New York Times*. March 15, 1985.
———. 1999. "Parental Approval Law on Abortion Survives Test." *New York Times*. September 24, 1999.
Norman, Michael. 1982. "Discordant Voices on Jersey Death Penalty Bill." *New York Times*. February 27, 1982.
North, Douglass C. 1990. *Institutions, Institutional Change and Economic Performance*. Cambridge, MA: Cambridge University Press.
———. 1994. "Economic Performance Through Time." *The American Economic Review* 84 (3): 359–368.
Nossiff, Rosemary. 2001. *Before Roe: Abortion Policy in the States*. Philadelphia: Temple University Press.
Novkov, Julie. 2011. "Legal Archaeology." *Political Research Quarterly* 64 (2): 348–361.
O'Connor, Debra; Mary Devine. 2000. "Abortion Waiting Period Passes, Goes to Ventura, Governor Won't Say How He'll Act on It." *St. Paul Pioneer Press*. April 11, 2000.
O'Connor, Robert; Michael Berkman. 1995. "The Religious Determinants of State Abortion. Policy." *Social Science Quarterly* 76(2): 447-460.
Oelsner, Lesley. 1972. "Court Voids Jersey Abortion Law." *New York Times*. March 2, 1972.
Orren, Karen. 1991. *Belated Feudalism: Labor, the Law, and Liberal Development in the United States*. Cambridge, MA: Cambridge University Press.
Orren, Karen; Stephen Skowronek. 2004. *The Search for American Political Development*. Cambridge, MA: Cambridge University Press.
Page, Scott E. 2006. "Path Dependence." *Quarterly Journal of Political Science*, 1(1): 87-115.
Parker, Glenn R. 1989. "Looking beyond Reelection: Revising Assumptions about the Factors Motivating Congressional Behavior." *Public Choice* 63 (3): 237–252.
Paul, Christopher. 2008. "US Presidential War Powers: Legacy Chains in Military Intervention Decisionmaking." *Journal of Peace Research* 45 (5): 665–679.
Perez-Pena, Richard. 2000. "'70 Abortion Law: New York Said Yes, Stunning the Nation." *The New York Times*. April 9, 2000.
———.2011. "Christie's Conservatism Is Not Just Economic." *New York Times*. April 17, 2011.
———. 1999. "State Senate Again Passes Ban on a Type of Abortion." *New York Times*. March 25, 1999.
Peters, Jeremy. 2007a. "Corzine Signs Bill Ending Executions, Then Commutes Sentences of 8." *New York Times*. December 18, 2007.
———. 2007b. "New Jersey Moves to End Death Penalty: Taking Aim at a Statute Not Exercised in 45 Years." *New York Times*. November 19, 2007.
———. 2007c. "New Jersey Senator Urges Delay on Repeal of Death Penalty." *New York Times*. November 21, 2007.
Peterson, Iver. 1976. "The Antiabortion Bill is Vetoed by Carey." *New York Times*. June 23, 1976.
Pew Forum. 2008. "U.S. Religious Landscape Survey." The Pew Forum on Religion & Public Life. Accessed Sep. 21, 2015. http://religions.pewforum.org/maps.
Pew Research Center. 2009. "Obama, Catholics and the Notre Dame Commencement." The Pew Forum on Religion & Public Life. April 30, 2009. Accessed Sep. 21, 2015. http://www.pewforum.org/Politics-and-Elections/Obama-Catholics-and-the-Notre-Dame-Commencement.aspx.
Pew Research Center. 2012. "The Complicated Politics of Abortion." Pew Research Center for the People & the Press. Accessed Sep. 21, 2015. April 22, 2012. http://www.people-press.org/2012/08/22/the-complicated-politics-of-abortion/
Phalon, Richard. 1973. "Dismissal of Abortion Cases Foreseen in Bergen: Indictment of Dr. Livingston Cited by Prosecutor." *New York Times*. January 24, 1973.
Phelps, Jordyn. 2016. "Chris Christie Blames His Spokesman for 'Misquote' About Planned Parenthood." ABC News. January 12, 2016.
Pierson, Paul. 2000a. "Increasing Returns, Path Dependence, and the Study of Politics." *The American Political Science Review* 94 (2): 251–267.

———. 2000b. "Not Just What, but When: Timing and Sequence in Political Processes." Studies in American Political Development. 14 (Spring): 72–92.

———. 2004. *Politics in Time: History, Institutions, and Social Analysis*. Princeton, NJ: Princeton University Press.

Pioneer Press. 1992a. "Candidates Speak: Minnesota House of Preresentatives." *St. Paul Pioneer Press*. October 13, 1992.

Pioneer Press. 1992b. "Candidates Speak." *St. Paul Pioneer Press*. August 25, 1992.

Planned Parenthood Affiliates of New Jersey. 2012. "The Consequences: Impact of State Budget Cuts to New Jersey's Women's Health Programs." Accessed November 2, 2012. https://www.plannedparenthoodaction.org/planned-parenthood-action-fund-new-jersey-inc/issues.

Polidata. 2002a. "County-Based Regions and Markets for New Jersey." Accessed July 1, 2013. http://www.polidata.us/pub/maps/rg2000/nj_reg.pdf.

Polidata. 2002b. "County-Based Regions and Markets for New York." Accessed July 1, 2013. http://www.polidata.us/pub/maps/rg2000/ny_reg.pdf.

Pollock, Stewart G. 1982. "State Constitutions as Separate Sources of Fundamental Rights." *Rutgers L Rev*. 35 707.

Preston, Jennifer. 1997a. "New Jersey Assembly Votes To Ban Abortion Procedure." *New York Times*. May 9, 1997.

———.1997b. "Bill Voted in Trenton to Ban Disputed Abortion Method." *New York Times*. June 17, 1997.

———. 1997c. "New Jersey's Senate Overrides Whitman Veto of Abortion Curb: Ban on Type of Late-Term Procedure Is at Issue." *New York Times*. December 16, 1997.

———. 1997d. "Judge Temporarily Blocks State Ban on Some Abortions: A Challenge Based on Imprecise Wording In the Language of the Law." *New York Times*. December 17, 1997.

Purnick, Joyce. 1996. "How Albany Avoids Stand on Abortion." *New York Times*. December 6, 1996.

———. 1980. "Legislators Back Death Penalty." *New York Times*. January 15, 1980.

Price, Richard S., and Thomas M. Keck. 2014. "Movement Litigation and Unilateral Disarmament: Abortion and the Right to Die." *Law and Social Inquiry*, 40(4): 880–907.

Quinnipiac. 2000. "New Jersey Voters Split on Abortion Limits, Quinnipiac University Poll Finds; 3 - 1 Support Parental Notification of Abortion for Minors." Quinnipiac University. December 7, 2000.

Ragin, Charles C. 2000. *Fuzzy-Set Social Science*. Chicago and London: University of Chicago Press.

Reagan Leslie J. 1997. *When Abortion Was a crime: Women, Medicine, and the Law in the United States, 1867-1973*. Berkeley: University of California Press.

Renshaw, Jarrett. 2012. "Gov. Chris Christie Signs $31.7B Budget with Spending Cuts." *New Jersey Star-Ledger*. June 29, 2012.

Richardson, Cynthia Watkins. 2011. "In the Eye of Power: The Notorious Madam Restell." *Khrinokos*. The University of Maine. Accessed March 23, 2012. http://www.library.umaine.edu/khronikos/html/restell/restell.htm.

Richer, Karine. 2008. "Abortion in Canada: Twenty Years After R. v. Morgentaler." *Parliamentary Information and Research Service*. Library of Parliament. September 24, 2008.

Robinson, Douglas. 1965. "Rockefeller Gets Bill on Abolition of Death Penalty" *New York Times*. May 20 1965.

Roh, Jongho, and Donald P. Haider-Markel. 2003. "All Politics is Not Local: National Forces in State Abortion Initiatives." *Social Science Quarterly* 84:15-31.

Rosenberg, Gerald N. 1991. *The Hollow Hope: Can Courts Bring About Social Change?* Chicago: The University of Chicago Press.

Rosenthal, Alan. 1986. "The Legislature." In *The Political State of New Jersey*, edited by Gerald M. Pomper. New Brunswick, NJ: Rutgers University Press, 118–159.

———. 2001. *The Third House: Lobbyists and Lobbying in the States*. Washington, DC: CQ Press.

Rosenthal, Cindy Simon. 1995. "New Party or Campaign Bank Account? Explaining the Rise of State Legislative Campaign Committees." *Legislative Studies Quarterly* 20: 249-68.

Roux, Theunis. 2009. "Principle and Pragmatism on the Constitutional Court of South Africa." *International Journal of Constitutional Law* 7 (1): 106–138.
Rule, Sheila. 1978. "Albany Leaders Favor Retention of Medicaid-Financed Abortions." *New York Times*. January 31, 1978.
Russo, John. 1976. "Death Penalty Is Favored." *New York Times*. August 8, 1976.
Salmore, Barbara G.; Stephen A. Salmore. 1998. *New Jersey Politics: Suburban Politics Comes of Age*. Lincoln & London: University of Nebraska Press.
———. 2008. *New Jersey Politics and Government: The Suburbs Come of Age*. New Brunswick, New Jersey & London: Rivergate Books.
Santi, Angela Delli. 2010. "NJ Senate Fails to Override Family Planning Veto." *Associated Press State and Local Wire*. September 20, 2010.
Santora, Mark. 2004. "'Morning-After' Pill May Be Sold Over the Counter, Assembly Says." *New York Times*. February 3, 2004.
Saxon, Wolfgang. 1992. "George Michaels, 80, Legislator Who Changed Abortion Law, Dies." *New York Times*. December 5, 1992.
———. 2000. "Former Gov. Malcolm Wilson, 86, Is Dead." *New York Times*. March 14, 2000.
Scheingold, Stuart. 2004. *The Politics of Rights: Lawyers, Public Policy, and Political Change*, 2nd Edition. Ann Arbor: University of Michigan Press.
Schmidt, C.W. 2008. "Brown and the Colorblind Constitution." 94 *Cornell Law Review*. 203-238.
Schneier, Edward V.; John Brian Murtaugh; Antoinette Pole. 2010. *New York Politics: A Tale of Two States*. Armonk, NY: M. E. Sharpe Incorporated.
Segal, Jeffrey A.; Harold J. Spaeth. 2002. *The Supreme Court and the Attitudinal Model Revisited*. Cambridge, MA: Cambridge University Press.
Segers, Mary C.; Timothy A. Byrnes. 1995. *Abortion Politics in American States*. Armonk, NY: M.E. Sharpe.
Sheboygan Press. 1996b. "24-Hour Abortion Wait OK'd." *Sheboygan Press*. March 22, 1996.
———. 1978. "Abortion Bill Vetoed." *Sheboygan Press*. March 9, 1978.
———. 1977. "Abortion Payments Continued." *Sheboygan Press*. August 6, 1977.
———. 1973. "Abortion Refusal Bill Passage Hailed by Otte." *Sheboygan Press*. October 27, 1973.
———. 1975. "Anti-Abortion Measure Draws Heated Censure." *Sheboygan Press*. June 5, 1975.
———. 1978. "Assembly Acts Quickly on Abortion Bill." *Sheboygan Press*. March 17, 1978.
———. 1990. "Assembly OKs Parental Consent Bill." *Sheboygan Press*. January 31, 1990.
———. 1985. "Compromise Reached on Teen Pregnancy Bill." *Sheboygan Press*. October 16, 1985.
———. 1996a. "Panel Backs Wait Period for Abortion." *Sheboygan Press*. January 9, 1996.
———. 1998. "'Partial-Birth Abortion' Ban Challenged." *Sheboygan Press*. May 1, 1998.
———. 1997. "Partial-Birth Abortion Ban OK'd by Assembly." *Sheboygan Press*. May 23, 1997.
———. 1974. "Senate Agrees States Should be Permitted to Outlaw Abortion." *Sheboygan Press*. February 13, 1974.
Shellum, Bernie. 1973. "Minnesota House Asks Congress for Amendment to Prohibit Abortions." *Star Tribune*. April 13, 1973.
———. 1974. "Senate Approves Limits on Abortion." *Star Tribune*. February 14, 1974.
Silver, Sheldon. 2007. "2007 NYS Assembly Significant Legislation." Press Release. December 27, 2007. Accessed April 2, 2012. http://nyassembly.gov/Press/2007Leg/.
Skocpol, Theda. 1999. "How Americans Became Civic." In *Civic Engagement in American Democracy*, edited by Theda Skocpol and Morris P. Fiorina. Washington, DC: Brookings, 27–80.
Smith, Rogers M. 1988. "Political Jurisprudence, the New Institutionalism, and the Future of Public Law." *American Political Science Review* 82 (1): 89–108.
Smothers, Ronald. 1976. "Bill Restricting Abortions Passed by Senate in Albany." *New York Times*. May 31, 1976.

Smyser, A. A. 2000. "Hawaii's Abortion Law: 30 Years Old." *Honolulu Star-Bulletin*. March 21, 2000.
Solinger, Dorothy J. 2005. "Path Dependency Reexamined: Chinese Welfare Policy in the Transition to Unemployment." *Comparative Politics* 38 (1): 83–101.
Solinger, Rickie. 2017. *Politics of Reproductive Rights in 20th-Century America*. Oxford: Oxford University Press.
Spriggs, James F. II; Thomas G. Hansford. 2001. "Explaining the Overruling of U.S. Supreme Court Precedent." *The Journal of Politics* 63 (4): 1091–1111.
Squire, Peverill. 2008. "Measuring the Professionalization of U.S. State Courts of Last Resort." *State Politics & Policy Quarterly* 8 (3): 223–238.
Srb, Arthur. 1978. "Senate OKs Restriction on Financing Abortions." *Sheboygan Press*. February 17, 1978.
Star Tribune. 1981. "At the Capitol" *Star Tribune*. May 7, 1981.
Sturdevant, Lori. 1981a. "Abortion Bills' Expected Easy Ride Hits Obstacle" *Star Tribune*. March 25, 1981.
———. 1981b. "Panels Include Fathers in Abortion Notification Bill." *Star Tribune*. April 8, 1981.
Sullivan, Joseph F. 1973a. "Jersey Eases Standards on Abortion Prosecution: Kugler Asserts Any Physician May Act to Preserve Health." *New York Times*. February 1, 1973.
———.1973b. "Assembly To Consider New Statute On Abortion: Cahill Has No Bill A Repository for Bills." *New York Times*. February 4, 1973.
———.1979. "Bill on Detailing Risk in Abortion Passed in Jersey." *New York Times*. November 14, 1979.
———. 1976. "Byrne to Sign Bill for Death Penalty if Legislature Acts." *New York Times*. October 8, 1976.
———. 1982. "Court Tells Jersey to Pay for Therapeutic Abortions." *New York Times*. August 19, 1982.
———. 1982a. "Death Penalty Bill Signed by Kean; He Calls for Execution by Injection." *New York Times*. August 7, 1982.
———. 1993. "Florio Signs Death Penalty Aimed at Terrorist Murders." *New York Times*. July 29, 1993.
———. 1982b. "Jersey Senate Approves Bill to Reinstate Death Penalty." *New York Times*. May 7, 1982.
———. 1991. "Judge Would Consider Life-at-Conception Issue." *New York Times*. September 7, 1991.
Sullivan, Ronald. 1970. "Abortion Reform in Jersey Stalled: Change in Law This Year Is Doubted by G.O.P." *New York Times*. March 13, 1970.
———.1965. "State Commission Recommends End of Death Penalty." *New York Times*. March 20, 1965.
Theimer, Sharon. 1998. "Abortion Bill Passes: Partial-Birth Ban Sent to Governor." *Sheboygan Press*. March 27, 1998.
Tushnet, Mark. 2006. "The Supreme Court and the National Political Order: Collaboration and Confrontation." In *The Supreme Court & American Political Development*, edited by Ronald Kahn and Ken I. Kersch. Lawrence: University of Kansas Press, 117–137.
Tyler, Humphrey S. 1975. "The Assembly Reforms: Easy Come, Easy Go." *Empire State Report* 1: 296–297, 311–313.
Vergeront, Susan. 1989. "Wisconsin Needs a Parental Consent Law for Abortions." *Sheboygan Press*. June 4, 1989.
Volden, Craig. 2002. "A Formal Model of the Politics of Delegation in a Separation of Powers System." *American Journal of Political Science* 46 (1): 111–133.
Waaldijk, Kees. 2000. "Civil Developments: Patterns of Reform in the Legal Position of Same-Sex Partners in Europe." *Canadian Journal of Family Law* 17 (1): 62–64.
Waggoner, Walter H. 1970. "New Jersey Sued on Abortion Law: Group Including Y.W.C.A Cites U.S. Constitution." *New York Times*. March 6, 1970.
———. 1974a. "Byrne Signs 'Conscience' Abortion Bill: Governor Signs 'Right to Conscience' Abortion Bill." *New York Times*. October 3, 1974.

———. 1974b. "Jersey Senate Curbs Use of Medicaid for Abortion." *New York Times*. June 18, 1974.

———. 1976. "Medicaid Stayed on Abortion Curb: Civil Liberties Union Gets a Temporary Injunction." *New York Times*. January 17, 1976.

———. 1977a. "Trenton Topics: Court to Hear Plea to Bar Abortions Under Medicaid." *New York Times*. June 25, 1977.

———. 1977b. "Medicaid Is Banned in Some Abortions: Judge Allows Jersey Law to Bar Payment." *New York Times*. June 28, 1977.

———. 1978a. "Court Orders New Jersey to Pay For Abortion for Medicaid Client: 'Equities Are Overwhelming.'" *New York Times*. June 17, 1978.

———. 1978b. "Abortion Financed by Medicaid Is Approved for Rape Victim, 12: Abortions Called Elective." *New York Times*. June 28, 1978.

———. 1974. "Jersey Senate Restricts Medicaid for Abortions." *New York Times*. June 18, 1974.

Waldron, Martin. 1977a. "Antiabortion Bill Stirs New Debate." *New York Times*. February 27, 1977.

———. 1977b. "Abortion Issue Flares Anew." *New York Times*. January 30, 1977.

———. 1978. "Byrne Pocket Vetoes a Bill to Restore Death Penalty." *New York Times*. March 4, 1978.

———. 1980. "Capital Report: Help for Newark: CAPITAL REPORT." *New York Times*. January 13, 1980.

———. 1978. "Chief Justice Hughes Reaffirms Right of Women to Early Abortion." *New York Times*. June 20, 1978.

———. 1977. "Death-Penalty Bill Goes to Byrne After a 58-to-16 Vote in Assembly: Jersey Assembly Sends Death-Penalty Bill to Byrne." *New York Times*. February 1, 1977.

———. 1976. "Death Penalty Bill Supported in Senate." *New York Times*. December 14, 1976.

———. 1979. "New Abortion-Law Proposal Sets Stage for Confrontation: Abortion Confrontation Due." *New York Times*. January 21, 1979.

Ward, Robert B. 2006. *New York State Government*. Rockefeller Institute Press.

Washington Post. 1971. "N.J. Will Not Pay For N.Y. Abortions." *The Washington Post*. October 1, 1971.

Wechsler, Philip. 1973. "Abortion Foes Mount Drive on Hospitals: Letter Drive Planned, Abortion Foes Push Drive on Hospitals." *New York Times*. April 15, 1973.

Wedeking, Justin. 2010. "Supreme Court Litigants and Strategic Framing." *American Journal of Political Science* 54 (3): 617–631.

Wefing, John B. 1997. "The New Jersey Supreme Court 1948–1998: Fifty Years of Independence and Activism." *Rutgers LJ* 29: 701.

Weiden, David L. 2011. "Judicial Politicization, Ideology, and Activism at the High Courts of the United States, Canada, and Australia." *Political Research Quarterly* 64 (2): 335–347.

Westfield Leader. 1968. "Dr. Spragg Attends Newark Hearings on Abortion Law." *Westfield Leader*. November 21, 1968.

Wetstein, Matthew E. 1996. *Abortion Rates in the United States: The Influence of Opinion and Policy*. Albany, NY: SUNY Press.

———. 1995. "Effects of Public Opinion on Abortion Policies and Use in the American States." *Publius: The Journal of Federalism* 25 (4): 91–105.

Wetstein, Matthew E., and Robert B. Albritton. 1995. "Effects of Public Opinion on Abortion Policies and Use in the American States." *Publius: The Journal of Federalism*. 25(4) 91–105.

Whereatt, Robert; Bill McAuliffe. 2000. "Abortion Measure Draws Ventura's Veto." *Star Tribune*. April 15, 2000.

Whereatt, Robert; Donna Halvorsen. 1992. "State Legislators May Have No Choice but to Confront Abortion Issue." *Star Tribune*. June 30, 1992.

Whitman, Christine Todd. 1997. "Statement of Gov. Christie Whitman Regarding the Override of Her Conditional Veto of A-2409/S-1668." *Office of the Governor News Release*. December 15, 1997.

Whittington, Keith E. 2007. *Political Foundations of Judicial Supremacy: The Presidency, the Supreme Court, and Constitutional Leadership in U.S. History*. Princeton, NJ: Princeton University Press.

Women's Health Policy Report. 2007. "Actions Taken on Women's Health-Related Legislation, Programs in Maryland, New Jersey." National Partnership for Women and Families. June 15, 2007. Accessed Jan. 16, 2018. http://split-square.blogspot.com/2007/06/weekly-medical-news
-newsletter-25-june.html.

Wright, Gerald C.; Robert S. Erikson; John P. McIver. 1985. "Measuring State Partisanship and Ideology with Survey Data." *Journal of Politics* 47 (2): 469–89.

Zemans, Frances Kahn. 1983. "Legal Mobilization: The Neglected Role of the Law in the Political System." *The American Political Science Review* 77 (3): 690–703.

Zorn, Christopher; Jennifer Barnes Bowie. 2010. "Ideological Influences on Decision Making in the Federal Judicial Hierarchy: An Empirical Assessment." *The Journal of Politics* 72 (4): 1212–1221.

Index

About the Author

Jonathan F. Parent is Assistant Professor of Political Science at Le Moyne College in Syracuse, NY. He received his PhD in Political Science at the University at Albany, SUNY in 2014 and his BA from the University of Alberta in 2004. His research focuses on law and reproductive rights, politics and sexuality, and the U.S. Supreme Court. His work has appeared in academic journals including *Law and Society Review*, *Justice System Journal*, and the *Journal of Law and Courts*.

www.ingramcontent.com/pod-product-compliance
Ingram Content Group UK Ltd.
Pitfield, Milton Keynes, MK11 3LW, UK
UKHW012037150926
475560UK00001B/58